Praise for *Mission High*

"Rizga delves deep into what is not often shown or known: what's working. She pulls back the curtain on test scores, painting a vivid picture of what a low-scoring, highly successful school looks like and why test scores shouldn't matter as much as they do."

—*San Francisco Chronicle*

"A thoughtful, well-researched account of her time [at Mission High], using it as a case study to explore the problems with education reform in the US. . . . In clear and cogent prose, Rizga makes a compelling case for allowing schools to direct their own learning. *Mission High* is both a breath of fresh air and an inspirational, practical model for struggling education communities around the country."

—*Shelf Awareness*, starred review

"A firsthand report on a 'failing' school system. . . . This skills-based model represents a shift in thinking that could very well establish a shift in results."

—*Kirkus Reviews*

"Recommended for parents, teachers, and administrators concerned with the problems in our educational system and looking for fresh ideas on how to fix it. Rizga is convinced that Mission High has found answers others can learn from, and she makes a compelling argument."

—*Library Journal*

"An intimate look at how an alternative, progressive approach to education works. . . . Accessible and thoroughly researched, Rizga's book covers a brief history of America's education reform and the path to high-stakes testing, and weaves in profiles of Mission's students and faculty. These profiles form the heart of the book, showing students who find community and success (even if not measurable by a multiple-choice test), teachers who provide encouragement, personalized instruction, and more meaningful assessments, and a principal who refuses to 'teach to the test.'"

—*BookPage*

"This book is a godsend. For years we at 826 Valencia have known how great Mission High is—its students, its teachers, its myriad innovations—and we've told everyone we could. Now Kristina Rizga has put it all together in a highly readable and moving portrait of a school that succeeds despite being often misconstrued or mislabeled or even dismissed. There is joy in the hallways of Mission High and daily academic triumph at Mission High, and this book explains how this extraordinary school gets it done. This book is a crucial primer for anyone wanting to go beyond the simplistic labels and metrics and really understand an urban high school and its highly individual, resilient, eager and brilliant students and educators."

—Dave Eggers, cofounder, 826 National and ScholarMatch

"Kristina Rizga writes for those of us weary of trendy ed reform dispensed from on high. Instead, she listens hard to the students and teachers who must deal with their daily consequences. And—with rigor, common sense, and empathy—she tells of the teachers and students confronting shifting tides of reform and profoundly stacked odds, and succeeding. The Mission High that Rizga describes is a beacon, and her deeply textured, heartbreakingly humane book also shines a beautifully clarifying light."

—Jeff Chang, author of *Who We Be: The Colorization of America* and *Can't Stop Won't Stop: A History of the Hip-Hop Generation*

"In *Mission High*, Kristina Rizga embeds at a San Francisco public school to show the high standards, professionalism—and even love—that belie the easy label of 'failing school.' A much-needed corrective to an education debate that often fails to ask how students and teachers experience reform on the ground."

—Dana Goldstein, author of *The Teacher Wars: A History of America's Most Embattled Profession*

"A clear-eyed, evidence-based, and wonderfully fresh understanding of what education 'reform' truly means."

—Katrina vanden Heuvel, editor and publisher of the *Nation*

"By introducing us to the struggles and triumphs of teachers and students, Rizga has redefined what success means in American education. It's not what testing reveals, but what lives are transformed. *Mission High* is one of the best books about education I've read in years. It should be a conversation changer."

—LynNell Hancock, professor of journalism, Columbia University, and director of Spencer Fellowship for Education Journalism

"Kristina Rizga's *Mission High* depicts an educational paradox: schools that perform poorly on tests, on average, can also be some of the most deeply engaging and productive learning spaces. Through vivid, compelling portraits of dynamic, resilient students and thoughtful, committed educators, Rizga captures beautifully how young scholars are encouraged and developed. This is a must-read for anyone who wants to understand the holistic nature of teaching and learning."

—Prudence L. Carter, professor of education, Stanford University, and coauthor with Kevin G. Welner of *Closing the Opportunity Gap: What America Must Do to Give Every Child an Even Chance*

MISSION HIGH

ONE SCHOOL, HOW EXPERTS
TRIED TO FAIL IT, AND
THE STUDENTS AND TEACHERS
WHO MADE IT TRIUMPH

◇◇◇◇◇◇◇◇

KRISTINA RIZGA

BOLD TYPE BOOKS

NEW YORK

Hardcover first published in 2015 by Bold Type Books
An imprint of Perseus Books, a division of PBG Publishing, LLC, a subsidiary of
Hachette Book Group, Inc.
116 East 16th Street, 8th Floor
New York, NY 10003

Paperback first published in 2016 by Bold Type Books

Bold Type Books is a co-publishing venture of the Type Media Center and Perseus Books.

Books published by Bold Type Books are available at special discounts for bulk purchases in the United States by corporations, institutions, and other organizations.
For more information, please contact the Special Markets Department at the Perseus Books Group, 2300 Chestnut Street, Suite 200, Philadelphia, PA 19103, or
call (800) 810-4145, ext. 5000, or e-mail special.markets@perseusbooks.com.

Designed by Jack Lenzo

Library of Congress Cataloging-in-Publication Data
Rizga, Kristina.
Mission High : one school, how experts tried to fail it, and the students and teach-
ers who made it triumph / Kristina Rizga.
pages cm
Includes bibliographical references and index.
ISBN 978-1-56858-495-9 (hardback)—ISBN 978-1-56858-462-1 (ebook) 1.
Mission High School (San Francisco, Calif.) 2. Academic achievement—Cali-
fornia—San Francisco. 3. Educational evaluation—California—San Francisco.
4. Educational sociology—California—San Francisco. 5. High school students—
California—San Francisco. I. Title.
LA245.S4R59 2015
371.26'20979461—dc23
2015007384

ISBN: 978-1-56858-567-3 (paperback)

10 9 8 7 6 5 4 3 2 1

To Mike Stern

To our greatest teachers: Fruma and Pēteris Rizga,
Yvette and Gerry Stern

To Mission High School students, teachers,
and staff, whose boundless capacity for inclusion,
generosity, and patience made this project possible

Contents

Preface   *ix*

Chapter 1: Maria   1
Chapter 2: Mr. Roth   27

THE PROGRESSIVES (1890–1950)   **63**

Chapter 3: George   73
Chapter 4: Mr. Hsu   89

DESEGREGATION (1957–1970)   **115**

Chapter 5: Pablo   123
Chapter 6: Principal Guthertz   153

**THE STANDARDS AND ACCOUNTABILITY MOVEMENT
(1980–PRESENT)**   **185**

Chapter 7: Ms. McKamey   193
Chapter 8: Jesmyn   223

Epilogue   *241*
Author's Note   *253*
Acknowledgments   *259*
Notes   *267*
Index   *281*

Preface

What motivates students to learn, work hard, and persevere through life's toughest challenges? Why is it so difficult for the world's wealthiest and most powerful country to build good schools in every neighborhood? This book started with a reporting assignment, when *Mother Jones* magazine sent me to answer these questions in a series of stories about public schools. The assignment was supposed to last for eight months, but as I immersed myself in the private lives of students and teachers, the surprising realities I discovered compelled me to stay at the school for four years. The more time I spent in classrooms, the more I began to realize that most remedies that politicians and education reform experts were promoting as solutions for fixing schools were wrong.

Like many Americans, I believe that democracy and the economy can't function without decent public schools that are free and accessible to everyone. It is also clear that our educational system is not working for too many children, particularly African American and Latino students. While there is no achievement gap between white and black infants,[1] studies show growing disparities beginning at age four in a variety of educational outcomes that over time morph into gaps in grades, graduation rates, and college enrollment numbers.[2] Until the United States can find a way to teach all students effectively, our country will continue to waste one of its greatest assets in the global economy: the huge reservoir of diverse and creative human talent. Why does America, a country that strives to be a moral leader in the world, have such stubborn racial and income gaps in education? And what can be done to fix this?

I have been obsessed with these questions as a journalist for over a decade, and when I started a job as an education reporter for *Mother Jones*, I brought them up in my first meeting with my editor, Monika Bauerlein. We were sitting in her office in San Francisco, talking about schools, educational reform, and a new, personally painful reality in my life. Most of my middle-class friends, whose kids were about to enter elementary school, were leaving San Francisco's public schools for the suburbs. Those who stayed sent their kids to private schools. "Why do our public schools have such a bad reputation?" I asked Bauerlein. "Why can't my hometown of San Francisco, one of the most affluent and progressive cities in the world, build excellent public schools for everyone?"

Bauerlein, who had covered education as a reporter in the past, suggested that I find a school that was struggling, convince the staff to let me spend a year with them, and find out. There are too many politicians, powerful bureaucrats, management and business experts, economists, and philanthropists making decisions about the best solutions for schools, we agreed. What do students and teachers think about the policies these experts are implementing, such as increased use of standardized testing, making it easier to fire ineffective teachers, or opening more charter schools? How do these policies compare with what actually works in the classroom? There are close to 50 million students[3] and 3 million teachers[4] in America's public schools, but we rarely hear from them, the very people we are actually trying to "fix."

I wondered at the time why I hadn't read many accounts of how these national issues were playing out on the ground. It turns out that there's a reason: it's easier for a journalist to embed with the army than to go behind the scenes at a public school. Schools are a home to minors, after all, and the degree of protection is greater than in most other public institutions. It took months to find a school that would let me be a fly on the wall. Finally, the principal of Mission High School in San Francisco, Eric Guthertz, opened his doors to me in late 2009. Even then, it took months more for some teachers—wary of media distortion and stereotyping of students of color—to warm to me. Eventually, after building trust among teachers and students, I gained full access to Mission High. One of the oldest and most diverse public schools in the country, Mission is an ideal microcosm for exploring the key challenges of public schools across the nation. The school has 950 students holding passports from more than forty countries. Latino, African American, and Asian American students constitute the majority of the school's population. Some 75 percent are poor, and 38 percent are English learners.[5]

The surprises began right away. When I first started reporting on education in 2006, I used to think that though imperfect, standardized test scores—the Big Tests students take once a year—are the most reliable markers we have to see how students and schools are doing. Test scores are the main set of data used by education experts, state officials, and many parents in our country. When I first entered Mission High, it was listed among the lowest-performing 5 percent of schools in the country. In 2010 President Barack Obama authorized a major intervention program in schools like these, ordering radical restructuring. Options included replacing the principal and either revamping the curriculum or replacing half the staff, closing the school, or turning it into a charter.[6] San Francisco's oldest comprehensive public high school, founded in 1890, would have to show dramatic growth in scores in the coming years or face dramatic interventions, including possible closure.

Yet while Mission High was labeled a "low-performing" school in 2010, 84 percent of the graduating class was accepted to college. In a student survey, 89 percent said that they liked Mission and would recommend it to others, a higher percentage of positive responses than the district average.[7] By 2013 the graduation rate for African American students was 20 percent higher at Mission and college enrollment for black students was 14 percent higher than the district average.[8] Grades, graduation rates, and attendance rates for all students went up. Suspensions went down by 86 percent from 2008 to 2014. "How can my school be flunking when I'm succeeding?" Maria, one of six students whose journeys I followed deeply in this book, asked me when we first met in 2009.

As I spent time at Mission, I came to realize that in every school there are many reliable markers that can give us a more accurate picture of how students and schools are doing. At Mission, teachers have their own system of accountability, which attaches most of the weight to other measures beyond test scores, such as grades and attendance data disaggregated by race, ethnicity, income, and special needs; student feedback about teachers; observations of many classes in a row to understand the intentions and sequencing of lessons; observations of the degree of work production in the classroom and student engagement with that work; detailed review of student work produced in the class; and extensive interviews with students and teachers. Though difficult to implement, these criteria are far more informative than standard measures used by education analysts and experts, such as yearly test scores and occasional observation by administrators.

After two years at Mission, I was forced to let go of another major assumption about education: that emphasis on individual students' test scores is the best way to monitor and promote individual learning. I have come to believe that this faulty logic harms learning. Some of the most important things that matter in a quality education—critical thinking, intrinsic motivation, resilience, self-management, resourcefulness, and relationship skills—exist in the realms that can't be easily measured by statistical measures and computer algorithms, but they can be detected by teachers using human judgment. America's business-inspired obsession with prioritizing "metrics" in a complex world that deals with the development of individual minds has become the primary cause of mediocrity in American schools. The focus on quantitative, standardized outcomes promotes standardized teaching: prepackaged delivery of content and instruction "in the middle," making it difficult to serve the individual needs of students with different levels of skills and motivation.

This realization also helped me get closer to understanding some of the root causes of the achievement gap and potentially how to fix it. The highly successful and experienced teachers at Mission High reduced or closed the achievement gaps through personalized instruction, teaching each student individually. They raised the bar above everyone's needs and then provided necessary supports for all students to reach that bar. The best teachers knew the individual strengths, interests, and challenges of all their students and refined their craft and approaches based on a variety of qualitative and quantitative markers. People in the education field often refer to this kind of teaching as "student-centered," but at Mission they just call it good teaching, as opposed to simply delivering standardized content and then sorting students into different groups of perceived ability.

For math teacher Taica Hsu, personalized instruction means that he doesn't look at his students from what educators refer to as "the deficit model." He doesn't focus on arbitrary standard performance expectations that his students aren't meeting at the moment. Hsu says that students want to know that teachers see them as individuals who are valuable right now, regardless of their grades or test scores or their knowledge of certain skills. A teacher's ability to see the strengths of individual students can cut through the anxiety and self-doubt, often caused by negative racial stereotypes in our society.

After three years at the school, I had to let go of yet another deep-seated notion. I used to think that successful education reform occurs when struggling schools adopt research-based practices from academic reports, case studies from other countries, or practices of high-scoring schools with similar demographics. As I observed the implementation of new teaching approaches in the math department for three years, I saw firsthand how copying and pasting blueprints from other places doesn't work. The recommendations of experts in academia or other schools are too general and don't take into account the most important variable: the unique ecosystem of each school and the individual needs of its diverse student body. Schools always need to seek out new ideas and learn from the wisdom of others, but much more important, each teacher and school needs to channel all outside recommendations through a daily process of individual and collective research and action: detecting student engagement in the classroom, checking for understanding and growth, collecting and analyzing student work, and making constant changes in lesson plans and school policies.

This book is about this other, messier, mostly qualitative and largely invisible side of the story about public schools in our national debate. After four years at Mission, I have come to believe that educational reforms won't succeed unless there is greater inclusion of the voices of students and teachers and the use of more complex, school-based markers that can give us a much deeper insight into what quality education means and how sustainable change can happen in all struggling schools.

Take the story of Darrell, a student I profile in this book. A reflective, brilliant young man, Darrell struggled in middle school. His father was the single provider for his large family of thirteen of his own and adopted kids. Darrell had a reading disability that wasn't detected until he started high school in 2008. Before attending Mission High, his academic confidence was low, and he didn't think of himself as a good writer. But by his junior year at Mission High, he was thriving: taking AP calculus, writing ten-page research papers in history and ethnic studies, and celebrating several college acceptance letters.

When I asked Darrell to reflect on what contributed to his success at the end of his senior year in 2012, he talked about his teachers and mentors. The best teachers at Mission worked hard to create intellectually engaging classrooms for every student, he said. They gave students "the freedom to think" and "taught you how to analyze different texts and express your ideas effectively." Because Darrell's teachers saw him as an individual with his own unique ideas, passions, and strengths, they knew how to use the content to tap his intrinsic motivation, pushing him to work hard, learn new skills, and overcome personal difficulties. With every piece of work, Darrell could hear his own thoughts more and take pride in his own voice. Over time he became addicted to that feeling. It is this sense of pride in his own intellect, more than anything else, that contributed to his resilience throughout high school, he explained, helping him overcome daily obstacles and self-doubt in social settings where other young adults had much more self-confidence and deeper social support systems.

That kind of personalized, rigorous teaching is rare in many schools with low and high standardized test scores. In too many schools, students are still primarily rewarded for showing up, listening to lectures without interrupting, filling out worksheets, passing tests, participating in some discussions, and writing occasional papers. "My middle school teachers seemed to just go through the standards and then test you," Jesmyn, another student I profile, recalled. "They don't seem that enthusiastic about what they are teaching." National teacher surveys show that educators struggle to teach students with varying levels of skills and motivation. In a 2008 national survey commissioned by the Fordham Institute, more than eight in ten teachers said "differentiated instruction"—educational jargon for personalized teaching—was "very difficult" or "somewhat difficult" to implement.[9] Many policy makers and parents say they want personalized, student-centered education, but all of the major incentives and penalties are attached to standardized outcomes.

This is because our country, as this book explains, has been on a century-long road toward increased standardization in education. The most effective teaching, the kind that values high intellectual and emotional engagement of every student, is not the fastest way to get to the highest standardized test scores. Hands-on projects, in-depth discussions, frequent written assignments, multiple drafts, and individual feedback take more time. The "bonus" skills that these activities teach—communicating complex ideas, debating, learning from one's mistakes, self-discipline, curiosity, resilience, integrity—aren't measured by standardized test scores and in many classrooms are often overlooked. The best way to get to higher test scores is for classroom activities to mimic the language, procedures, and requirements of the test. It's no surprise then that a 2013 Gallup Poll, which surveyed over 600,000 US students, found that student engagement drops precipitously between grades five and twelve.[10]

The latest research by psychologists, economists, and neuroscientists tells us that these "bonus" skills are hugely important.[11] Many students I profiled talked about the importance of a broad range of intellectual, social, and emotional skills. In the hundreds of hours I spent in Mission High classrooms, I observed how many of these skills are taught. I found that while such complex skills resist easy quantification by standardized test scores, they have been effectively detected and measured by assessments designed by skilled teachers for decades. A comprehensive, critical review of the latest research on learning by the University of Chicago Consortium on School Research in 2012 came to similar conclusions. The report, "Teaching Adolescents to Become Learners," found that grades given out by teachers, unlike test scores, measure many more of these cognitive, social, and emotional skills.[12]

Mission High School, like many other public schools across the country, has resisted pressure to teach to the test and is going in the opposite direction of our country's standardized approach to education. This book is an intimate portrait of how such an alternative, progressive approach works at one school, and how its successes—and many continued struggles—can be detected using more nuanced evidence, including the judgment of skilled teachers. Many of our country's most powerful individuals, like Education Secretary John King Jr. and education reform experts, such as Bill Gates and Eli and Edyth Broad, have big plans for the future of American public schools.[13] These ideas include new standardized online tests and increased use of these tests to grade students and schools, more charter schools, and increased governance by management and business experts rather than educators. This book is an attempt to elevate the largely invisible voices of students and teachers in the larger conversation about education in America today and to allow their wisdom and expertise to expand our imaginations about possible solutions and to stretch our definitions of quality education.

Chapter 1

Maria

"Speak English, taco," a heavy girl with a giant backpack yelled when Maria asked her in Spanish where to find a bathroom. The pink backpack bounced as the girl stomped down the hall. It had been hours since Maria began looking for a bathroom. Anger boiled up inside her, but she didn't know any words in English to yell back at the girl. That was the hardest part. Even though Maria was tiny, probably the shortest girl in her seventh-grade class, she had always stood up for herself back in El Salvador. She'd always had something to say back. *Please don't let them see me cry,* she thought while her lower lip trembled.

The bell rang. A flood of backpacks, shoulders, and sneakers swirled around her. She couldn't see anything until the sea of strangers streamed back into classrooms. She stood alone in the hallway. She wasn't going back to class. It was late 2006, Maria's first day at school, and her first week in the United States. Maria's new middle school in San Francisco's Mission District was the biggest building she had ever seen in her life. It was bigger than the entire Best Buy department store Maria had walked through the previous week. At the school, Maria was in a class for Spanish-speaking newcomers, practicing English words for colors and numbers, learning how to say "thank-you" and how to introduce herself. She struggled with more advanced subjects. It didn't help that her math teacher started each class by saying, "Okay, my little dummies." He spoke too fast. Maria never raised her hand in his class and never asked him any questions.

One day Maria stopped by the administrative office, looking for someone to help her with multiplication. She got in line behind a middle-aged woman, who asked her some questions in Spanish. Maria said school was really difficult for her. The woman told her not to worry. "Latinas usually don't finish high school," she said. "They go to work or raise kids." The woman was right, statistically speaking, and Maria's middle school experience all but ensured she would join the 52 percent of foreign-born Latinos who drop out of high school.[1] She graduated from eighth grade without learning to speak English, struggled with writing in Spanish, and didn't know how to multiply. And then everything changed.

At Mission High, the troubled school she had chosen against the advice of her friends and relatives, Maria earned high grades in math and on some days found herself speaking English even with her Spanish-speaking teachers. By eleventh grade she was writing long papers on complex topics like the war in Iraq and desegregation. She became addicted to winning debates in class, despite her shyness and heavy accent. In her junior year she became the go-to translator and advocate for her mother, her aunts, and other Latino kids at school. In March 2012 Maria and her teachers celebrated her receiving acceptance letters to five colleges, including the University of California at Davis, and two prestigious scholarships. But on the California Standards Tests—the yearly multiple-choice tests mandated by the federal government from 2001 to 2013—Maria scored poorly.[2]

According to the results of these state tests, which were given to all students, Mission High was among the lowest-performing 5 percent of schools in the country.[3] And the tests, as Maria understood all too well, were the basis upon which her school was evaluated by the government. "How can this be?" she often asked herself. "How can my school be flunking when I'm succeeding?"

∞∞∞∞∞∞∞∞∞∞∞

When Maria turned three, she stopped hearing her mother's voice in the mornings. Her mother disappeared one day, and no one said a word about it. Finally, when Maria was seven, her grandmother explained that her mom had crossed three borders to find work in California. Maria and her older brother were raised by her grandparents in the village of San Juan Las Minas in El Salvador. Their aunt Angelica came to visit when she could. Maria doesn't remember much from those early days, except for her aunt's soothing voice. Maria would often sit on her lap, enveloped in a large bear hug, listening to her tender whispers. Angelica had two children of her own, but she didn't mind when Maria started calling her mom.

Around the age of seven, Maria learned how to climb the mango trees in the nearby groves. Together Maria and

Angelica would scramble up, racing to reach the thickest branches at the top, where they would bite into the orange flesh of sweet mangoes and watch the juice flow down their legs to their naked, dangling feet. The mangoes were sweetest when the air was heavy with rain. After Angelica left, Maria spent the rest of the day by herself. Her grandparents were busy working in the vegetable garden, watching four kids, and looking after cows, pigs, and chickens.

Angelica and her two children lived a few hours away in San Salvador, the capital of the most densely packed nation in Central America. Angelica ran a small corner liquor store and sold homemade tamales on the side. In her native Las Minas she could go outside after dark, but in San Salvador she avoided doing that. Angelica feared the members of the Mara Salvatrucha gang, or MS-13, as they are commonly known. Formed in the 1980s by Salvadoran youth in California who were being victimized by other gangs, MS-13 became one of the most violent gangs that now operate in Central America, Mexico, and the United States.[4] Its members roamed the city streets of San Salvador, fighting for money, territory, and control of the drug trade. Angelica was paying off MS-13 every month, and for the most part they left her alone, except the day they shot one of her customers in the store. Maria was there. It was the first time she saw a human body break up into chunks like a ripe mango hitting the ground. A piece of the man's head dropped on her foot.

Angelica loved escaping the violence of the big city for Las Minas. "I'm like you, Maria. Like a little girl," she used to say when they played soccer together. Maria felt like Angelica's daughter. Her light brown skin and long chocolate-brown hair were just like her auntie's. She always washed and brushed her hair thoroughly. That was what told the outside world how close they were.

Maria remembers the day her auntie died more clearly than most days. She remembers Angelica's tall body lying in a light, wooden coffin beside the kitchen table. Candles had been burning since the morning. As the sun climbed up in the sky, the scent of candle wax gave way to the smell of beer and sticky sweat. There were more than twenty strangers in the house. Shirtless, their shiny bodies were covered in black tattoos depicting letters, numbers, and devil's horns. Maria knew that these men were in MS-13. Angelica's boyfriend had once pushed one of the MS-13 members out of her store. Now that member came with his friends to Angelica's funeral, hoping to teach the boyfriend a lesson. As the house got hotter, the men's voices grew louder. They started playing poker, roaring at their violent jokes.

Maria was praying near the coffin. She could see her auntie's dark hair through the white lace covering her face. It had been a week since Maria last heard Angelica's voice. "Don't worry," her auntie had said on the phone. "I'll take care of everything. I'll pay off MS-13." But she couldn't. She didn't have enough money. Three days after that call, Angelica was found in a San Salvador hospital without any clothes on. The doctors said she had been raped and tortured for days. There was nothing they could do to save her.

Maria tried to focus on praying, but the men in the house got louder, throwing cards across the table and spitting on the wooden floors. Maria gathered her courage and walked toward them. Her head barely reached the tabletop.

"Be respectful or get out of my house!" she shouted as loud as she could. The men turned their heads toward her, cards suspended in their sweaty hands. For a few moments, the house was as quiet as Maria thought it should be during prayers for the dead. Then the men started laughing, pointing their fingers at Maria and stomping their feet. A quiet girl in their midst walked toward Maria and tried to touch her tear-covered face. Maria dodged her and ran outside. When she returned, the MS-13 men were still there. They left only after Angelica's body was buried. They took all of Maria's grandparents' money.

"Why don't you come to America?" Maria's mother, who lived in San Francisco, asked her on the phone a week after the funeral. "Your brother and aunt Olivia are already here." Maria's mother had been talking to her about coming to the United States since she was seven. "I'd always say no," Maria recalls. "I loved my auntie more than anything. I didn't want to be in any other country but mine. But when my auntie died, I had no one close left. What could I do?"

At the age of twelve, Maria was the youngest passenger among the twenty people on the bus crossing El Salvador, Guatemala, and Mexico toward California. They called their driver "coyote," slang for a person who smuggles immigrants across the American border without official permission—which can take up to a decade to obtain. Maria's ride was easy. She had her own seat the whole time. Dinners were the best part of the trip. The coyote bought his passengers chicken every night. At home, her grandparents cooked chicken only when they had relatives over for a Sunday meal.

◇◇◇◇◇◇◇◇◇◇◇◇◇◇◇◇

It was a gorgeous spring afternoon in 2008, and the lush green expanse of Dolores Park near Mission High School was dotted with people. From the park, Mission looked like a church. The facade and doorway were decorated with intricate Spanish baroque moldings. Heavy iron chandeliers adorned the ornate ceiling above the entrance hall. The light glittered on spotless yellow linoleum. As Maria and her middle school classmates toured the school's library, courtyards, and cafeteria, she noticed that most people seemed friendly. Even the security guards were joking around. Eric Guthertz, the school's principal, couldn't stop talking about Mission High's history. The musician Carlos Santana and the writer Maya Angelou went to Mission, he proudly informed his visitors. The school featured after-school programs like the Latino student club, soccer games, and creative writing classes. Maria asked a few Latino students if they liked Mission. To her surprise, all of them said they did. But everyone Maria knew outside of Mission told her not to go there. Her mother's friends said that she should go to a "better school." Maria's friends in her middle school told her that Mission had gangs.

Guthertz took Maria and some Latino classmates to the classroom of Amadis Velez, who spoke to them in fluent Spanish. He told them that he would be their English teacher. Maria noticed Velez's college diploma from the University of California at Berkeley on the wall, surrounded by photos of Frida Kahlo, César Chávez, and Salvador Dali. "He was so welcoming," Maria remembers. "He kept making jokes about our English, making us laugh. After I met Mr. Velez, I knew I'd be going to Mission."

"Maria didn't speak a lick of English when she started in my ninth-grade English class," Velez recalls. "That year, there were only two students whose English was worse than Maria's." Velez also noticed that Maria's skills in Spanish grammar and in math were at least two years behind her Latino classmates'. Maria was less than five feet tall and weighed about seventy pounds. "She was tiny," Velez tells me, "but very spunky, and her leadership and popularity among students stood out to me right away."

Maria loved that she had a class with Mr. Velez every day. He taught her English and geography in the ninth grade, and history in the tenth. He checked in with her after class every afternoon. Maria didn't realize how many things she had on her mind. All kinds of worries kept pouring out in their conversations. Could Mr. Velez explain the word *tariffs*? What's this thing, *analysis*? Who could finally teach Maria how to multiply? "I thought of myself as a really bad student back then," she recalls. "I didn't believe in myself. But Mr. Velez always told me not to give up, to keep going, keep pushing."

When Maria was a sophomore, Mr. Velez started charting her path to college. He said that she needed to transfer into regular English classes as soon as possible, since classes for English learners weren't credited by many universities. He also explained that California was one of twelve states that allow undocumented students like Maria to pay resident tuition rather than out-of-state tuition, which can be twice as much.[5] Velez said that Maria was not eligible for any government grants or student loans, but there were private scholarships, and he would help her get them. All of this was possible, he said, if Maria kept her grades up, did all of her homework, and worked twice as hard as her classmates who already knew English. He said he would be there for her no matter what. He told her to have fun and to laugh a lot.

Most days she did well and felt good about her progress. She met with Mr. Velez after class to review her grammar. He urged her to write more complex sentences. By the end of the year, she was writing essays that didn't fit on one page anymore. She earned an A in his modern world history class. Then one morning, over breakfast in the small studio that Maria shared with her mother, two brothers, her auntie Olivia, and a younger cousin, she found an envelope on the kitchen table. Inside were the results of the standardized tests she had taken a few months before. Her stomach dropped. She had done much worse than she had anticipated. In history, her score was "far below basic"—the lowest ranking.

What Maria didn't know was that according to the California Department of Education, only 19 percent of Mission High's Latino students scored "proficient or above" in history in 2010.[6] The vast majority of Latinos, at Mission High and *statewide*, had scores similar to Maria's.[7] She knew that Mr. Velez thought she was smart. But this was the first grade she had received from people outside of Mission, and it made her wonder: Was Mr. Velez wrong?

"Multiple choice kills you, Maria," Mr. Velez said to her when he saw the score. He told her the test didn't measure her intelligence and understanding of history. Mostly it just pointed to the differences between her language skills and those of a native speaker.

All Maria could think about as they talked was the woman at her middle school who had told her that Latinas usually don't finish high school. She also remembered another thing from their exchange three years before: the woman had advised her to stop speaking Spanish at home. She said that Maria would have to leave El Salvador behind if she was ever to become an American, that the United States had higher standards than her homeland.

Maria had blocked all of that out of her mind. She had kept speaking Spanish with her mother and some friends, and her performance in Mr. Velez's classes had given her confidence in that decision. Now she had doubts.

◇◇◇◇◇◇◇◇◇◇◇◇◇◇◇◇

Every spring from 2002 to 2013, students in the third to eleventh grades sat down to take standardized tests required by the federal No Child Left Behind Act of 2001 (NCLB). The law mandated that each state come up with its own list of curriculum standards that every student had to master in each grade and a set of its own tests. These tests were meant to measure mastery of basic knowledge that was deemed necessary for success in the workplace or college. In most states, standardized tests consisted primarily of multiple-choice questions.[8]

The people who fought for these standards and tests wanted to raise expectations for all students. They knew that for decades Latino and African American students, children with learning disabilities, and low-income students weren't being intellectually challenged, were often stuck in segregated and underfunded schools, and were routinely shuffled into vocational training. The proponents of standardized testing argued that school-designed tests, grades, and other feedback by teachers were not reliable data to get an authentic picture of what was going on in the schools. As more states started using standardized testing in the 1970s and 1980s, urban education researchers were able to flag the outliers: schools that were reducing the achievement gap between white, middle-class students and students of color and the poor.[9] Larry Cuban, historian and professor emeritus of education at Stanford University, told me that the data collected from these tests helped to dismantle the idea that students of color, poor students, and disabled students were unable to learn.[10]

In 2001 the Bush administration pushed the No Child Left Behind Act through Congress. For the first time the federal government required states to pay attention to achievement data disaggregated by race, ethnicity, and class. Congress also mandated that schools raise achievement among all subgroups by 2014 or face radical consequences, including restructuring or closure. By this time, testing had undergone a political transformation. Now it was at the core of a business-inspired approach championed by a coalition of odd bedfellows, including business leaders like Bill Gates; idealists like Wendy Kopp of Teach for America; politicians like the Republican governor of Florida, Jeb Bush; and education officials like former Washington, D.C., schools chief Michelle Rhee. Standardized tests, many of these reformers believed, could bring accurate metrics and hard-core sanctions to the complacent, ossified world of education bureaucrats and teachers' unions. Closures or mass firings at low-performing schools and bonuses for high-scoring teachers were supposed to disrupt a system that, in the reformers' view, had failed students and the companies for which they would one day work.

Supporters of NCLB argued that the law adds empirical data to the conversation about achievement and keeps schools accountable for educational outcomes. The law was animated by this faith in metrics. It mandated that states use test scores to determine whether schools were succeeding or failing, with the latter required to improve or be subjected to punitive measures. The law passed with broad bipartisan support among the political elites, and many civil rights groups—such as the Education Trust and the National Council of La Raza—were behind it.[11]

After just one year in the country, Maria had to take the same standardized, multiple-choice tests as students who were born in the United States, even though studies show that non-native speakers take four years on average to become proficient in English—and that's with constant focus.[12] In 2010 Latino students made up the majority of California's public school students for the first time in the state's history.[13] At Mission High, close to half of all students are immigrants, primarily Latino. Principal Guthertz notes that more than 20 percent have been in the United States less than two years. Maria scored "proficient" in history for the first time in the eleventh grade. In her six years in the United States, standardized tests showed where Maria stood in relationship to mainstream students, who grew up on a steady diet of American culture and middle-class social norms. But such tests didn't measure how much Maria grew as a learner before she reached the arbitrary mark of "proficiency" set by the state.

Standardized tests didn't measure higher-order thinking skills, such as Maria's ability to synthesize information in a coherent essay, analyze it in the broader historical context, make connections to the present day, and express an informed and original point of view while she was strengthening her grammar skills.[14] The latest research by psychologists, economists, and neuroscientists tells us that achievement tests can't measure important social and emotional skills either, such as Maria's growing confidence in her intellect, the courage to speak up in class and defend her views, the tenacity to keep rewriting her papers and work on her weaknesses, the social skills to form new relationships and to ask for help, and the resilience to come to school every day even when deportation notices arrive.[15]

A look at Maria's schoolwork over the course of a year, on the other hand, can show this much broader range of her intellectual, social, and emotional skills. In the frequent quizzes designed by Maria's teachers, in her essays, multidraft research papers, art projects, and presentations, what we see is clear evidence of an intellect battling to find its voice. In her first year in Mr. Velez's class, Maria's essays rarely ran beyond two paragraphs. By the end of tenth grade, while still scoring "far below proficient," Maria's writing couldn't fit on one page anymore. She often crammed sentences with her own ideas about the topics into the margins and wrote long after the bell rang. She also started speaking out in class more and helping other newcomers with their classroom work. Velez might have moved Maria's reading and writing skills in English and history from the sixth-grade level to the ninth in one year, but standardized test scores don't take that into account. As far as federal and state education officials and reform experts are concerned, Maria was not at the tenth-grade level with the students in the rest of the country, and as a result, a school like Mission and a teacher like Velez are considered "failing."

Linda Darling-Hammond, professor of education at the Stanford Graduate School of Education and one of our country's preeminent testing researchers, has found that assessments and tasks designed and scored by skilled teachers, such as essays, science projects, research assignments, and presentations, are far more effective than standardized tests at promoting learning and diagnosing how students are doing.[16] In 1998 British education scholars Paul Black and Dylan William surveyed 580 studies by leading researchers in the United States, United Kingdom, Australia, Switzerland, and Hong Kong and concluded that frequent, lower-stakes, meaningful verbal and written assessments created by teachers (called "formative assessments" in educational jargon) produced larger learning gains than most instructional interventions that had been implemented and studied.[17] The push toward centralized data has left behind many of these old-fashioned, commonsense markers. Even the godfather of standardized testing, the cognitive psychologist Robert Glaser, warned in 1987 about the dangers of placing too much emphasis on standardized test scores. As reported by the *New York*

Times, Glaser called them "fallible and partial indicators of academic achievement" and warned that any standardized tests would find it "extremely difficult to assess" the key skills people should gain from a good education: "resilience and courage in the face of stress, a sense of craft in our work, a commitment to justice and caring in our social relationships, a dedication to advancing the public good."[18]

◇◇◇◇◇◇◇◇◇◇◇◇◇◇

It is nine in the morning, and the lights are off in Robert Roth's classroom, in which twenty-three juniors in the US History class are sitting. Winter rain taps on the windowsills, and warm moisture fills the room. In the flickering light from a television screen, Maria can see her friend Jesmyn breaking small pieces from a muffin and popping them into her mouth. Maria lowers her chin into her hands. Her right leg, sheathed in tight, dark, blue jeans, lightly bounces on the linoleum floor.

On the screen an actress portraying education reformer Paula Crisostomo is arguing with her father, a Filipino immigrant wearing a blue work shirt. "I told you to stay away from these agitators!" he yells at Paula, after seeing her on TV waving a protest sign in the face of a police officer. Based on a true story, *The Walkout* (2006) captures the events of the 1968 protests in the public schools of East Los Angeles. About twenty-two thousand Latino students participated (one of them was Antonio Villaraigosa, who later served as mayor of Los Angeles, from 2005 to 2013), inspired by a teacher named Sal Castro. Back then, most Latinos were forbidden to speak Spanish in class. Curricula largely ignored Mexican and Central American history, and Latinos were steered toward menial labor.

In the film Crisostomo can be seen with her fellow students, shaking the metal gate of her school, locked shut by officials to prevent students from walking out. The students rattle the bars, chanting "Viva La Raza!" while police stand on the other side. The gate breaks. Maria's entire class erupts in applause as Crisostomo and her peers flood into the street. After the film ends, Mr. Roth switches on the lights and turns to his class sitting in motionless silence. "Any thoughts, anyone?"

"It's incredible to see how courageous Paula was," says a student from Nicaragua named Catharine. "She lost confidence so many times, but whenever she lost it, her friends were there to support her."

"In middle school, I was told to speak only English at home," Maria says next. "I think that's wrong. I already do at school. They shouldn't tell me how to live my life."

Juan, who just wrote a paper on assimilation among young Latinos, agrees. "A lot of Latino kids at Mission don't speak Spanish, and that's stupid. If you don't know where you come from, you're lost."

"I can relate to Paula, how people don't believe Latinos are smart enough for college," adds Yesennia. "These stereotypes make me want to prove them wrong."

"Speaking of stereotypes," Jesmyn jumps in, "I was in the bathroom with five black girls, and we were fixing our hair. Two Asian American girls come in and they run out right away, thinking that we are going to bully them. I want to fix that. I'm a nice person!"

Roth waits a few seconds and jumps in, "Michelle, you were talking to me about this kind of stereotype the other day. Do you mind sharing what you said?"

"When we moved to St. Louis from China," says Michelle, "we went to an all African American school. My parents were telling me to stay away from black students. But African Americans were all really nice to us." She pauses for a moment. "A lot of times, it's coming from parents. But they just don't know. My parents never met any black people in China," she adds.

"Most parents," George, a recent immigrant from China, adds quietly.

"That's exactly right," Roth adds. "George chose not to go to Lowell [a prominent public magnet high school in San Francisco], because he wanted to go to a diverse school. His parents supported his decision."

"It's not about the ethnicity, it's about the person," George exclaims, in a slightly more confident voice.

"I love George," Jesmyn says with a hand on her heart. "I'm about to cry here."

The bell rings. Jesmyn and her friend Destiny come up to Maria. "What's 'Viva la Raza'?"

"It kind of means being proud to be Latino," Maria explains, smiling.

"How do you say it?" Jesmyn asks, and Maria tells them. "Viva La Raza! Viva La Raza! Viva La Raza!" all three chant, fists in the air, laughing.

As students shuffle past them leaving class, Roth reminds them, "A short reflection on this film is due next time. And please! Don't summarize, analyze. Why is this important? How does it connect to other things we learned?"

The following week, Roth passes back his students' homework essays. On Maria's he has written, "It's a B this time! See me about this, OK?"

Maria shows up in the doorway of his office the next day. "Some of the stuff you've been writing is so powerful. You are really getting there, Maria," Roth says, lowering his reading glasses and putting down a folder.

"Why isn't it an A, then?" Maria half-smiles, and pulls out her homework. "Is this really bad grammar?"

"Look, writing is primarily about ideas," Roth tells her. "Language, grammar, and style are important tools to express those ideas. But don't start by focusing on a few grammar mistakes, or you'll get stuck on that and ignore the bigger issues." He had adjusted the spelling and punctuation errors in one paragraph, and explains what he did, but he spends most of the time talking to Maria about other issues, the skills he deems essential "to getting your thoughts out" and "speaking out in the world." These include thesis, evidence, analysis, conclusion, and an original point of view. "Did you organize your thoughts in a way that made sense?" he asks her. "Did you back up your opinions with evidence? Did you go deep enough?"

Roth explains to Maria that she summarized and discussed *The Walkout* effectively, but when it came to analysis and conclusion, her writing seemed rushed. "What are the connections between these protests and the African American struggle for civil rights?" Maria gives him a few examples. Roth suggests that she think some more about why these efforts were ultimately successful. "How did these walkouts change things? Why are we studying this?"

A few weeks later Maria presents a research paper on equal access to education in front of her classmates. While rewriting her essay about *The Walkout*, she had discovered that some Latino parents were organizing school boycotts even before the launch of the civil rights movement. Discovering how school boycotts by Latino parents in the 1930s and 1940s helped contribute to the African American civil rights movement and the Supreme Court decision in *Brown v. Board of Education* (1954) was her favorite finding of the year. She couldn't wait to tell her friends Jesmyn and Destiny about it. When Maria wrote about it, she forgot all about her challenges with grammar. She had so much to say about why the courage of these parents to speak out mattered, how it changed everything in America and can be felt at Mission High to this day.

"Did you know that *Mendez v. Westminster* happened seven years before *Brown v. Board of Education?*" Maria proudly announces to her class. In the 1946 case, Latino parents won the first-ever antisegregation lawsuit in federal courts. "It helped the *Brown v. Board* attorneys to win their arguments before the Supreme Court," she explains to her classmates. "The *Mendez* case was the beginning of the end for *Plessy v. Ferguson* [1896], which said that 'separate but equal' is fine."

When she gets to the section about walkouts, Maria spends the largest portion of her presentation discussing the main reason walkouts succeeded and providing evidence of progress. "*The Walkout* shows that nothing happens if people don't make their demands loud. Nothing changes if people just sit quiet and cry," she argues. "In the movie, they said that as these protests spread in the next few years, Chicano college enrollment increased from 2 percent to 25 percent."

A few months later, Roth makes an announcement at the beginning of the class. "One more day before the big bad test, everyone!" he explains and passes out a practice version of the California Standards Test (CST), the final exam in US history as far as the state is concerned. Teachers don't have access to the actual multiple-choice questions, but the California Department of Education releases a few samples so that students can practice.

"Are they all just multiple-choice again this year?" Darrell asks. "That's it," Roth replies, "but it doesn't show exactly what you know—just what you remember. This is not how it will be in college."

"All I'm asking you to do is to take it seriously," Roth says. "Do it for the school. Let's do a quick review together."

"Who was the first Catholic president? Give me three things about the New Deal." Dozens of students shout out answers before Roth has a chance to pick a respondent. Darrell has his hand in the air permanently. The back and forth turns into shouting, and laughter takes over the classroom. "You are going to nail this test. Don't let them trick you!"

As Roth retreats to his desk, Maria stares at the rows of empty circles on her sample test. Her heart feels like it is climbing out of her chest. She feels a sharp, pounding pain in her head. The first multiple-choice question reads:

During the late 19th and 20th centuries, urban immigrants generally supported local political machines that:

(a) diminished the role of new immigrants in civic affairs

(b) were usually supported by urban reformers

(c) provided essential services to the immigrants

As always, Maria starts translating the English into Spanish. Then she gets to the word "diminished." She has seen this word many times before, but it was usually contextualized by many other words, and she could guess the meaning of the passage without knowing every term. In this short sentence, though, there are no hints. Maria tries to remember the word's meaning for a few minutes. Nothing.

"Affairs" is another word she has heard before, but can't remember the meaning of. She translates the rest of the sentence—"the role of new immigrants"—but that doesn't help. She takes a deep breath and translates the rest of the answers. B is a possibility, she thinks to herself. There are some connections, but something feels off. C seems right. But what about A? What if that is even closer to the right answer than C? There is no way of knowing. She fills in C for now.

"Five more minutes, everyone," Roth interrupts. Maria has spent too much time on the first five questions, and now she has to rush. She translates another page and randomly chooses answers for the rest.

She switches to the written section of the exam, and her leg stops bouncing. Roth always includes written sections in the tests he designs. He doesn't believe that "teaching to the test"—matching the curriculum to the format of the standardized tests, which are mostly multiple-choice—amounts to authentic learning.

When the bell rings, Maria keeps writing, and she doesn't stop until Roth collects the pages from her. Roth waits until the last student leaves the room, and they look over Maria's test together. She gets most of the answers wrong on the practice multiple-choice section, the only one that would have counted for the state. On Roth's essay question, she gets an A+.

∞∞∞∞∞∞∞∞∞∞∞∞

"Why doesn't my opinion about my school matter?" Maria asks me one late afternoon, as a senior, in her studio apartment in the Mission District. "Why does the government get the final say on whether my school is good or bad? Some people in my middle school told me that I'll never go to college. Then I came to Mission, and Mr. Velez made me feel so welcome. Mr. Roth expects more from me than anyone. How can they call our school 'bad'?" As we talk about her work at Mission, Maria tells me that discussions like the one about *The Walkout* were her favorite part of being in school.

"I'm shy. I don't speak that much in other classes, but Mr. Roth teaches me how to do it. He taught me that it's okay to argue even when I still have a lot of questions. Before, I would give up easily, and not defend my point of view. Now, I argue, and I love winning," she says, beaming, while her little cousin bounces on the bunk bed next to us. While debating is one of Maria's favorite things about school, she spends most of her time in Roth's class researching and writing papers. "That's how I prepare for the debates and learn how to express myself clearly."

"Mr. Roth tells me that I will get an A, if I am dedicated to working on my weaknesses and showing improvement. What I really like about his teaching is that he shows me exactly how I improve each time," Maria adds.

Maria says she prefers the documentaries and long articles Roth brings to class to her history textbooks and the standardized tests for which they are written. "Our textbook doesn't even mention the Civil War in El Salvador," she informs me. She uses the textbooks to make an outline of important dates, names, and events, and to look up definitions of new words like "laissez faire." She then uses the outlines to study for tests. But Maria doesn't remember many of these facts from year to year. What she recalls are topics she studied in-depth through her research papers, presentations, and art posters. She plugs a small flash card into my laptop to show me what she has learned.

"Oh, I really liked this one," she exclaims, opening a paper titled "Latinos in America in the 1920s." When her class focused on the Roaring Twenties, Maria discussed how Latino dances like the borero, cha cha cha, and tango entered mainstream American culture during this time. This led her to research Hollywood, where she made her favorite discovery. "Dolores del Rio was the first Mexican movie star to gain interest among white audiences," she wrote in her paper. "Dolores also showed the world that height does not matter at all if you want to be an actor. She was very famous and beautiful even though she was very short like me!"

"Last year, I became really interested in African American history, and their struggles," she explains, clicking through presentation files on Ida B. Wells, Frederick Douglass, Ella Baker, and W. E. B. DuBois. "Learning about this motivates me not to give up." She opens a paper from the previous year titled "Reconstruction Defeated." "I wanted to find out how the government justified treating African Americans unfairly with Jim Crow even though the Constitution said that all men and women were equal," she tells me. In the conclusion of her paper, Maria argued that local and state governments were using *Plessy v. Ferguson* to establish a "separate, but equal" doctrine that allowed them to treat people of color unfairly. "Through this paper, I became really interested in the 14th and 15th Amendments," she explains.

As I hand Maria's flash card back to her, she says that she will soon be applying to seven colleges and was recently elected Latino Student Club president. She is now helping new immigrant students at school. She is volunteering at a Mission senior housing project through the Latino Club, helping older immigrants in her neighborhood. "And in my free time, I babysit my little brother and my auntie's daughter," she tells me. "From now on, I only have time to talk with you over lunch at school."

Midway through Maria's senior year in 2012, she was watching *Waiting for "Superman"* (2010) in Mr. Velez's college expository writing class. They were learning about achievement gaps, test scores, teachers' unions, charter schools, and different solutions offered to "fix" schools like Mission. In one scene, D.C.'s then school chancellor, Michelle Rhee, is shown firing the principal of a low-scoring school, and then the film cuts to scenes of teachers and parents protesting school closures.

Maria sat in the back and seemed distracted. Her aunt Olivia had received a letter from US Immigration and Customs Enforcement (ICE) demanding that she leave the country within thirty days. Maria was worried about her aunt. She had recently read an article about suicides in detention centers. She found out that one of the major causes was sexual abuse of female detainees. Yet unlike the troubles at her school, this was an issue Maria felt equipped to handle. She recalled a paper she had written about the 14th Amendment and its guarantee of due process. She used her research skills to find out about the appeals process and to find a lawyer. The lawyer didn't speak fluent Spanish, so she acted as a translator.

"Which facts in the movie shocked you?" Velez probed as the movie ended.

"What we spend on prison inmates," one student called out.

"Why is it so hard to fire a bad teacher?" said another.

"I was shocked how *low test scores* are in California and D.C.," added a student with big headphones around his neck.

"California test scores are low, but the movie didn't mention we have the most immigrants here," countered a classmate. "Our English scores are bad, but that doesn't mean our school is bad."

"What would you do to make schools better?" Velez asked. Students took turns calling out responses as Velez wrote down their suggestions on a whiteboard: Make the tests more meaningful. . . . Allow our teachers to write these tests. . . . Don't test immigrant students in the first two years. . . . Give more money to public schools in

California. . . . Ask students which schools are good and bad.

"Could they close Mission like those schools in D.C.?" Maria asked.

The shouting stopped.

"We won't let them," another student responded, and the class burst out laughing.

Chapter 2

Mr. Roth

"Your essay on the *Mendez v. Westminster* case was so powerful," Roth says as he rests his arm on Maria's shoulder in the hallway one chilly winter morning in 2011. "You really nailed it this time." He concentrates on Maria's face. Roth is dressed in a black, long-sleeved shirt, black jeans, and black shoes. His closely cropped hair has lost most of its pepper.

"Huh? Me? Thanks, Mr. Roth." Maria stops for a brief moment to soak in the praise before she walks through the classroom door. Clenching a thick bundle of tissues in her hand, she looks out an open window for a moment, smiling.

The J-Church train outside shrieks along the rails near the school. Maria closes the window before settling into her desk. Propping the classroom door open with his right hand, Roth scans every face in the morning rush of students flowing through the hall.

"Have you been avoiding me, Pablo?" Roth shouts. "I saw you near the cafeteria yesterday and you didn't even say hello." Pablo smiles reluctantly. "Am I going to see you after school today to look over your outline?"

"Yes, I will be there," Pablo heaves a long, dramatic sigh, with arms akimbo.

"How are you doing, Darrell?" Roth turns his head toward a tall student walking into his classroom. "Are you coming to see me after school today for a test review?" Darrell nods in agreement as he joins the rest of the students.

Ten minutes after the bell rings, Jesmyn slowly cracks open Roth's classroom door, peeking through with one eye before she tip-toes inside. The class is quiet. Students are writing. Everyone is working on the "Do Now," a fifteen-minute review exercise on topics students studied in the last class. Today there are three "short identifications," events or ideas students have to describe in their own words in no more than three sentences. There is also a short, one-page essay in which students have to discuss the significance of a historic event and connect it to other topics they have already studied.

"I'm late. I know, I know," Jesmyn whispers to Roth as she moves toward her desk in the front row. She sits down, planting her legs widely on the floor. She puts her red glasses on and reads the instructions on the board, "Test Review. Twenties and the Start of the Great Depression (15 pts)."

"Look at you, kiddo!" Roth walks over to Jesmyn and says quietly, "Showed up even though you are upset about being late," he smiles. Her pinched lips relax into a smile.

Roth gives Jesmyn a sheet with instructions and whispers, "Respond to each of these questions. Briefly explain the Scopes Trial, who was Henry Ford, and the assembly line. Then a short essay on who supported Prohibition and why."

"Whoa, this is too much, Mr. Roth!" she exclaims out loud. "How much stuff do I need to write for each?"

"As short as you can," he whispers back. "Just include the most relevant information. You can look in the textbook, but you must use your own words. If you copy, you don't learn. But you don't need the textbook. Just get started, and you'll see that you know much more than you think." Jesmyn exhales a long breath and writes her name on a blank piece of paper. Roth is setting up the projector while students are writing.

"Two more minutes, everyone!" Roth interrupts.

"No!" Destiny and Jesmyn protest.

"See, this is my problem." Roth enters the middle of the classroom. "You don't listen to me. I say two more minutes and you say, 'Leave me alone, I'm writing!'"

"OK, Destiny," Roth says five minutes later. "Tell me one group that supported Prohibition and why."

"Women's groups concerned with domestic violence," Destiny replies confidently.

"Great. Jesmyn?"

"Businesses."

"Why?"

"They didn't want drunk workers."

"That's exactly right. Who else?"

"Church groups, because they felt it was a sin to drink," Maria adds.

Jesmyn jumps in with her hand up: "Oh, gangsters rise in Chicago because of Prohibition."

"That's a really good point. Why is this happening?" Roth probes.

"They get into the business of bootlegs, and Al Capone had the law on his payroll," Jesmyn rushes to explain.

Darrell raises his hand and adds, "Anti-immigration groups also supported Prohibition."

"That's true. Why are they doing that?" Roth inquires.

"They say immigrants are drunks and are destroying American morals and should not be allowed here," Darrell explains.

"That's right," Roth nods his head.

"Mr. Roth, what's a bootleg again?" Marvin jumps in.

"Emilio, could you answer Marvin's question?"

"Selling something illegally."

"That's right. And I know that none of you are bootleggers," Roth smiles. "Oh, no. You don't copy CDs. No, I've never seen that."

"All kidding aside," Roth continues, as he moves back to the center of the room again. "We've been studying the Twenties for a while, and this will be on the test in a few weeks. Remember, if we are doing something in class, it will be on my test. I'm studying with you. You have my e-mail and my phone number. Come see me after school if you need help with any of these topics we went over today."

Roth turns on the projector and a black-and-white photograph appears on the projection board: Dorothea Lange's *Migrant Mother* (1936).

"What do you see here?" Roth asks while students flex their wrists.

Darrell raises his hand and answers, "A mother who is moving around and struggling to feed her children."

"There is something very thoughtful about this picture," Marvin says.

"That's so true," Roth chimes in. "What do you see that makes you say that?"

Darrell raises his hand again. "Children are tired and hopeless, but the mother doesn't look hopeless."

"What makes you say that?" Roth probes.

"Children turned their heads away, like they are ashamed," Maria comments. "But the mother is not ashamed. You see perseverance and determination in her eyes."

"Exactly," Roth jumps in. "As Maria pointed out, this photo is not exploitative. Lange shows us both the struggle and the inner strength of the mother." More of Lange's photographs appear on the projection board. As students take turns describing what they see, Roth reviews previous material—the Dust Bowl, the Bonus Army, the beginning of Social Security—and connects it to the faces students see in the black-and-white stills. After the Lange introduction, he moves into the center of the classroom.

"OK, Emilio, you gotta sit down," Roth scans the room quickly. "And put the phone away, please."

"Jesmyn, are you ready to present?" She nods and comes up to the front of the class.

"How many of you have heard of the Tulsa Race Riot of 1921?" Jesmyn asks her classmates. Two hands go up. A few weeks earlier, Roth had offered students their choice of preselected research projects that were not in the textbooks or required by the state standards. The Tulsa Race Riot of 1921 had jumped out at Jesmyn right away. She admired her boyfriend's grandmother, Edna Tobie, and knew that she was originally from Tulsa, Oklahoma. So one Sunday Jesmyn had spent the whole day at Tobie's house talking to her and her sons about life in Tulsa before the violence broke out. Tobie had described how despite the legacy of slavery and the Jim Crow laws, black people in Tulsa created a proud, self-sustaining community with jobs, churches, and two newspapers.

The next day Jesmyn had stayed up until 2:00 a.m. summarizing her findings and preparing for the presentation. She wanted her classmates to know that despite centuries of slavery and exclusion, black people always found ways to survive and thrive. She wanted them to care about Edna and the Tulsa community as much as she did after hearing Edna's story. As she wrote, she looked up more precise words in the thesaurus, trying to craft more moving sentences. She reviewed drafts on lined, three-hole-punched paper and threw them on the floor if she wasn't satisfied. Each new draft felt a little better, more refined, and engaging, and sounded more like her.

"Tulsa had the second-largest African American community in the United States at the time," Jesmyn says to the class. "More than ten thousand African Americans lived in the Greenwood District. There were black-owned businesses, two newspapers, churches, and a real sense of pride in people. The riots started with a rumor that an African American man had raped a white woman. These rumors were typical at the time. Hundreds of white men attacked the community. They burned it down. Mrs. Tobie's mother was ten at the time, but she remembers holding her mother's hand, looking at their burned-down neighborhood filled with white ash, smoke, and people crying. . . . The local government didn't come to defend Tulsa residents from the violence. No justice was served then or later. Mrs. Tobie explained to me that because no justice was served, some older folks blame it now for the young men's distrust of the government. Young men don't trust that the police are there to protect them either. It made me realize that even though it happened a long time ago, there are deep, deep scars in Tulsa. Mrs. Tobie and her sons couldn't stop talking about it even though they weren't even alive then."

"I want to be a social worker one day and work in my community," Jesmyn reflects in the conclusion of her presentation. "It is important for me to understand where deep scars come from."

∞∞∞∞∞∞∞∞∞∞∞

It's 7:40 a.m. on a Friday, two weeks later, and junior Darrell cracks open the door of Roth's classroom. Dressed in a Mission High football jersey, Darrell looks nervous. Like many African American students Roth encounters, he doesn't think of himself as a good "test-taker." Darrell has arranged two review sessions with Roth to prepare for the upcoming test later today.

"I'm ready for you, Darrell!" says Roth.

Darrell nods and takes off his headphones as he enters the room. Tall and slender, he towers over his teacher. He takes his usual spot in the back of the class, gets his notebook out of the backpack, and looks for the right page.

"OK, what's the Monroe Doctrine?" Roth begins.

"The US policy in early nineteenth century that established, hmm . . . Latin America as its sphere of influence," Darrell responds in a calm, quiet voice.

"That's exactly right!" Roth says and smiles at Darrell, who takes a bite out of his bagel. "Who was Lili'uokalani?" asks Roth.

"The Queen of Hawaii who was overthrown at the end of the nineteenth century," Darrell replies.

"You are going to ace this test," Roth tells Darrell after an intense, twenty-minute drill. Soon after, the bell goes off and twenty-six juniors shuffle into the US history class. They pass a white dry-erase board where Roth has written in large, blue letters: "There will be an essay on the test today. I didn't want it, but an evil spirit took control of me and made me do it!"

Roth, like many teachers across the country, doesn't believe that the multiple-choice tests that constitute the majority of state standardized tests promote or measure learning, but he is not against *all* tests. In fact, Roth has written articles, published by the Bay Area Writing Project, arguing for the importance of tests created by teachers to promote retention of knowledge and academic confidence. But the tests Roth and his colleagues in the social studies department design don't look anything like the standardized ones students take once a year.

In Roth's class this morning, students are spending the entire hour writing. First, they are asked to construct two- to three-sentence responses identifying key historical events and concepts. In the second half of the test, students answer an essay question in which they are required to show evidence of their understanding of why a particular historical event took place and how it connects to other themes they have studied, then analyze the significance of the event today.

To get an A on this written test, Darrell can't just get away with relying on his memorization skills and "test-taking" strategies, like including exact words from the question in his first few sentences or detecting questions that are meant to "trick" him and eliminating the least likely answers first. Remembering dates and names of individuals and significant events is very important, but not sufficient for an A, either. Not only does he have to construct an essay providing accurate content, effective summaries of key events, and clear organization, Darrell also has to form his own thesis, provide the most relevant evidence, interrogate the points of view of others, and sustain an argument to bolster his point of view. Darrell has to integrate all of these different pieces and state something that he has considered deeply.

Even the most sophisticated multiple-choice questions can't measure these skills, and yet, when Roth was teaching at Thurgood Marshall High School in San Francisco, a state official came to meet with the social sciences department in 2004 and told Roth and his colleagues to eliminate writing from their classrooms. Standardized tests didn't include writing, the state official said, as he encouraged teachers to "teach to the test" or spend more time creating worksheets that mimicked multiple-choice questions students would encounter at the end of the year. Roth and his colleagues ignored the advice of the state official, but studies show that teaching to the test has increased across the country since the NCLB was implemented in 2001. In *Hugging the Middle*, Cuban found that more lesson time is spent preparing students for tests, and the curriculum is being narrowed to what is on those tests.

This means many teachers are cutting out writing and hands-on projects to focus on lower-level skills emphasizing rote memorization. Over 70 percent of nearly fifteen thousand districts in the nation have cut back time spent on social studies, science, art, and music in order to have more time for teaching reading and math, which was used by the federal and state governments to grade schools.[1]

Before Darrell took classes with Mr. Roth, he struggled with tests in social sciences and humanities. He thought of himself primarily as a "math and science" person. "I had a reading disability that we only found out and started working on in the ninth grade," Darrell explains to me. Until then, tests that required reading with a time limit were very challenging for Darrell, and because he struggled with reading, he didn't think he could be a good writer. Instead, he focused all of his energy on math and science and usually felt ahead of his classmates in those subjects.

By his junior year, Darrell started to feel a little less anxious about the tests Mr. Roth was giving in his US history class. "Mr. Roth's tests were some of the toughest at school, but he didn't leave you hanging," Darrell says. He feels that he had plenty of opportunities to engage with the material and make sense of it all before the test came around. And unlike some other classes, which offer a few high-stakes tests and an occasional paper, Roth's tests were not the only way students gathered points for a final grade. Every "Do Now," classroom essay, homework, research paper, and art poster contributed to Darrell's final grade. Roth's final was an in-depth research paper.

"Standardized tests pick away at students with the apparent goal of uncovering the gaps in student knowledge," Roth explains the difference between a standardized test designed by a psychometrician in some distant testing company and his own. "I try to create tests that allow students to demonstrate what they know about a subject we have deeply studied, what they understand about why an historic event took place, and what connects the past to their own lives. My tests ask students to draw from all that they know. They have an opportunity to shine, and it builds their commitment and confidence."

Neuroscientists have found that such an approach to learning leads to "consolidation" or actual physical changes in the brain, which rote memorization doesn't produce. Eric R. Kandel, a Nobel Prize–winning neuropsychiatrist who pioneered research in the development and persistence of memory, suggests that we learn best by association, rather than through memorization of disconnected concepts and random phrases detached from meaningful context. Associative learning, which consists of engaging with concepts from slightly different angles, working with them in different formats, and investigating related questions, is essential for *consolidation*, a key element in the process of building long-term memory. "For a memory to persist," Kandel writes in *In Search of Memory*, "the incoming information must be thoroughly and deeply processed. This is accomplished by attending to the information and associating it meaningfully and systematically with knowledge already well established in memory." Without proper encoding and consolidation, Kandel suggests, we are unable to then store and retrieve those memories, a key function for permanent learning. Kandel and other researchers discovered that the process of deep learning changes the physical structure of the brain itself, strengthening the synaptic connections that facilitate learning, a process known as neuroplasticity.[2]

Henry L. Roediger III and Mark A. McDaniel, professors of psychology at Washington University in St. Louis and authors of *Make It Stick: The Science of Successful Learning*, have come to similar conclusions in their own research and synthesis of other studies. They write that passively listening to lectures; re-reading, highlighting, and underlining texts; and then cramming a week before a high-stakes midterm or final exam don't work. These most common practices, researchers argue, create the illusion of mastery, but gains from such learning fade quickly.[3] Long-term learning occurs when students are consistently asked to apply their knowledge in a variety of daily formats, such as quizzes, regular discussions, projects, and essays.

"Any last-minute review questions?" Roth asks on this Friday morning, as he passes out the tests he designed last night. "Why was the crushing of the Philippines so brutal?" Darrell's seatmate asks. "Great question. Anyone in the class wants to tackle that?" Roth asks. Many hands go up. "Remember: don't summarize, analyze. Why is this important? Why are we studying this? How does it connect to other things we have learned?" Roth reminds students, as the testing clock starts ticking.

Students hunch over their papers; quiet scribbling takes over the room. The ear-piercing screech of an ambulance siren invades the room. Darrell calmly flexes his wrists. He then gets out of his chair, stretches out his slender frame, and walks over to the electric pencil sharpener. The sound of the pencil sharpener blocks out the ambulance siren

for a moment. Maria has a question and raises her hand.
Roth walks over to her and they talk in a low voice. Josh is
scrawling something on the back of his classmate's chair.
Roth spots him and walks over to him next.

"Test-taking is a tenuous process," Roth explains to me.
"Students can get stuck on little concepts or the spelling of
a complicated word. If you completely disengage, they trip
and fall, and many don't get up. At the same time, I also
work hard not to intervene too much. Not to mess it up."

Another ambulance flies down the street. Jesmyn
drums her fingers against the wooden desk, then lowers
her head and keeps writing. Rosa finishes first and proudly
walks over to Roth with her test. "Congratulations," he
says as he staples the pages together. Rosa is standing at
the front, behind Roth's desk, quietly dancing and beaming at the other students.

The bell rings an end to this hour-and-a-half-long test.
Some students get up and hand their tests to Rosa to sta-
ple. The sound of quiet scribbling speeds up.

"Mr. Roth, how do you spell Guantanamo?" Jesmyn
asks.

Roth writes it on the board.

Mario gets out of his desk and jumps around in a quiet
celebratory dance. "Mr. Roth, you need to make this test
shorter next time," he says as he drops off his test. He
leaves the room with his right hand raised in a salute.

"Will you have to grade these all weekend?" Rosa asks.

"I know! That's what I'm freaking out about right now,"
Roth replies.

Five minutes after the bell, Darrell is still scribbling
furiously, occasionally shaking out his wrists. Maria comes

back to the classroom with a lunch tray in her hands and offers Darrell a piece of orange.

"No, thank-you," Darrell politely declines. "Can I have another piece of paper, Mr. Roth?"

"Darrell is going for the world record this time," Roth tells Maria.

"I think I'll do pretty well on this one," Darrell says with a deadpan look on his face, and keeps writing.

∞∞∞∞∞∞∞∞∞∞∞∞∞∞∞

I visited Roth during Mission's spring break in 2013. He was sitting by a gas fireplace in the living room of the two-bedroom home he shares with his longtime partner, Judith Mirkinson. In the hallway the photos of their children—Ona, Gemma, Max, and Jack—take up most of the walnut-paneled wall space, marking different phases in their lives. "They all graduated from San Francisco public schools," he says with a smile.

Before Roth became a teacher in 1988, he had been an activist for decades. Growing up in New York City in the early 1960s, he was part of a generation of white youth profoundly influenced by the civil rights movement. He joined the student branch of the Congress for Racial Equality (CORE) when he was fourteen years old and demonstrated outside of his Queens high school to protest de facto segregation as part of a one-day school boycott called by a coalition of civil rights groups.

When Roth arrived at Columbia University as a freshman in 1967, he found himself in a center of student rebellion. He became engaged with Students for a Democratic

Society (SDS), which in his second year on campus helped to bring the university to a grinding halt over two main issues: Columbia's participation in military research that supported the war in Vietnam and its plan to build a university gym that was encroaching on the neighboring Harlem community. When black students took over one university building in the spring of 1968 and renamed it Malcolm X University, the predominantly white SDS took over other buildings on campus. In his book, *Bringing the War Home*, historian Jeremy Varon notes that as national and international media descended on Columbia, student protests all over the country gained unprecedented recognition and influence in the United States.[4] Varon argues that the Columbia protests were most significant for the connections they made between the issues of racism, militarism, economic inequality, and "student power." Columbia eventually called in the New York City police to clear out the buildings. They arrested seven hundred people and injured dozens, Roth informed me.

"That year radicalized me," he remembers. "I learned a lot about power and privilege, black leadership, and building complex alliances. The Columbia protests were so effective because black students in the Student Afro-American Society (SAS) made the gym a central issue and connected the campus organizing to the Harlem community. This was the key to the Columbia strike, but white radical kids got all of the attention and became the national figures in the media. The leading role of black students was written out of the story." Roth's time at Columbia also gave him his first taste of teaching. While in college, he worked as a counselor for middle school–aged kids at the

YMCA in Manhattan and at the Project Double Discovery, a program that brought high school students from Black and Puerto Rican communities onto the campus to take classes and live in the dorms.

By 1969 Roth had dropped out of Columbia in the wake of another year of student protests, a thirty-day jail sentence for his participation, and pending disciplinary action by the university. While organizing with SDS in Chicago and at the time of the assassination of Black Panther leader Fred Hampton, Roth joined the Weather Underground organization, a more militant arm of SDS fighting to stop the violence in Vietnam and killings of civil rights activists. For the next seven years Roth lived underground, resurfacing in 1977. He pled guilty to a series of misdemeanor charges connected with a demonstration in Chicago in 1969 and received two years' probation.

Roth moved to San Francisco in 1977 and became a member of the anti-imperialist group Prairie Fire Organizing Committee. His future partner, Judith Mirkinson, worked for the organization and was one of the first people he met there. Roth later joined the Pledge of Resistance, a Central American solidarity group, traveling four times to Central America during the US-backed wars in El Salvador and Nicaragua. Throughout this time, Roth moved from one job to another to pay the bills. He worked as a waiter, a preschool teacher, and a medical transcriber. In 1992 he helped found the Haiti Action Committee, after the coup that overthrew the democratically elected government of President Jean-Bertrand Aristide, and since then has been involved with the nonprofit, which now supports locally operated schools, hospitals, and community-based earthquake relief organizations. In 1982 he decided to go back to school and become a history teacher. He raced through San Francisco State University, taking extra credits each semester so that he could finish his BA and then get his teaching credentials. At San Francisco State, most classes Roth took focused on lesson planning for teaching history; in retrospect, they were not helpful without real classroom context. The traditional content felt dry. Discussions of significant historical changes were centered around one famous individual, such as Franklin D. Roosevelt or Dr. Martin Luther King Jr., overlooking what Roth believed was the fascinating nuance and complexity of history and the role of everyday people in social change.

Roth firmly believes that teaching history should be all about helping students realize how many different people shape it. When students see that historical change is not about one famous person or event, "they see the potential power of their own voices in the process of changing their own world," he explains. When students learn about the many ordinary people who have found ways to resist oppression, colonialism, and slavery, they are inspired to engage more deeply with the academic subject and their own communities. Roth never stops looking for vivid narratives that can illustrate how something happened in a more nuanced way and why it matters to this day. This lifetime learning process has always kept him engaged with the subject he loves to teach. If he was relying entirely on prepackaged curriculum designed by someone else or recycling what he created himself year after year, he would lose his connection with history. If he lost his engagement with history, he couldn't guide his students in creating their own.

"The content defines who I am as a teacher," he explains. "I'll research the topic until it hits me as a teacher. I'll have something particular to say. It's about finding an ability to connect with students about history. It's very different from handing in a worksheet, grading it, giving it back. Then doing a project, an activity. That's good, but if you don't have that other part where you are really engaged with the content yourself, the class doesn't spark. In our social studies department at Mission teachers spend hours at home researching, filling in the gaps in the textbooks, building new curriculum, discussing and sharing it with each other. It's an exciting intellectual process."

Despite Roth's very personal connection to history and the lessons he learned as an organizer, he didn't feel fully prepared when he first walked through the doors of Luther Burbank Middle School in San Francisco in 1988. "Can I really teach thirty students at the same time?" he recalls thinking to himself, completely overwhelmed as he walked through the hallway enveloped in the cloud of teen shouting and laughter, disrupted by the occasional squawking of walkie-talkies. "Can I survive?"

In his first years as a teacher, his peers and two decades of activist experience helped him much more than his formal educational training. "The most important thing I learned as an activist was to really listen to other communities," he says. "Just listen, not see myself as the center of everything. When I started teaching at Burbank, I'd never been to Sunnydale, Oakdale, Double Rock neighborhoods in San Francisco. I'd heard about them. Now I was teaching students from those areas. They had a tremendous amount to impart to me. So did their parents. That sense of humility is completely connected to equity. That process changed me, and it deepened my own understanding of what fighting for social justice means."

In his first year at Burbank, Roth invested a lot of time in building deep relationships with students, parents, and successful teachers. Burbank was a large inner-city school, and many teachers struggled with discipline. But there were also veteran teachers who ran tight classrooms and a core of younger teachers who were determined to learn. Roth observed the classes of veteran teachers and absorbed their techniques.

Roth knew right away he was happy teaching. He felt he had found his calling. His classes often crackled with energy and excitement. But there were also many challenges. The lesson plans he taught didn't go over as smoothly as he expected. Some of the content wasn't clicking. He didn't always know how to break it down in a way that made sense for students. A few students looked bored, and some were disruptive. As Roth replayed the entire lesson in his head at the end of each day, he would rewrite his plan for the next day to try out something different. Some days it worked, and his students seemed more engaged. But just as he got comfortable, some new issue always seemed to appear out of nowhere.

When Roth was in his second year of teaching, he met Pirette McKamey, a young, energetic African American history teacher and a writer in her first year. Her sense of humor, intellectual curiosity, directness, and lack of pretense stood out right away to Roth. The two teachers started meeting informally to share their trials and triumphs with each other. Soon after, McKamey invited Roth to observe her class. "I was stunned," Roth recalls almost twenty-five years later. "Whenever a student answered something, Pirette would stop the whole class for a second. 'That is so interesting!' she would say. I could tell that she was really hearing her students. She found her thirteen-year-olds intellectually fascinating. She was the opposite of a teacher who runs around with predetermined notions. She was very clear about what she was teaching, but she was completely present, responsive to students right from the beginning. I learned to step back and listen to students more from Pirette."

While many teachers planned their lessons in isolation, McKamey and Roth started meeting more formally after school to plan lessons together. In 1990 McKamey suggested that they co-create a whole new "unit" together, one that would be more fun and intellectually stimulating than some of the prepackaged lesson plans and textbooks many teachers used. Units are typically a collection of lesson plans organized around a central theme or a book that students will investigate in-depth for several weeks. Engaging units typically cross disciplines, such as McKamey's unit "Quests," in which students study different characters through fiction and nonfiction and venture into geography, psychology, history, and anthropology to examine the deeper meaning behind different types of quests while developing their reading and writing skills.

Drawing from her knowledge as a writer, McKamey felt that units should be planned and taught as coherent stories. She argued that the daily lesson planning approach, which introduced separate bits and pieces of content and skills, wasn't the most effective way to teach and learn. Thinking of units as stories would allow teachers to point out connections between different lessons and identify the many nuanced shadings and overlaps of different concepts, McKamey argued.

"Pirette was the impetus for our big projects, like the West Africa Project," Roth recalls their first four-week unit focusing on the history of Mali, Ghana, and Senegal, among other countries. The project included hands-on group projects, like building a three-dimensional, four-foot replica of the Western Sahara desert out of clay and rocks; creative writing assignments; and research papers. It culminated with presentations in front of the whole school and parents. The unit was a success, and the district asked McKamey and Roth to present it to other teachers.

The West Africa Project was a turning point in Roth and McKamey's early partnerships, but the process of creating their own unit raised a new series of difficult questions. While units with hands-on projects and more intellectually rigorous content engaged students in visible ways, did this translate to measurable increases in learning and skills? What was the best way to teach content for both mastery and measurable growth in intellectual skills, such as ability to synthesize information, analyze different texts, interrogate the arguments of others, and communicate complex ideas effectively? And then there are skills that independent thinkers have. They don't just follow the conventions of correctness; they bend rules and use their own voice.

McKamey says that at some point during their second year of working together, Roth took the lead in the argument that writing was the best tool to teach and assess content mastery and intellectual growth. Literacy can't just be about reading, he argued. Every educated person in the modern world has to have strong writing skills to succeed in the workplace and academia and to fully participate in society. Writing can also provide a powerful platform for students to "talk back" to the texts and their teachers. "As they talk back, they engage with their knowledge in a variety of formats and extract their own meaning," Roth explains.

Writing also helped Roth and McKamey teach each student individually. Rather than simply identifying "wrong" and "right" answers in worksheets or multiple-choice tests, teachers could use a student's writing to trace the thinking that led to specific "knots" in understanding, identify missing skills, and connect them with targeted feedback or tools that would help students learn.

Educational psychologists and theorists call this kind of practice teaching in the "zone of proximal development": that place where we can't yet learn by ourselves, but we can with targeted assistance, modeling from an experienced coach, and constructive feedback.[5] With frequent practice, students internalize these tools and eventually can use them independently.

Today there is a broad research-based consensus that effective writing instruction is key to literacy: it teaches us to think more deeply and speak more precisely. But teaching writing outside of an English department was not the norm at Burbank and continues to be rare in schools today, because No Child Left Behind placed greater emphasis on testing in reading rather than writing.

In 1992 Roth became the chair of the social studies department at Burbank. He initiated collaborative meetings between history and English teachers to promote a systematic approach to teaching writing across disciplines. Roth and McKamey started developing curriculum on how to teach analysis: a key skill for expository writing, which helps students make the necessary leap from subjective opinion and generalizations to detailed and thoughtful consideration of the evidence and different points of view. Teachers still developed their own units, but a typical eighth grader now finished the school year at Burbank having thoroughly practiced and produced twelve different pieces of writing: essays, analysis of primary documents, short research papers, and some creative assignments like poetry or short stories.

When Roth and McKamey proposed writing as a systemic approach to learning and assessments at Burbank, some teachers accepted these changes; others did not. So Roth and McKamey did what committed teachers all over the country have been doing for years: they formed their own, informal group and set their own agenda for classroom reforms. Within a few weeks, a group of six teachers started meeting after school and discussing specific learning goals using writing. "What constitutes good academic writing?" teachers asked each other and started making collective lists: thesis, topic sentences, textual evidence, and conclusion, among many others. They then created additional lists describing precise skills that would be introduced, practiced, and explored in each grade to help students master strong academic writing, including the following: "write cogent paragraphs; respond to quotes from the text; use effective vocabulary; articulate author's purpose; write a multi-paragraph essay; read grade-level texts." The teachers could now identify how they needed to support students to succeed in each of these skills.

Such systemic, collective planning is far too rare in American schools today. Teachers need time to do it, but schools don't have a consistent mechanism in place to prioritize such processes. Teachers in high-achieving countries like Japan and Finland teach about six hundred or fewer hours each school year, leaving them ample time to prepare, revise their lessons, and learn from their experiences. By contrast, American teachers are near the top of the list when it comes to instructional time and spend about 716 hours in the classroom a year, leaving them with significantly less time for planning and analysis of student outcomes.[6]

As McKamey, Roth, and their colleagues struggled to implement the early version of their own teacher-led classroom reforms at Burbank, they enrolled in an African American–led summer program in 1996 geared to black teachers and educators working with African American students. Organized by the Center for Applied Cultural Studies and Educational Achievement (CACSEA), the program was designed to introduce teachers to a long history and rich body of research on effective teaching practiced by African American educators.[7] While many of the techniques Roth and McKamey learned through CACSEA had been used by African American teachers for decades, these methods were overlooked by most education schools.

Rather than emphasizing educational theory, as most education schools do, CACSEA scholars offered research-based instructional strategies that work.

During the summer Roth and McKamey learned about the importance of four Rs: rhythm, repetition, recitation, and relationships. Rhythm of the class refers to the importance of alternating teaching activities among a lecture, reading, writing, individual practice, and group work. Teachers learned about the importance of pacing the class: not spending too much or too little time on any activity. Several workshops led discussions about effective classroom management, emphasizing the importance of maintaining structure and routines and providing clear instructions on what students need to do and how to do it. When teachers don't have clear structure and don't provide explicit instructions, too often "classroom management" defaults to prison-like crowd control: endless comments like "don't do this" or "behave this way," and noise management. Sessions were provided on how to build academic relationships and how to spot engagement—rather than presume misbehavior or "acting out"—and connect it to work in a disciplined way.

CACSEA scholars argued that drilling grammar and vocabulary in isolation doesn't work. McKamey took additional summer classes in phonology and morphology at the University of California at Berkeley shortly afterward. She spent the next twenty years refining curriculum that integrates teaching of grammar, vocabulary, and language development in social studies.

Language and literacy scholar Noma LeMoine led workshops on the origins of African American English—a form of communication with distinct grammar, patterns, and roots in West Africa—to help teachers in the program shed stigmas associated with black English. She presented studies in which participants associated black English with illiteracy, slang, or substandard English. She argued that teachers can't succeed in their craft if they look at the home languages of their students as a deficit.[8] Teachers also read work by Arnetha Ball, professor of education at Stanford, whose research focuses on specific teaching strategies on how to effectively build on the home cultures of students to teach formal English writing. She argues that effective teaching means adding to the home cultures of students, rather than trying to replace them.

The CACSEA summer program opened up a world of research, with specific tools teachers could put in their pockets and use in the classroom tomorrow, McKamey says. Most important, the program highlighted the importance of viewing all students as intellectuals, noticing their individual brilliance rather than seeing "problems" or "empty vessels." "Often, the discussion of African American students begins with a model of deficits: list of students that are giving teachers a hard time," Roth recalls. "And we miss this level of black students who perform well and contribute a high level of intellectual exchange. It's very important to notice and name that. If you don't, all the negatives dominate and despite all that talk of high expectations, your expectations slowly become lower and lower."

Around the same time, in the mid-1990s, McKamey and Roth connected with the National Writing Project (NWP), based at the University of California, Berkeley. The nonprofit put on a workshop at Burbank and stated its support for classroom educators who taught writing. In its book for teachers, *Because Writing Matters*, the NWP argues that until the 1970s, the teaching of writing was rooted in a nineteenth-century model of language development and pedagogy of memorization and skill drills. It focused on essential skills: building vocabulary, identifying parts of speech, diagramming sentences, mastering grammar and punctuation, and following conventions. There was very little attention paid to the more conceptual side of writing, one that focuses on the ways writers construct meaning and develop a writing process that allows them to think more deeply. In addition, during this time most educators also assumed that reading should be taught before writing, and emphasis on mechanical errors overshadowed all other conceptual skills.[9]

Eventually decades of research concluded that isolated skill drills failed to improve writing and new schools of thinking emerged that swung the pendulum of teaching to another extreme. By the early 1990s teachers mostly focused on free-writes, creative expression, and journals, often overlooking grammar and formal writing skills.[10] At the time when Roth and McKamey joined the local chapter of the NWP—the Bay Area Writing Project (BAWP)—NWP aimed to promote a more balanced approach to teaching writing: providing opportunities to practice basic skills and learn how to think and write critically and creatively.

At BAWP, Roth, McKamey, and their colleagues had an opportunity to hone in on what works in teaching writing. They brought multiple drafts of their students' writing to talk about grading and the science behind commenting on student work. When teachers provide feedback on writing, many default to a "what's wrong with this paper" commenting strategy, Roth says. They are competent critics of student writing, but they struggle to form their critical responses to facilitate growth in skills. This requires the ability to read student work as a person who is open-minded to the writer's voice and unique strengths as an intellectual. When students can sense that a teacher has the skills to hear their voices and see their strengths, they are much more likely to push themselves academically and work on their weaknesses and basic skills at the same time.

Making a shift from being a proctor to being a teacher requires empathy for the individual writing process, McKamey says. This means teachers have to write themselves and be closely familiar with all of the challenges that come with the craft of writing. McKamey and Roth wrote articles for other teachers through BAWP in which they merged the teaching strategies they had learned through various workshops with their own knowledge and practical wisdom from their classrooms.

In 1999 Roth and McKamey decided to leave Burbank. The school had hired its fourth principal in a short span of time, and the situation at the school felt chaotic. The teacher-led research and action committee that Roth and McKamey had built up with their colleagues was fraying at the edges due to instability at the administrative level and increasing pressure from the district to raise test scores. They both wanted to teach high school and work at a school with a significant population of African American students. There weren't that many options to choose from.

Even though they wanted to teach at the same school, they each took one of the few available jobs at different schools.

Roth took a history position at J. Eugene McAteer High School in San Francisco. McKamey went to work as an English teacher at Thurgood Marshall High School. When McAteer was shut down in 2002, Roth went to work at Marshall—which had even less stability than Burbank—making it difficult to build and maintain teacher-led school reforms. Marshall High went through one principal after another in the span of six years, Roth says. McKamey ended up leaving for Mission High in 2004, and Roth joined her there in 2007.

Transitions between schools are never easy, Roth says. Stability is very important for quality teaching and learning. "I told myself, Mission will be my last stop. It takes years to build up relationships and a certain reputation. People at the school know you. Families know you. Students know you. Their brothers and sisters know you. When you move, you have to re-establish everything. The first three months you feel like a newcomer. I remember going to Pirette in my first month at Mission and saying, 'I don't think I'm doing well here.' And she said, 'You are doing just fine.'"

For the past six years as the social studies department chair at Mission, Roth and his colleagues have tried to build up the same kind of "bottom-up," "teacher-led" work that he and McKamey tried to grow in every school where they worked. At Mission, an evolving group of teacher-leaders organize opportunities for their colleagues to plan lessons together, analyze student outcomes, and review the latest research together. Roth and McKamey also coach at least seven teachers every year, and they are focusing on helping other teachers bring more writing into every classroom. The social studies department now has higher grades and attendance among African American and Latino students than any other department at Mission.

The professional partnership between Roth and McKamey that started in 1989 has continued for nearly three decades. Both teachers say that it helped them grow more than any other professional development outside of school.

∞∞∞∞∞∞∞∞∞∞∞

On a late afternoon in February 2014, Roth is meeting with a senior named Kendrick. Kendrick had written an essay in his ethnic studies (honors) class that caught Roth's attention. It was a reflection about Michael Sam, the defensive football lineman from the University of Missouri who had publicly come out as gay earlier that week.[11] Roth had brought a few articles on Sam's coming out to class and after a discussion, asked students to write a one-page reflection at the end of the class. When Roth was collecting assignments, Kendrick—a bright student who frequently struggled with written assignments—asked Roth if he could take it home to finish. "I want to say more," he said. "I want to read more sources at home and say more about what Sam wanted."

"You and I have been working on your writing for two years," Roth begins this informal conversation. "You have ideas, you can get your words out, but you don't always elaborate or write in paragraphs."

"I know, I don't," Kendrick nods in agreement, looking down at his white sneakers.

"But here, you really elaborate," Roth points to specific paragraphs. "You write in paragraphs. You structured it like a formal essay even though I said it's just a one-page reflection in class. How did you organize it?"

"I was reading all of these articles at home, watching Sam on TV, and I was already subcategorizing it in my head," Kendrick explains, his voice becoming more confident. "I was thinking about it and I just saw it."

"I spent two years looking at your writing, and there is real progress," Roth continues. "There is more of a discipline to this essay, you know what I mean?"

Kendrick nods.

"Did you notice how you started with 'evolutionary step' in the first sentence of your essay and then ended with 'revolutionary step' at the end?"

"Not really," Kendrick responds.

"That's real craft," Roth points out. "It's a small step, but it can create this 'boom!' That's really good."

"I didn't notice that. It was just flowing out."

"And then, the very last sentence, where you say you are looking forward to watching Sam on Sundays, which of course implies that you are convinced that he'll be in the NFL," Roth adds. "See what I mean? It's one subtle choice of words and you create this powerful ending."

Kendrick is looking at his conclusion, smiling.

"Why didn't you type it?" Roth inquires.

"I feel like I limit myself when I type. It looks so small. I just had to get into the habit of doing this: allow myself to flow, not think about the length and grammar problems."

"Sure! I know what you mean," Roth comments. "I know you've been watching recordings of Sam's playing for a long time. What did you see?"

"What stood out to me right away is that he is a little too small, a little too slow, but he is so fierce," Kendrick responds. "Bloody nose that he is not even feeling is what I remember. And he just keeps going. He has that special something."

"Sure, he is not the biggest player, but he has a very high motor, right?"

"Exactly, that something special."

"You should add that," Roth says. "You can do it without going on and on about it. Just one paragraph. And you can make the intro a little stronger, too. It's a little light right now. I think you should add to it, type it, and this should be your portfolio piece [a yearly collection of completed classroom assignments that students deem their strongest work]."

"Thank you, Mr. Roth. Let me work on that," Kendrick responds quietly, smiling.

"These one-on-one conversations about students' writing are so important," Roth comments after Kendrick leaves. "It's through these brief conversations that you can see interest, confusion, disconnect, motivation, road blocks," he says while preparing his classroom for the next day: straightening desks, putting books away, and picking up small pieces of paper from the floor.

"Kendrick extended the assignment rather than shrink it," Roth continues, buffing every desk with a cleaning spray and paper towel. "He worked on it at home, looked up extra sources. You don't need to have these conversations all of the time. They are never more than five minutes. I've maybe had four with Kendrick in my two years. But when you see something like this, you have to say something. It's so much more powerful than writing long comments on assignments."

Roth says that sometimes teachers know much more about their students' personal lives than they do about their intellectual skills and academic work. "Students' personal lives, their emotional lives shouldn't be the center of the conversation or the relationship. We have to allow students to be vulnerable, provide support, but the essay is due. 'We are going to meet tomorrow during fourth period when you don't have a class and we are going to do it together.' And they will come because over the course of the year, you were working with them. And they know you are taking them seriously and they are in a real process with you as a teacher."

"If you just go, check, check, check, you are missing opportunities." Roth says as he gathers written assignments in a folder to grade later tonight. "If you grab students quickly on a small assignment and comment on it in writing or raise a question—it only takes two more minutes—it creates an intellectual exchange and builds your relationship."

"Sometimes, my written comments or this kind of conversation works," he adds, locking his classroom for the day. "Other times, it doesn't. It's fine. It's not about being perfect. It's about a sustained intellectual dialogue that students can feel."

◇◇◇◇◇◇◇◇◇◇◇◇◇◇◇◇

Darrell still remembers the essay that made him feel like a writer, he recalls as a senior in 2012, over an iced coffee in the Maxfield's coffee shop near Mission High. It was an analysis of primary and secondary sources on the Reconstruction that he wrote in Mr. Roth's US history class in 2010. For days, he read and re-read the essays of W. E. B. DuBois, as well as Lorraine Hansberry's play *A Raisin in the Sun*. "I just remember thinking about the topic for weeks and weeks, reading every book on Reconstruction I could find," Darrell says. "I talked to my football teammates about it for hours and hours."

"Mr. Roth was very good at giving you that necessary space and encouragement to think," he explains. "In other classes that teach writing, sometimes there is too much talk about the form and the structure of it. 'Do this and do that.' Mr. Roth said, 'Don't stress about the grammar. Give yourself some space to think. Write. Then, we'll think about the grammar together.'" Darrell ended up developing an essay arguing that economic opportunities alone— without an equal political voice at every level—will never lead to freedom for African Americans. "The legacy of slavery is still with us," says Darrell, who was born and raised in the Fillmore, San Francisco's historic African American neighborhood.

A reflective, brilliant young man, Darrell struggled in middle school. Darrell says that before Mission High, his academic confidence was low and he didn't think of himself as a good writer. By his junior year at Mission High, though, Darrell was thriving: taking AP calculus and writing ten-page research papers in his social science classes, in addition to playing football and basketball.

When I asked Darrell to reflect on what contributed to his successes, he talked about how the best teachers at Mission worked hard to create intellectually engaging classrooms for every student, he says; they gave students "the freedom to think" and "taught you how to analyze different texts and express your ideas effectively." Because Darrell's teachers knew his intellect and his interests, they knew how to use the content to tap his motivation, to push him to work hard, learn new skills, and persevere through some of his toughest days, as he grieved over losing two of his brothers to gun violence in the previous five years.

Darrell was accepted to several colleges after graduating from Mission. He credits many of his teachers at Mission High for helping him improve his reading, writing, math, and science skills, but it was Mr. Roth who helped him develop skills to express his "thinking voice," as he refers to it. "Mr. Roth would always say, 'Write in your own voice. Don't try to imitate anyone. Personalize it.'"

"I couldn't do this kind of work at home," Darrell explains, adding that he would often bring his drafts to Mr. Roth to discuss before or after school. He grew up in a small apartment where his single dad struggled to raise thirteen of his own and adopted children. "It was too chaotic at home. I did all of my homework at school."

With every one-on-one session with Mr. Roth, Darrell says, he could hear his own thoughts more and take pride in his own voice, and over time he became addicted to that feeling. "Writing for the grade just wasn't satisfying anymore," he explains. It's this sense of pride in his own thoughts and ideas, more than anything, that fed his resilience as he moved through high school.

"There is no other feeling like a sense of accomplishment, when you know that you honestly pushed yourself and you got to some new place, because of your own hard work, and your own thoughts," Darrell says. "It's the highest high."

THE PROGRESSIVES

(1890–1950)

The founding of Mission High School in 1890 occurred at the beginning of one of the most powerful and far-reaching education reform movements in American history. The Progressives, as these varying strands of reformers were called, were responding to radical changes in the United States caused by industrialization and the influx of immigrants from Southern and Eastern Europe. At the turn of the twentieth century, the United States had emerged as the world's most powerful industrial nation. The invention of the telephone, phonograph, electric lighting, and automobile increased the scale of production and commerce and fueled rapid growth. The new industrial economy created many jobs, but the rapid growth—prone to boom and bust cycles—also dislocated thousands of workers. Many of the new jobs were paying very little, resulting in growing inequality and labor strikes.

The Progressives emerged as a political response to the social upheaval. They wanted to create new institutions for a society that was now urban, industrial, corporate, and multicultural. Some Progressive reformers focused on improving living and working conditions in cities. Others focused on making schools and other government institutions more efficient and accessible to a larger population. In addition, many Progressive education reformers worked toward ending child labor and making school attendance compulsory. They strove to abolish corporal punishment in the classrooms and make schools more humane and intellectually engaging for students. In the process, Progressives expanded schooling to millions of working-class and poor students; by the 1950s, the United States had become a leader in universal education. In 1911 only about 7 percent of American teenagers were enrolled in high schools.[1] By the 1950s, close to 80 percent of teenagers attended high schools.[2]

Most historians identify two major strands in the Progressive education movement: "Administrative Progressives," who focused on the top-down organizational reforms to create "efficient" schools to produce productive workers, and "Child-centered Progressives," who prioritized transforming learning and teaching at the classroom level to make schools more intellectually and emotionally engaging for students.

Administrative Progressives were inspired by the corporate factory model, which was viewed as a very successful economic institution. Following its organizational model, they wanted to divide the labor for efficiency in schools and create "scientific curriculum," which was meant to prepare students for their most "useful" social roles. In *The One Best System: A History of American Urban Education*, Stanford education historian David Tyack writes that similar to education policy elites today, Administrative Progressives were convinced that there is one best system for educating all urban students. All they had to do was discover it and then scale it up in the rest of the country.[3]

Many Child-centered Progressives were inspired by the ideas of John Dewey, an educator and philosopher, who was horrified by what he called the "medieval" teaching practices of traditional schools. In a 1909 survey of school dropouts in Dewey's hometown of Chicago, children said that they preferred to work in a factory than go to school, where teachers routinely beat them, reduced learning to rote memorization and recitation of boring curriculum, and made them feel incapable of academic achievement.[4] Child-centered Progressives argued that schools must promote student interests and initiative, create opportunities for active and engaged learning, and organize learning around projects that drew on student interests and taught skills at the same time. Deweyian educators, like many teachers today, argued that schools should act as mini-democratic societies, modeling values of inclusion, cooperation, and integrity. Child-centered reformers also invented the concept of a "community school," a tradition many progressive schools like Mission High continue today. This view holds that school should be the educational and social center of each neighborhood, focusing on academics, while also providing family support, health, and social services.

In 1896 Dewey founded the Laboratory School at the University of Chicago, attended mostly by the children of professors or other professionals affiliated with the university.[5] As James W. Stigler and James Hiebert document in *The Teaching Gap: Best Ideas from the World's Teachers for Improving Education in the Classroom,* at the Laboratory School classroom teachers collaborated with academic scholars to find the best educational practices, shaping a unique bottom-up, student-centered process for improving the quality of education. Rather than following one-size-fits-all, top-down curriculum created by the technocrats, they paid close attention to the interests and abilities of their students, experimented with different strategies and lesson plans, and then judged the efficacy of their teaching methods based on student responses in the classroom.[6]

Tyack describes an Italian principal of Benjamin Franklin High School in East Harlem in the 1920s, Leonard Covello, who became inspired by the ideals of community schools and child-centered education practiced at the Laboratory School. Benjamin Franklin had students from twenty-five ethnic groups, the three largest of which were Italian, Puerto Rican, and African American. The school was located in a crowded slum in which only 9 percent of the population was native-born whites. Covello turned Benjamin Franklin into a community school, similar to Mission High today. He chose to live within walking distance of the school and organized a community advisory council to bring people in from the neighborhood to the school. Parents could take English classes at their kids' school, and parent association meetings were held in several languages. Like at Mission High, the curriculum emphasized American unity and cultural pluralism at the same time as a way to fight against negative ethnic stereotypes. This experiment, Covello wrote, came closest to fulfilling the dream of a school that was an authentic representation of its community.[7]

According to Theresa Perry, professor of Africana studies and education at Simmons College, many historically segregated black schools that had successfully educated black students long before the civil rights era were also organized around the culture of the community and centered on the needs of its students.[8] Even though leading Administrative Progressives desired and expected black teachers to provide a standard vocational education to African American students, many of these educators taught nonrequired Greek literature, Latin, and higher math and celebrated the rich intellectual history and traditions of African Americans to instill self-respect and racial pride in their students. In the pre–civil rights era, getting a high school or college diploma rarely led to more job opportunities in a racist society, Perry writes, but despite this barrier African Americans always insisted on getting an education, because developing one's intellect meant "to be a human," "to be the opposite of a slave," to seize denied citizenship, and to take control of one's own life.[9]

Anna Julia Cooper, the daughter of a North Carolina slave who became one of the first African American women to earn a PhD, was one such teacher, as noted by author Dana Goldstein in *The Teacher Wars: A History of America's Most Embattled Profession*. Cooper taught at and later became the principal of the M Street High School in Washington, D.C. M Street was one of the most prestigious black public schools in the United States, whose students scored higher on a district-wide exam in 1899 than

students at any white school in the city.[10] Cooper was an
early critic of the use of IQ testing, resisted the pushing of
poor students into vocational training, and advocated for
more equal funding in black schools. Goldstein writes that
at the turn of the century, the primarily black and segregated D.C. public school system was the only one in the
nation that received notable federal funding and had no
pay gap between white and black teachers. Like her coun-
terparts in other community schools, Cooper provided
additional services to the community—such as parenting
classes for young mothers, a library, a savings program,
and music and arts classes—in addition to rigorous, intellectual education. Like many other teachers who served
poor communities, Cooper saw such antipoverty efforts as
an essential part of effective schools.[11]

In Chicago in 1904, Dewey left the Laboratory
School, and an Administrative Progressive named Charles
Judd took over in 1909. Judd's vision inverted the student-
centered, bottom-up school reform process and the ideals
of "community schools." Inspired by the top-down corporate factory model, he replaced the observations and
research by classroom teachers with scientific observations
and curriculum created by college-educated bureaucrats.[12]
In Judd's vision, university-based experts would focus on
finding the best ideas. Teachers were meant to implement
them. The ideas for school reforms were now coming to
schools from the outside. Researchers moved to universities, and teachers stayed at schools. Under Judd, the University of Chicago became the major center for education
policy, which then spread its so-called scientific approach
to public schools and policy makers.

Judd was not alone. Other academics, such as Ellwood Cubberley (Stanford University) and Edward Thorndike (Teachers College, Columbia), and other Administrative Progressives made their universities major centers for education policy, which also promoted its scientific methods to the school policy makers and practitioners. Education historian David F. Labaree notes in *Someone Has to Fail: The Zero-Sum Game of Public Schooling* that like major education reformers of today, Administrative Progressives enjoyed more support from the business leaders and major philanthropists, who had less patience for the minutia of daily teaching practices and were much more interested in bringing business and management models to schools. The Administrative Progressives considered the approach of child-centered teachers a romantic pursuit that was not based in "rigorous science."[13] They wanted to create an efficient structure of school governance and curriculum that would prepare students for their most useful future roles, which back then meant that students of black, Latino, and Eastern and Southern European immigrant parents should get a curriculum geared for vocational training rather than one that emphasized rigor and intellectual development.

Ultimately the Administrative Progressives won the battle of ideas, and many education historians argue that they were the most powerful—and controversial— reformers of public education in American history. The ideas of the Child-centered Progressives were never broadly and deeply integrated into the formal structures of American public schools. Cuban examined the impact of student-centered Progressives from 1880 to 1990 and found minimal influence.[14] Labaree concluded that justifying spending on public schools is easier when reformers talk about practical goals like "promoting economic growth" and "job skills" than romantic goals like intellectual engagement of a student. He argues that one reason for the failure of Child-centered Progressives was that they discounted the importance of engaging with the structural part of schooling, focusing solely on learning and teaching. Certain ideas and values of Child-centered Progressives are practiced by many schools and individual teachers today. These ideas appear in contemporary phrases such as "whole child," "social and emotional growth," "intrinsic motivation," and "project-based learning." But the top-down views of the Administrative Progressives won the day and continue to impact public schools and the national debates surrounding them more than any other education reform movement since then.[15]

The most important legacy was the change in the decision-making process and terms of the debate about school reforms. Modeled after the top-down management process of factories, the decisions concerning teaching and learning were now flowing from the outside, with policy makers and university researchers designing new rounds of "tougher" curriculum standards and tests, to the teachers implementing them, and finally to the students learning them.

Another lasting reform was the creation of "tracking," a widely used practice in American schools in which teachers separate students by skills and ability into different classes. Administrative Progressives wanted to expand access to high schools to absorb the influx of working-class immigrants. These newcomers had to learn English and skills for the new, industrial economy. On the other hand,

Administrative Progressives also struggled to satisfy the demands of the middle-class families who had long enjoyed elite access to high schools and with that, a social advantage over working-class students. Labaree writes that the "tracked" high school became the institution that embodied the grand political compromise at the time between working-class parents, who demanded access to education as a form of social mobility, and middle-class parents, who sought to preserve their social advantage. The creation of the new "tracked" high schools satisfied both demands: it allowed all students to attend, but then channeled working-class students into different paths based on their perceived ability and future social role.[16]

To do this kind of sorting "scientifically," Administrative Progressives introduced another major reform that is still very much with us today: intelligence testing and standardized achievement tests. Testing came to prominence after World War I. IQ tests were first used during the war to determine which solders were fit for desk jobs and which would be sent off to trenches,[17] with African American recruits often taking a different version of the test, for illiterates, regardless of whether they could read or write.[18] As author Anya Kamenetz eloquently documents, some of the creators of these early tests were racists, driven by ideology about the roots of inequality more than science, and were using these tests as "scientific" tools to argue that intelligence and merit were fixed, genetically inherited qualities. One of the creators of the IQ tests, Lewis Terman, the chair of psychology at Stanford University, argued that the low test scores of "negroes," "Spanish-Indians," and Mexicans were racial characteristics, and he was a proponent of forced sterilization.[19]

Soon after World War I test makers found a new market in public schools that were trying to make efficient decisions about where to place students based on their achievement and intelligence test scores. Critics of the tests, including emerging teachers' unions, argued that such examinations revealed differences in educational opportunities rather than innate intelligence. Despite these concerns, IQ tests became widely used in public schools and became the foundation for the Scholastic Aptitude Test (SAT), introduced in 1926 as a way to screen college candidates. By the 1930s two-thirds of Mexican American students were identified as "slow learners" or "mentally retarded" on the basis of the IQ test.[20]

Teachers began to organize politically because they didn't like being reduced to mere functionaries and testing proctors. As they gained more power through unions and professional associations, they demanded better working conditions and higher pay, but they also wanted more autonomy in the classroom and less testing and standardization. In 1904 Margaret Haley, a paid organizer for the Chicago Teachers Federation, said in a meeting of the National Educators Association, "Across the country teachers are denied job security, underpaid, jammed in overcrowded classrooms, and denied a voice, because of 'factorizing education,' making the teacher an automaton, a mere factory hand, whose duty is to carry out mechanically and unquestioningly the ideas and orders of those clothed with the authority of position."

"How can the child learn to be a free and responsible citizen," Haley continued, "if the teacher is bound? How can an autocratic school teach the process of democracy?"[21]

Chapter 3

George

When George neared the end of his middle school education in Taishan, China, he took one of his homeland's most grueling standardized tests, which would determine his future. The Senior High School Entrance Examination (or Zhongkao)—a precursor to The National Higher Education Entrance Examination (or Gaokao), China's notorious college entrance exam—is given to all middle school students. It tests various subjects, including math, Mandarin Chinese, and a foreign language. Students who score high on the test go to elite high schools, advancing them toward college and middle-class comforts. Students who score low go to other high schools which can limit their opportunities to lower-paying industrial, agricultural, or service jobs. This is the only metric government officials in China use for making high school placement decisions.[1] If George didn't do well on the Zhongkao, his chances of getting into China's best universities would be close to zero, unless his parents had a lot of money for bribes or powerful connections among government officials, which they didn't.

George always did well on tests. He wasn't too worried about getting into a college-oriented high school, but he wanted to score high enough to qualify for scholarships. Chinese high schools are not free, and although George's family was better off financially than the parents of his friends who worked in agriculture—his father was a businessman and his mother worked at the post office—they could still use the extra help.

When the Zhongkao results arrived and were posted at the school for everyone to see, George and his parents were relieved. Out of about ten thousand students who took the exams in George's native province of Guangdong that year, he ranked number 12. Soon after, George and his family were wooed by the best high schools in his region, offering George scholarships and other perks. But similar to increasing numbers of other Chinese families, they rejected these offers and chose American schools instead.[2]

Like many students across the globe, George wanted an American college degree. At home and abroad, it would mean more job opportunities. In addition, Chinese universities are not that strong in mechanical engineering, George says, a field he always wanted to study. George and his parents reasoned that going to a high school in America would add more skills to his resume that are not as available in China: improved English, critical thinking, and the ability to navigate different cultures.

In 2008 they flew to California, leaving their old lives behind. When they arrived in San Francisco, George and his family settled with their relatives. His aunts and uncles who lived in San Francisco advised him that smart students usually went to Lowell High, the city's top-performing magnet school. George would have to take an English-language placement test given by the district, but he didn't think twice about it, since he had scored at the top of his country on the Zhongkao exam in English. A week later George took the exam, and his whole world turned upside down.

The school district official told George that he couldn't go to Lowell. While George had passed the reading and writing portions of his language placement exam, he struggled to communicate in English—understanding what the testing officials were asking and responding effectively. He would have to choose among several other options for schools, including Mission High, one of several schools in the district designated to support immigrant students. George was devastated. He felt like a failure for the first time in his life. He always got top grades and test scores in every subject, and that formed the core foundation of his self-esteem.

On his first day at Mission High, George felt completely disoriented by his new place in the world. In his English class, he looked at the whiteboard and couldn't understand most of the words on it. He remembers searching for the translation of "HW" (shorthand for homework) in his small, electronic dictionary, but it returned no results. George's relatives told him not to worry. As soon as his English improved, he could transfer to Lowell. But within a few weeks at the school, he started changing his mind about leaving Mission. Despite the school's negative reputation among George's relatives, he found that all of his classes were academically challenging. George and his parents even went to interview teachers at Lowell and found that teachers were equally strong in both schools. In his Algebra I class, George felt that he was ahead of most of his peers, but his teacher, Ms. Betty Lee, was very good at noticing and teaching all students despite their diverse skills and motivations, he says.

A few weeks into his math class with Ms. Lee, an African American youth named Lorenzo introduced himself to George. Lorenzo asked him to clarify a concept he had just presented in front of everyone. George agreed to help out, and the two kept talking as they walked to their next class. When Lorenzo found out that George was new to Mission High, he said he would look after him. Over the next few days, Lorenzo and his friend Jaleel showed George around the school and the neighborhood, told him where to get the best lunch, introduced him to their friends, and told him which people to avoid. Lorenzo invited George to play basketball with his friends at lunchtime and soon afterward invited him to try out for the school's team. George made the team and met even more friends, including Darrell.

George says that after a few weeks at Mission, he felt at home at his new school, and his new friendships helped him realize that he wanted to be in a diverse school like Mission.

"Education should be about expanding your world, making it bigger than your home and family," George reminisces one cold April afternoon in 2012. Early spring rain is drumming at the windowpanes of the small computer room.

"Until I moved here, I didn't know any African Americans or people from Central America, Argentina, Mexico, or Thailand personally," he says softly, running his hand through his closely cropped, spiky black hair. "There are so many different people and interesting stories here."

Tall and slender, dressed in a dark grey sweatshirt and blue jeans, George is a senior now, and an editor of the new Mission High magazine he cofounded with his friends.

"Every school I went to in China had a newspaper, and Mission High should, too," he says, while showing off various magazine stories in progress: a story about Mission High's Mock Trial team; a photo essay about alumnus Carlos Santana's recent concert at Mission; a profile of "Mission High School students' dream school," the University of California at Berkeley, with survival tips from a recent graduate who just spent a year there.

The school hasn't had funding to support a student-run newspaper for many years. George and his friends are raising money to change that, he says. "In a big school, students are too often separated by their interests, like basketball, Dragonboat, Latino Club. Magazines capture the entire community and help bring everyone together, and that's what Mission is all about."

The stories of his classmates changed him, George says.

"If I went to a school like Lowell, I'd spend my entire high school prepping for tests and college. When you are constrained by grades and that competitive atmosphere around you, you lose relationships and connections with others. You lose freedom. Life becomes about competition rather than finding a way to do what you are good at and be useful for the planet."

George says he wants to work in healthcare robotics in the future. Some day, he wants to start and run his own lab, where talented people from all over the world could collaborate on developing better artificial arms and limbs for people with serious injuries. Such work requires that George communicate with people from different cultures, he says, knowing their personal stories, culture, and history—beyond superficial television narratives that often perpetuate stereotypes.

"I understand why people from Central America risk their lives to come to the United States," he adds. "I came here to go to college. Central Americans come here because they will get killed if they don't. Maybe it's illegal in terms of some local laws, but it's not illegal according to human laws. You can't really understand their decision unless you know such a person and hear their story personally."

"When I came here, I didn't hear any positive comments about Mission," George says. "But I met so many smart and interesting people at Mission. Test scores don't tell you much about who is a genius and who is not."

◇◇◇◇◇◇◇◇◇◇◇◇◇◇◇

Around the time when George and his classmates in Taishan took the Zhongkao exam, a delegation of American education and business leaders traveled to China hoping to unearth the miracle ingredients of its educational system. Chinese students have been outperforming their American peers on standardized international tests in math and science for decades, the delegates later wrote in a

2005 report, *Education in China*. The study called on US schools to adopt some of China's approaches, including a stronger emphasis on math and science and higher-quality national curriculum and textbooks.[3] The successes of Chinese students on international tests inspired many similar American delegations, reports, documentaries, and books looking for ways to emulate schools in the People's Republic.[4] A documentary, *Two Million Minutes: a Global Examination* (2008), compared the lives of high school seniors in the United States, China, and India, implying that American students are spending too much time socializing and playing sports at the expense of academics.[5]

While most reports praising China's educational system highlight different strengths and weaknesses in the system, all are driven by the same logic. If the United States could just figure out the secret formula that leads to higher performance on standardized tests, it could apply the same principles at home, which would reduce our educational achievement gaps and help American schools produce strong, competitive workers in the global economy. Many education scholars, such as Tony Wagner, Yong Zhao, Lisa Delpit, and David F. Labaree, point out that such a narrow view of educational purpose overlooks a host of important skills that quality education should provide, such as critical thinking, creativity, resilience, and the ability to navigate different cultures.[6]

Zhao, a Chinese-born professor of education at the University of Oregon, is concerned that America's desire to copy China's successes on international tests is harming its greatest strength: a public school system that promotes independent thinking and celebration of individual

differences.[7] He observes that despite America's mediocre
performance on international tests since the 1960s, it still
files more patents and wins more Nobel Prizes than any
other country in the world.[8]

Zhao, who went to schools in China and worked there
as a teacher, notes that the problem of "high test scores
but low ability" (*gaofen dineng*) is a widely recognized issue
in Chinese society, referring to students who score well on
the tests but have few skills that are useful in real life.
In *Catching Up or Leading the Way*, Zhao describes how
English-language proficiency among Chinese students is
often mentioned as an accomplishment of its educational
system. But most young people who do well on the English
tests in China can't use it for the most important purpose:
communication. In another study Zhao cites, the China
Alumni Net traced the careers of *zhuangyuans*, students
who receive the highest scores in their province on the
National Higher Education Entrance Examination. The
study looked at the career achievements of *zhuangyuan*
from 1977 to 1998 and concluded that their names do not
appear on the lists of distinguished scientists, entrepre-
neurs, scholars, or engineers.[9]

Zhao has documented that countries in which students outperform American peers in international assessments—China, Singapore, and South Korea—are all
implementing reforms to have less standardization of
curriculum and fewer tests.[10] These countries do that, he
argues, because they are struggling to cultivate creative,
autonomous, and self-driven individuals, whom they view
as the strengths of the American public school system.
And while American leaders are working to transform

schools into institutions that will produce better test takers, Chinese parents are increasingly leaving their homeland to send their kids to American schools instead. From 2005 to 2013, the United States issued fifty times more visas to Chinese students planning to attend high schools in America, and these numbers don't even include students like George, who came to the United States on an immigration visa.[11] Many families who leave China for American high schools report that the American educational system is better at teaching students skills that are essential for participating in the global economy in the twenty-first century: critical thinking, creativity, initiative, and leadership.[12]

Wagner, the expert in residence at Harvard University's Innovation Lab, is also convinced that the US drive to transform students into better test takers is a misguided approach to improving schools or reducing achievement gaps. In *Creating Innovators*, Wagner argues that content knowledge alone is not sufficient in today's world.[13] Students need a broad range of intellectual and emotional skills, such as critical thinking and the ability to solve problems creatively, and they need to be engaged with their learning. Wagner is calling for classrooms to teach concepts and creativity rather than facts. The United States can accomplish this, Wagner writes, by giving fewer multiple-choice tests, allowing schools to judge teachers on a broad range of students' work produced over the course of a year, supporting teachers to design classrooms that are personalized, and teaching higher-order thinking skills.[14]

Jo Boaler, a professor of mathematics education at Stanford University, argues in *What's Math Got to Do with It?* that America's obsessive use of standardized tests encourages "procedural" teaching of math that emphasizes rote memorization over deeper, conceptual understanding. She has observed and studied hundreds of math classes in Europe and the United States and finds that the procedural approach to teaching math leaves too many students cold, uninterested, and traumatized by the subject.[15]

Salman Khan, the founder of the popular educational organization Khan Academy—a nonprofit that provides free online tutorials, primarily in math and science, to students all over the world—worked as a hedge fund manager in his previous career. In *The One World Schoolhouse* Khan describes meeting clients who couldn't solve the basic eighth-grade algebra needed in the financial world, because they were taught to remember x's and y's, but not how to apply them in real life. "The difficulty, of course," Khan notes, "is that getting to this deeper, functional understanding would use up valuable class time that might otherwise be devoted to preparing for a test." Khan criticizes America's overreliance on testing and doesn't think it is an effective strategy for school reform. Instead, the United States should be asking, "Why do students forget so much of what they supposedly 'learned' as soon as an exam has been taken? Why do grown-ups sense such a disconnect between what they studied in school and what they do in the real world?"[16]

∞∞∞∞∞∞∞∞∞∞∞∞∞∞

When George was a junior at Mission High, he took a precalculus class with Mr. Taica Hsu. George asked Mr.

Hsu to explain the mathematical concept of "exponential functions," a widely used mathematical expression that illustrates growth or decay of numbers. He called Mr. Hsu over during class and asked him to show the fastest way to get to the answers using the formula. "After Mr. Hsu started explaining the concept to me," George recalls one late afternoon in a café in Berkeley, "I realized that he wasn't going to just show me how to get to the answer quickly. He gave me an exercise that was forcing me to try different things out with this concept, run into walls, deal with difficulties, feel my way around math. Rather than showing me how to get to the answer quickly, he was asking me to find the answer by myself."

"I hated that exercise," he says with a smile as he runs his hand through his hair. "'Just tell me how to get to the answer as quickly as possible,'" he recalls thinking to himself. "It was really annoying. I wasn't used to approaching math this way."

It's a few weeks before the end of the spring semester at the University of California at Berkeley, where George is a sophomore now, majoring in mechanical engineering. It's a sunny May afternoon, and we are sipping iced tea. The room is hot, and every window is open. George stands up for a minute and waves at a few friends outside. Two students next to us are leaning on their elbows, motionless, their eyes glued to a dense textbook.

As a student in China, George was used to looking at math as a list of procedures and rules, he explains. His main job was to memorize formulas and the right sequence of steps and then practice these steps often in order to increase the speed of calculations and be able to use them in an increasingly more complex way. Students like George—who could recall and execute the right steps quickly—were considered "good at math" in China. Those who were slower weren't considered as smart. So, when Mr. Hsu asked George to slow down and struggle with math, George thought the whole exercise was a waste of time. "He was making it harder to get to a precise answer quickly," he recalls.

Months later, he started seeing the point behind Mr. Hsu's approach. The more exercises like these George did, the more he noticed patterns, relationships, and how exponential concepts worked in real life. In one exercise, George and his classmates explored how the value of a savings account grew. In another exercise, he calculated how the population of rabbits increased over time and later compared its relative growth to that of wolves. After awhile a clear pattern of growth and decay in numbers emerged, and he could visualize how the mathematical expression of exponentials represented different mechanisms behind such growth.

"This is how we discovered and discussed the exponentials," George explains. "The way Mission High School teaches math is not just about memorization, so you can get a good grade and pass the test. They taught in a way that math could make sense to you. And it makes sense when you see how different concepts relate to each other and how it works in the real world. When you discover things, you truly get math. By high school, you just can't remember all of the math. There is so much of it. It's better to try to understand fewer concepts but more deeply."

A month later, Mr. Hsu asked George to discover "an inaccurate solution with graphing." "This really pissed me off," he recalls laughing. "If the graph starts out wrong, you can't get the right answer out of it. But the point was to talk about approximations. The concept still works at the end. And that's how you eventually discover those things. He was just making us comfortable with that idea, pushing us to use something that is not perfect."

Classroom interactions were also different at Mission High. George and his classmates sat at rectangular tables in groups of four and spent part of their class discovering or solving math problems together and part of it practicing skills on their own. In China, as in many traditional schools in the United States, students work mostly on their own, and looking at the answers of other students is considered cheating. But in Mr. Hsu's classes, students were required to ask questions, participate in discussions, show their approaches to classmates, or help others, George says.

"The most important thing I learned from group work in math is that if I can't explain a math concept to my classmate, I don't understand it well enough. When I explained something to others, I often obtained a new perspective on it, saw the world from a different angle, or came up with an easier, better explanation."

"This is how it works in the real world, in engineering labs," George adds. "You need to work together, explain your approaches, sell your ideas." In addition to encouraging work in groups, most teachers at Mission High also don't support "tracking" or separating students according to their perceived ability into different classes.

In his first year at Mission, George felt skeptical of such a system, but he has reconsidered his views now. "Mixing students with different math knowledge and skills is good for everyone," George says. "The students who master the concept before others learn more because they are forced to explain things."

Working in mixed groups also helped George expand his views on human intelligence. The human brain is a complex thing, George adds, and everyone learns at a different pace. Just because someone bombed one test last year doesn't mean he or she should be separated into a different class. A student who might struggle with the basics of arithmetic could be a genius with higher concepts and really good at explaining them to students who excel at acing the tests. George used to think that people who think slowly are not smart, but close work with his classmates made him realize that rushing to answers is not always the best way to solve problems. It was often the slower thinkers who forced everyone to deliberate on the relative advantages of various ways to get to the answer. "Human brains are too weak to appreciate the full beauty of the world, and rushing through any process makes you miss out on important parts," he says.

As he reflects on his education in China and California now, George says that he is lucky that he got his elementary education in China and his high school education at Mission High. He thinks the schools in China are better at teaching all students—rich and poor—foundational knowledge and giving everyone plenty of opportunities to practice and master basic concepts. But by high school,

George was hungry for Mission High's approach, which promotes more complex skills and deeper understanding of the substance behind texts and numbers.

This semester, George is taking several upper-level math and physics classes, and he says Mr. Hsu's way of teaching math prepared him better than many of his college peers from "better schools" to take advantage of college, academically and socially. In his classes, George and his classmates work on complex, open-ended problems that require students to think of them conceptually and visually. Before students pick a particular path to a solution, they have to make a lot of guesses and estimations and debate the pros and cons of the different methods and approaches. Most of his peers come from schools with much higher test scores in math than Mission High, but these students struggle in upper-level classes, because they are not used to explaining their work or approaching math in a more conceptual way.

"Here at Berkeley, you can't survive by memorizing the answers. You need to dig into math and use it a little bit to see what constraints it has and under what conditions you can use the concepts and how things are derived before you start solving for anything. It's very visual and conceptual." But teaching math in a more personalized, conceptual way that allows students to discover things on their own, make connections, and get plenty of practice in procedural fluency is difficult, George admits. "Teaching math the way Mr. Hsu does requires a lot of knowledge, dedication, and patience," George says. He had been in some math classes at Mission in which group work and complex problem solving didn't work. Teachers need to have a lot of skills and more time to make personalized education and group work effective, he says.

"Many students at Mission give up really easily," he explains. "They don't think of themselves as good at school. 'I won't do this!' they will say. I don't think it should be the students' responsibility to motivate their classmates. Many students at Mission just need more math classes and opportunities to practice."

"Mr. Hsu understands what the others think and what the students want, and he is really clear on what he wants students to do," George says as we walk out of the café together. "He is always there at lunch and after school to help anyone who has questions. And students do the work, even if they don't know everything. They do it for him. But it doesn't work with teachers who are just there nine-to-five and go home."

Chapter 4

Mr. Hsu

The first time Taica Hsu tried to teach math, he was eight years old. Sitting cross-legged on a light brown carpet in the middle of his room in 1992, he was writing out numbers with a white piece of chalk on a blackboard. His best friend's little sister Megan, who was six, was sitting across from him. At a time when kids of her age started learning addition and subtraction, Megan was already working on multiplication and some advanced algebra with Taica.

Before meeting Taica, this was not Megan's idea of having fun after school. She lived across the street from him and started visiting to swim in his family's outdoor pool and to play video games. But as Taica and Megan started to spend more time together, she would often confess that she struggled in her math classes. She didn't have the brain for it, she said. Taica had heard similar comments from his older sister, and this puzzled him. Playing with numbers, using different tricks and shortcuts as he hunted for the answer, was fun for him. In the third grade his teacher, Ms. Rubin, called him the "human calculator."

Taica couldn't help his sister with math; she was seven years ahead of him. But the next time Megan told Taica about her challenges with multiplication, he decided to help. He told her that she would remember her multiplication tables better if she could visualize how these numbers worked first. She could then use shortcuts every time she got stuck and move along. Taica used some oranges from the kitchen to illustrate what he meant. If Megan forgot the answer for 3 x 4, for example, she could remember 3 x 3 and then add 3. If Megan couldn't remember 3 x 3, she could keep adding three to itself three times and figure out the answer. Whenever Megan became overwhelmed, she could break down the problem into smaller chunks and solve it one step at a time, Taica explained.

As Megan's enthusiasm for math grew, she started telling other kids on their block about her sessions with Taica. Her older brother and four other neighborhood kids joined their study group. Soon a group of seven kids started meeting once a week in Taica's home in the small suburb of Florida. No one called it school or learning. They were just playing games and doing puzzles, sharing tricks with each other, joking around, and arguing about the best ways to get to an answer.

As Taica progressed through his school years, he continued his informal workshops and dreamed about becoming a math teacher. In high school he organized a formal after-school program for students who struggled with math. But when he got to Dartmouth College, he was on the premed track to make his working-class parents proud and less anxious about their long-term safety net. Taica's father, Stanley Hsu, didn't go to college. He moved to the

United States from China in his early twenties and ran several Chinese restaurants with his wife, Karen. Taica's parents worked twelve-hour days, six days a week, hoping their son and their daughter would have more comfortable lives with regular vacations.

In his freshman year at Dartmouth, Taica confessed to his parents that he wanted to become a teacher. His father disapproved. "Why would you waste your Ivy League degree to become a teacher?" he asked. Americans didn't respect teachers or pay them well, he argued. In his second year at Dartmouth, Taica enrolled in one class at the School of Education, and he felt at home right away. Within a week, he switched his major to education and Spanish.

In his education classes, Taica was deeply influenced by the work of Jonathon Kozol, a teacher, author, and civil rights activist, best known for his searing critiques of funding inequalities and racial segregation in American schools. As Taica immersed himself in Kozol's writings, he learned that two decades after the *Brown v. Board of Education* (1954) ruling that outlawed school segregation, more than 90 percent of black children were attending desegregated schools by the early 1970s. As a result, the achievement gap between black and white thirteen-year-olds was cut roughly in half nationwide during the 1970s and 1980s.[1] By the time Taica was reading Kozol's book *The Shame of the Nation: The Restoration of Apartheid Schooling in America* that progress had eroded. In 2001 only 28 percent of black children were attending majority-white schools, and 40 percent of black and Latino students attended deeply segregated schools at which 90 to 100 percent of the student body was poor and nonwhite.[2]

Such high-poverty, segregated schools struggle to offer high-level classes like calculus and to attract math and science teachers like Taica to teach them. He knew he loved teaching, but learning about the differences in funding between rich and poor school districts and growing racial segregation in American schools infused Hsu's passion for teaching with a sense of social justice. This needs to change, he thought to himself when he graduated in 2006.

After college Hsu enrolled at the Stanford Graduate School of Education to get his teaching credential in math, hoping to acquire the tools to help him reduce educational gaps and racial segregation in American schools. When Hsu enrolled in "math pedagogy" classes at Stanford, he didn't expect too many surprises. But within a few weeks he felt that he had to learn math all over again. Hsu's professors, Jack Dieckmann and Emily Shahan, presented him with an entirely new way of looking at and thinking about math. The traditional way of teaching math focused too much on rote memorization of formulas, rules, and procedures, they argued. It wasn't working for most students, leaving them uninterested in the subject and resulting in too many students—especially students of color and women—failing math classes and not choosing math or science as their profession. These ineffective ways of teaching math also made it difficult for teachers to personalize their instruction, resulting in "tracking"—separating students by skills and ability in different classes—and increasing racial segregation, Taica's professors said.

Professors Dieckmann and Shahan said that their approach to teaching math allows students to make sense of concepts, see how different mathematical expressions connect to each other, and explain an infinite number of phenomena in the real world. According to this approach, students need to have foundational knowledge and practice basic skills, but they also need to spend time discovering math's procedures, working with similar concepts from slightly different angles, and investigating questions surrounding them. When students can understand what they are memorizing and see connections between concepts, they retain math knowledge longer.

"I loved thinking about math this way," Taica recalls now, sitting in his math class at Mission High School one late afternoon in the fall of 2014. "I always liked math and was good at it, but this new way of thinking about it made me really fall in love with it," he recalls. "We would leave after doing a task at Stanford really understanding the mathematical concept rather than having a cursory view of it."

Taica came to Mission High right after graduating from Stanford in 2007 and has been teaching math for seven years he says, sitting in front of a large bookshelf that contains a small microwave, a sewing machine, and rows of books on algebra, CI math, statistics, and precalculus. He taught math more "procedurally" in his first two years at Mission and then more "conceptually" in the next five. Taica is convinced that the approach he learned at Stanford—which also informed the new Common Core Standards—is a better way to learn math and help more students like the subject.

"Approaching math conceptually is not just about doing calculations quickly or memorization," Hsu explains. "You are still learning procedural fluency, but you are also seeing connections, patterns, choosing your own strategy in solving something and justifying it. You are seeing how it interprets and explains the world around you. It allows students to develop a more intuitive understanding and a deeper connection with math."

∞∞∞∞∞∞∞∞∞

It is nearly ten in the morning at Mission High, and a stream of eighteen freshmen has just entered the classroom for their Algebra I class. Rasheed, a tall young man with a head full of long, black braids, drops his backpack on the table. The desks are organized in rectangles, and students sit in groups of four. Rasheed sits down near Jenny, who noticed her friend as soon as he walked through the door.

Jenny is wearing thick sweatpants over her light blue jeans on this cool, grey February morning in 2011. She has been out sick for a week and has asked Brandon to help her finish her homework. "I believe you multiply first before you add here," Brandon is explaining patiently while writing out every step of the solution on a separate piece of paper. "Jenny, you are really smart," he adds. "You can do it. You just need to take your time." Joaquin, a young man with a pink, boyish face partially covered by an oversized "Golden State Warriors" hat, walks in and stretches out on the two chairs at his desk. He puts his hat over his face and closes his eyes. Joaquin is about two heads shorter than Rasheed, who is a about a foot taller than the rest of his ninth-grade classmates.

Warm and charming, Rasheed is a formidable social force in the classroom. He can pull his friends away from work in an instant, but when class is in session, he uses that power to engage them with math. For now, before the bell rings, Rasheed puts his large headphones on Jenny's ears and plays some songs for her. Shipra is trying her earrings on Jenny's ears. Brandon throws a little paper ball at Shipra's head and turns away sharply to hide his prank. Unlike their peers in the twelfth grade across the hall, these freshmen are buzzing with electricity as they are settling in their seats—shouting, joking, flirting, and fidgeting.

"And that was our bell," twenty-seven-year-old Hsu says as he starts the class. He is dressed in a grey T-shirt, dark blue jeans, and turquoise Puma sneakers. "Happy Friday, everyone," he greets the class as the noise drops. "I want to thank many of you who came to see me after school if you had any questions. I really appreciated that."

"Please sit at the same table as on Wednesday," he continues. "Start with the 'Do Now' and then continue to work on the 'group challenge' from last week. Remember, everyone needs to participate in the challenge. What are some ways in which we participate?"

"Asking questions," students take turns answering. "Justifying steps. Answering questions of others. Asking for help. Plugging in numbers. Using resources from previous classes. Listening to someone else's ideas."

"Smart, smart, smart! Let's get to work," Hsu responds and starts walking around the classroom, gliding between the desks. Hsu's colleague, special education teacher Blair Groefsema, checks in with the other tables that need attention. This class has seven students with special needs, including one student in a wheelchair who communicates through a voice-activated electronic device.

Within a few minutes, Hsu notices a common error as students work through the 'Do Now' exercise, in which they are reviewing skills and knowledge from their previous lessons. Several students have mixed up distribution steps today and solved $3(x + 2)$ incorrectly, as $3x + 2$. Hsu sits on the edge of his desk and reviews the correct sequence of the steps with his students. Joaquin gets up to view what Mr. Hsu is demonstrating more closely.

As the students get back to work, Hsu continues to move around the classroom quickly, with a calming presence—asking questions, naming different skills students are exercising, praising effort. "I see Jenny and Brandon are drawing boxes," Hsu comments. "That's a really good technique. I really like how Irene is referencing her homework to help her solve this problem."

"Check your answers with everyone in the group before you finish," he reminds them.

"Mr. Hsu, are these 'like' terms?" Jenny asks with her hand raised.

"Yes, they are. Can you combine them?"

"Yes."

"What do you think you should do here, Joaquin?" Hsu walks over to the next table. "How did you get that answer?"

After the exercise, Hsu moves on to the group challenge, a multistep, "open-ended" math problem that students are asked to solve in a workshop-style group of four. Such exercises may or may not lead to a single answer, but they always allow for different paths to various solutions. Hsu says that open-ended problems illustrate the real depth of math for students and show them that math—like most things in the real world—requires multiple skills and approaches. "If you are only solving for x," Hsu explains to me after the class, "the problem has only one path and one solution. Students who get stuck on one small step throw their hands up and say that they are not good at math. In open-ended group problems, students are more likely to keep trying. They realize that there are many ways to approach problems, and if you are not good at one part of math, it doesn't mean that you are not good at all of it."

Today's group challenge is asking students to analyze and graph different types of lines—parallel, perpendicular, and intersecting—and solve for points of intersection. Students are asked to interact with each line as multiple representations—as a graph, equation, and a table—as well as to make a connection between solutions and visually represented points on the graph. The same lesson in a traditional classroom would be taught in a narrower way, Hsu notes. Students might be asked to memorize the equations of the lines and a few conclusions without visualizing them as multiple representations. When students are only asked to solve the equation, they may not completely understand all of the connections. When students don't make such connections, Hsu says, they are not learning deeply, but simply memorizing equations that are mysteries to them. Such knowledge is more likely to fade quickly.

Research by Jo Boaler, a professor of mathematics education at Stanford University, shows that students learn more when they interact with math in a variety of formats like these, such as engaging with multiple representations of the same concepts, talking to their peers about it, justifying their own thinking, or presenting to their classmates.

In *What's Math Got to Do with It?* Boaler notes that many students often think they have comprehended math when a teacher is explaining a new concept or procedure on the board and then students repeat the methods in their practice. But that doesn't mean that students understand it—that they can use it a month later in different ways. Long-term learning occurs when students have plenty of opportunities to apply the knowledge in a variety of formats.[3]

Following the group challenge, students do individual exercises in which they are asked to practice their skills and knowledge. As students do the work, Hsu walks around and provides personalized coaching. Individual practice time in Hsu's classes is typically followed by a low-stakes "mini-quiz" without any help from the teacher. He reviews these quizzes at the end of each day to make notes on which students need extra help and adjust his lesson plans for the next day.

Traditional classrooms typically don't follow this format. In most American classrooms, students watch their teachers lecture and model exercises at the front of the room. After a lecture or demonstration on the blackboard that many don't fully absorb, students are then asked to practice tasks individually, some in class but most at home.[4] Students who can get help with homework at home usually progress smoothly. Students whose parents work long hours or who can't afford expensive tutors typically fall behind.

Such teaching allows for an efficient delivery of the standardized content. The problem is that this standardized approach doesn't work, because no one is "standard," Hsu argues. That's why Hsu—along with his co-chair of the math department, Mary Maher, and other math teachers—has spent the past several years working to update the traditional script. Hsu's classrooms function more like group-style workshops than like lecture halls. Students spend most of the time producing work, alone and in groups, talking about math to their teacher and peers, while Hsu provides individualized coaching.

"Who would like to present their findings?" Hsu asks.

The students in Rasheed's group raise their hands.

"First of all," Rasheed begins, pointing to equations on the projection, "how did we know that these lines are perpendicular? We saw that the line is crossing. Second thing we noticed is that slopes are switched around."

"What's the only solution?" Hsu asks.

"Four and minus one," Jenny answers.

"Why?" Hsu probes.

"It's the only place where the lines cross," she adds.

"How did you know to go down three, and over two?" Joaquin asks.

"This part of the formula," Rasheed points at the board.

"Does this make sense? Are we convinced?" Hsu turns to the class.

"Yes," several students respond.

"Does anyone disagree?" he asks.

No hands go up.

"Time for a quick, individual check-in, everyone," says Hsu, who calls tests and quizzes "check-ins" to help ease the testing tension.

"I'm not prepared for this test," Shipra admits, clearly upset.

"I've seen you do these problems many times, Shipra," Ms. Groefsema reassures her.

The students get to work. A young man trained in working with students who use electronic devices for communication is helping a student in a wheelchair.

A few minutes later Jenny exclaims that she is done. So does Rasheed. Hsu walks over to them. Joaquin gets stuck and asks for help. He has forgotten how to pick numbers for the table to draw a parabola. Ms. Groefsema reminds him with a series of questions. He gets back to work. Hsu looks over Shipra's quiz. She has mixed up the steps: added first, rather than multiplied, he tells me quietly. She was asking for help more than anyone today. She will need extra one-on-one work with Hsu and a lot more individual practice to help her develop self-reliance and more confidence.

The bell rings, and Hsu finishes collecting the rest of the quizzes.

"I am so smart, I can teach this class," Rasheed says with a slight smirk on his face, as he looks back at Jenny.

◇◇◇◇◇◇◇◇◇◇◇◇◇◇◇◇

In June later that year, Hsu and I are at his home—a two-bedroom apartment in San Francisco's foggy Twin Peaks neighborhood—which he shares with three roommates and two cats. School ended for the summer two weeks earlier. Dressed in shorts, a white T-shirt, and flip-flops, Hsu has a fresh, restful glow on his face. He has just finished packing, getting ready to go to a math conference in Napa in a few days. The school district hasn't had money for teachers' professional development outside of school for several years, but Hsu applied for grants during the school year to pick up new skills over the summer. The conference will highlight project-based teaching of statistical modeling, Hsu explains excitedly. It's hard to find good curriculum that is engaging for students and teaches math in a way that is connected to the real world.

Ever since Hsu got to Mission High, he has been on a quest to find teaching approaches that can increase engagement with math for all students, especially students of color and women, who are vastly underrepresented in the fields of math and science. A 2005 Associated Press–America Online news poll showed that four out of ten adults said they hated math in school, twice as many as hated any other subject.[5] When Hsu first met Rasheed as a freshman, he said he didn't enjoy math, like many other students Hsu encounters. During the first few classes, when he got stuck on a math problem, he would put his head on the desk and stop working. Rasheed actually had more knowledge and skills than most of his classmates, but he often told Hsu that he was "not good at math."

Students will sometimes make lifelong decisions about their abilities based on just one class experience, Hsu explains. Psychologist Carol Dweck discovered that even though students often don't say it out loud, many often think of intelligence as a fixed, binary commodity—you are either born smart or "good at math" or not, and that is set for life.[6] Dweck found that small interventions can dispel this self-view, such as consistent communication from teachers, mentors, or parents that the effort and work on one's skills contribute more to academic achievement than innate intelligence.[7]

Many Mission students come in with large gaps in their math skills and low confidence in their abilities. In Rasheed's freshman class, about half of his classmates didn't know how to multiply without a calculator. As Lisa Delpit, professor of education at Southern University, has observed during her classroom research, students who assume that their lack of skills is an accurate measurement of their intelligence usually try to either check out of class—hoods over faces, looking at their phones, headphones on—or act out to avoid any public classroom performance that might reveal their gaps in knowledge or ability.[8] To make matters worse, once students start engaging with math, many students of color and women experience a form of anxiety called the "stereotype threat." Claude Steele, a social psychologist and former dean of the Graduate School of Education at Stanford, found that this form of distress arises in certain situations—during tests for African American students or math classes for women, for example—when an individual has the potential to confirm a negative stereotype about his or her social group. In some studies, when researchers ask students if they are anxious about their performance on an upcoming test, they say that they are not. But physiological tests show that their blood pressure and heart rate are increasing. In other words, they don't even realize that the "stereotype threat" is happening—it's often subconscious.[9]

Hsu sees such anxieties and self-doubt play out in his classrooms every day. To combat this, he spends a lot of time finessing learning environments in which students can see that everyone is "smart" in some way and has value to contribute, and that effort, resilience, humility, respect, and communication skills propel individual achievement more than a person's IQ score.

When Hsu started out as a math teacher, he struggled with sustaining student engagement with the material. Back then, he taught math the way he had learned it in high school and as an undergraduate: in a more "procedural," traditional way, focusing more on the memorization of formulas and the order of steps. He also lacked skills to detect knots in students' understanding or present material in a way that included his students' ideas and strengths. Even though Hsu supports the conceptual math approaches he learned at Stanford, teaching math conceptually is harder, he says. It requires specialized skills, an alternative curriculum, and ample time to plan lessons and analyze student work—all of which are in short supply among American teachers.

When Hsu taught procedurally, more of his students were passing California's standardized tests, but too many were bored or intellectually disengaged. And that kind of alienation had the worst consequences for struggling students. When students who think of themselves as high achievers become disengaged from the content, they tend to check out emotionally, but continue to push themselves to get good grades and pass the tests. When the hardest-to-reach students don't have a connection to the subject or their teacher, too often they stop coming to class or drop out altogether. That's why Hsu and his colleagues have been trying different research-based strategies to increase engagement.

In 2010 Hsu became co-chair of the math department and embraced a school district–funded voluntary program called Complex Instruction. This approach was based on over twenty years of research by Elizabeth Cohen, Rachel Lotan, and their colleagues at the Stanford School of Education, who argued that traditional methods of teaching failed too many students or made them feel intellectually incompetent.[10] Complex Instruction researchers suggested incorporating more conceptual math and group collaboration, among other changes. Around the same time, Mission High received some extra money from the federal School Improvement Grant (SIG) that allowed teachers to design their own school-based training program, including extra coaching. Taking cues from Japan's successful teacher training programs and working closely with a local nonprofit, the Coalition of Small Essential Schools, Hsu and Mary Maher gradually implemented different teacher support programs and new curriculum that incorporated the Stanford recommendations.

As a part of this program, some math teachers started meeting to identify yearly learning goals, plan units and individual lessons, name specific skills students would have to master, and share best teaching strategies to help students learn various skills. Many math teachers met to review student work together and analyzed their grading policies. Teachers started observing each other and discussed what they saw as strengths and areas that needed changes. Some teachers worked with experienced coaches. In addition, Hsu and some of his colleagues started administering regular student surveys, in which they asked students to report on what skills they were learning and where they were struggling and to grade themselves on their effort and participation. The math department also strengthened its commitment to creating more integrated classes without "tracking," which Hsu says perpetuates inequities and racial segregation and makes teaching students who struggle with math even more difficult.

In schools that use tracking, white and Asian American students typically take more advanced and honors classes, while most African American, Latino, and low-income students are in remedial courses. A 2013 study by the Brookings Institution, "How Well Are American Students Learning?," found that tracking in the United States today primarily occurs in high schools and some middle schools, with about three-fourths of the eighth-grade students attending tracked math classes. Brookings senior fellow Tom Loveless writes, "In tracked classes, students are assigned to different classrooms, receive instruction from different teachers, and study a different curriculum. The names of high school courses signal curricular differences. Advanced math students in tenth grade, for example, may take Algebra II while others take Geometry, Algebra I, or Pre-Algebra. Advanced tenth graders in English language arts (ELA) may attend a class called 'Honors English' while other students attend 'English 10' or 'Reading 10.'"[11]

Steele's research found that tracking causes more harm than good, because public sorting stigmatizes students and for many confirms their own doubts about their intelligence.[12] Chronic experiences with such settings leads to "disidentification" or moving oneself away from the academic setting as a source of self-esteem.[13] Research by other scholars, such as Jo Boaler, has shown that when teachers track, they assume everyone in that group is more or less the same.[14] It promotes standardized teaching: prepackaged delivery of content and instruction "in the middle," making it difficult to serve the needs of lower- and higher-achieving students.

Hsu has seen Steele's findings play out in tracked classrooms and believes that teaching heterogeneous groups makes him a more effective teacher because he has to teach individuals who are all developing at different rates and reveal different interests and strengths at different stages. He believes that when implemented well, heterogeneous classes can teach students to get along with people from different backgrounds and viewpoints, take criticism, ask questions, and solve problems collectively. Such skills proactively reduce conflict and teach students the value of intercultural communication and collaboration, aptitudes that many employers say they'd like to see more of in recent college graduates.[15]

As Mission High's instructional reform facilitator—a person tasked with coaching teachers and improving curriculum—Pirette McKamey has been poring over various measures of student achievement for years, and she rarely sees sustained, high grades for African American and Latino students in any classes, let alone math. For many students, their progress in heterogeneous classes continues into other grades with other teachers. Rasheed, for example, received an A in Hsu's class in ninth-grade algebra and two Bs in the next two years with other math teachers.

Rasheed started out disengaged, Hsu recalls, but he came alive in challenging group settings. He liked being able to ask questions. When his classmates needed help, he enjoyed explaining math concepts to them, which reinforced his knowledge and communication skills. Every time he helped his classmates out, he gathered more evidence of his math abilities. Over time, his self-esteem became attached to his work with math.

While some students thrived in a group setting, others didn't. For students like Joaquin, group work with limited guidance from a teacher didn't help. "The main lens in Complex Instruction is that the teacher is absent during group work, standing back to promote autonomy and independent work," Hsu explains. "But with many of our students, if they get stuck, there is complete shut down. It's important to recognize what's going on with the whole class and then modify your approach." Other students told Hsu in their surveys about his class that they wanted more time to work alone. They told Hsu that if they spent too much time working in groups, they didn't have enough time to practice their skills. "Just because you understand something conceptually, doesn't mean you are better at it procedurally," Hsu explains why he increased the time students spend in his classrooms practicing individual skills.

After eight years of working to create more effective math classrooms, Hsu says he has come to the conclusion that guidelines that come from the outside and promote new approaches are helpful, but copying and pasting structures from academic studies or other countries doesn't work. The recommendations of researchers are too general and don't take the most important variable into account: the unique ecosystem of each school and the individual needs of its diverse students.

McKamey, who mentors and observes Hsu, has seen multiple waves of well-intentioned, district-wide approaches like Complex Instruction in her nearly three decades as a teacher that often end up creating more problems than solutions. Because teachers' workloads are so heavy in the United States, many end up using most of their limited time copying new systems and structures, at the expense of thoughtful lesson planning and daily analysis of student work. "Teachers can get caught up in the ideologies of new approaches," McKamey explains. "And rather than asking, 'How can I be reflective? How can I grow as a teacher?' They ask, 'How do I set up these structures to organize students in groups and make sure they know their roles?'"

Teachers always need to seek out new ideas and learn from the wisdom of others, McKamey explains. But much more important is that teachers need to learn how to improve their craft in a way that works for all students. This means each teacher needs to feed recommendations from the outside through a daily process of his or her own individual and collective research and reflection. "Teaching is not a little bag of tools and strategies," McKamey explains. It works more like a three-dimensional, precisely arranged jigsaw puzzle, with the different parts operating together and reinforcing one another. Conceptual approaches to math and some group work are good strategies to increase student engagement, McKamey says, but they are not sufficient for effective learning.

McKamey says Hsu's biggest strength as a teacher is his ability to see and hear all of his students and refine his craft and approaches based on that information. His classrooms function more like workshops in which students produce a lot of work, which he uses to find just the right mix of activities for engagement and mastery of skills. "Taica is so aware of each student," McKamey comments. "He is never a self-aggrandizing talking head, like some teachers can be sometimes: 'Look how much math I know.' Taica always says, 'Yeah, you got it. Look how much math *you* know.'" When I tell McKamey that people in the education field refer to this kind of teaching as "student-centered," "personalized," or "differentiated," she says she doesn't use terms like that. For her, it just means good teaching, as opposed to just delivering standardized content and then sorting students into different groups of perceived ability.

For Hsu, personalized instruction means that he doesn't look at his students through what educators refer to as "the deficit model," focusing primarily on arbitrary standard expectations a student is not meeting at the moment rather than seeing each individual's unique strengths and brilliance. Hsu, a voracious reader of Claude Steele's research, says that students want to know that teachers see them as individuals who are valuable right now, regardless of their grades or test scores or their knowledge of certain skills. A teacher's ability to see the individual strengths of each student can cut through all of the other anxiety-ridden internal messages of self-doubt.[16] "Seeing every student as an intellectual is different than having high expectations," McKamey stresses. "It's about an equal partnership. As a teacher, I do know a lot more than my students, but I don't own their intellect. You are not looking at other students as empty vessels that need to be filled. You are looking for a little light in them."

Such personalized teaching with high expectations for all students is rare in the United States. National teacher surveys show that teachers "track" students because they struggle with teaching students who have varying degrees of skill and motivation. In a 2008 national survey commissioned by the Fordham Institute, more than eight in ten teachers said "differentiated instruction"—educational jargon for personalized teaching—was "very" or "somewhat difficult" to implement.[17]

Historian Larry Cuban has found similar data. Student-centered classrooms that personalize instruction require a lot more time for planning meaningful assignments, looking at student work, and individual tutoring and grading of student work. Cuban says that most teachers in the United States teach math procedurally, and some borrow freely from nontraditional approaches, but teaching math conceptually requires much more time and extra resources, while the bonuses that come with that— like student engagement or depth of understanding—are not necessarily detected by standardized and especially multiple-choice tests.

Many policy makers and parents say they want personalized, student-centered education, but all of the major incentives and penalties are attached to standardized outcomes.[18] As a result, a small percentage of highly skilled teachers are able to satisfy both mandates, usually by working many extra hours. But most struggle somewhere in the middle, on some days able to prioritize engagement and student-centered approaches, but on other days resorting to more efficient, top-down content delivery. As long as standardized tests have high stakes attached to them, teachers will continue to resort to the most efficient ways to satisfy federal mandates, Cuban told me.[19]

Many Mission High School teachers struggle with similar challenges. "If I don't have enough time to plan, I will end up just delivering information," second-year Mission High math teacher Dayna Soares says. A recent Columbia University Teachers College study found that American high school educators spend about 11 percent more time teaching in classrooms than the OECD (Organisation for Economic Co-operation and Development) average in 2012. This means that American teachers have less time left in their day to prepare for lessons and analyze student outcomes. But the author of the study, Samuel E. Abrams, notes that the biggest difference between higher-achieving countries, such as Finland and Japan, and the United States is how much school time is spent on preparation for standardized tests.[20] The United States administers far more standardized tests than any other industrialized nation.[21]

Instead of teaching five classes each day, Soares and Hsu wish they could teach three or four classes a day. This would leave more time to plan yearly goals, sequence effective lesson plans with meaningful assignments, provide personalized instruction, and comb through student work every day to make changes in the next day's lesson plan. Students also need extra classroom time, Hsu believes. It's been a challenge finding the right balance between teaching math conceptually to increase engagement and finding enough time to practice new skills, especially when many students are already two or three grades behind.

Hsu says he had the most success—with student engagement, enough time to practice, grades, and test scores—when Mission High had enough funding for a few years to support "double block": teaching two classes of Algebra I for all of his freshmen. Having this extra time allowed him to teach deeper, more conceptual content to students of mixed abilities, have plenty of time for individual practice, and include more real-world projects that students loved. He is hoping some foundation will choose Mission High for a pilot program in which teachers will have three classes each day and then spend the remainder of the day looking at student work and planning for the next lesson. "I think the results would be huge, but I'm worried most of the money will go toward computers in every classroom and new textbooks that are aligned with the new Common Core tests."

◇◇◇◇◇◇◇◇◇◇◇◇◇◇◇◇◇

"I'm pretty good at math now," Rasheed boasts one morning two years later, in Mr. Hsu's classroom. He is a junior now. After he got an A in his Algebra I class, his progress in math continued, with steady Bs over the past two years. "In middle school, I failed every math class," he says, pushing his thick, black glasses up on the bridge of his nose. "But Mr. Hsu made math fun." Rasheed liked the fast-paced energy of the class. "Mr. Hsu was always switching things up, there was some review, practice, but also lots of group projects and challenges."

Rasheed says working in groups helped him learn more. "In my middle school, we all sat separately at our own desks, and I couldn't ask my classmates to explain something to me if I got stuck. My middle school teachers would explain something on the board once, and then give us a piece of paper, and we would just work, work, work." When Rasheed watched his teacher model a new exercise on the board, he'd often think that he understood it. Then he would repeat the steps on his worksheets and realize that he didn't fully absorb everything. "If I had questions, the teacher tried to be helpful, but there were so many of us. I was completely lost. My dad had to get me a private tutor, and I felt bad. It's very expensive. And even with that tutor, my grades weren't good in middle school."

Rasheed says that talking out loud about math—with his teacher, with his classmates in front of the class—is a good way to learn, too. "If you wanted to get a good grade in Mr. Hsu's class, you had to ask a lot of questions and participate in discussions. I liked working in groups more than anything, because whenever I got stuck, I didn't have to wait for anyone. I would just ask someone next to me. Two heads are always better than one." He says that he often felt a little ahead of other classmates during group work, but he wasn't bored, because he enjoys helping his friends. "Every time I explain math to someone else, I get better at it myself. It sinks in more deeply."

I ask Rasheed what he remembers learning the most from his class with Mr. Hsu. "I became really good at linear functions, graphing different types of lines," he replies without a pause. "I could graph from tables or use graphs to make a table, or make a table from an equation. I got that down really well, and it's helping me a lot in other classes now."

Mr. Hsu gave a lot of homework, Rasheed recalls, but he was able to finish it most days without additional help, because he was able to ask so many questions in class.

"Some days I still had to see Mr. Hsu at lunch, or come early to class, but my dad doesn't have to pay for expensive tutors anymore," Rasheed says, smiling.

DESEGREGATION

(1957–1970)

In 1957 the superintendent of San Francisco, Harold Spears, was at the United Nations Educational, Scientific and Cultural Organization (UNESCO) meeting in Paris, where the news of Soviet Russia's launching of *Sputnik*—the first-ever artificial Earth satellite—shocked the assembled representatives. Within a few months prominent public figures came to San Francisco to blast public schools, which they viewed as responsible for the fact that the Soviet Union was ahead of the United States in science and math, as Larry Cuban describes in *Urban School Chiefs Under Fire*. Even though child-centered education had limited influence in the classrooms, by then critics of public schools associated the term "progressive" education and the name of Dewey with everything that they viewed as wrong with American schools: curriculum that wasn't hard enough, lax discipline, and too many classes focused on life skills. All four local newspapers ran front-page news articles, editorials, and weekly series with titles like "U.S. Schools—Can They Win the Science Race?" and "What's Wrong with Our Schools?"[1]

Just as some of today's prominent education reformers, such as Bill Gates, are worried about foreign rivals like China beating America's economy, power elites at the time were propelled by similar fears over the growing power of the Soviet Union. And just like today, they argued that schools were responsible for the fact that the Soviet Union was pulling ahead of the United States, and schools should spend more time on the core subjects of math, sciences, and reading, even at the expense of time spent on history, music, arts, or sports. Historian Joel Spring describes this period in *Schools: The Story of American Public Education*: "A teacher in my classroom pointed a finger at me and said, 'There is Ivan in the Soviet Union studying math and you are studying math and if you don't do well, we are going to lose to communism.' And I was forced out of history courses into math and physics programs as a result of Sputnik."[2] In 1958 President Eisenhower signed the National Defense Education Act, which sent federal monies into public schools to get more students to take math and science courses and train teachers in those subjects.

While Spears was dealing with the aftermath of *Sputnik*, civil rights organizers, students of color, and parents all over the country were demanding more control, access, and equity within a school system set up and run by the Administrative Progressives at the turn of the century. Echoing the views of African American educators like

W. E. B. DuBois and Anna Julia Cooper a generation earlier, the student activists, their parents, and many teachers called for alternatives to the centralized system run by
"expert" professionals, who in their view created schools
that were reproducing racial and class inequities.

In 1957 in Little Rock, Arkansas, Melba Pattillo
Beals—one of the first African American students to
attend a previously segregated, all-white school—found
herself trapped in a bathroom stall as white girls threw
flaming wads of paper over the top of the stall door,
attempting to set her on fire. The flames singed her face
and burned her arm before she freed herself by throwing
her heavy books over the door and escaped. At another
point in the school year, a white boy threw acid in her
eyes.[3] Beals was one of nine African American teenagers
chosen by the National Association for the Advancement
of Colored People (NAACP) to integrate Central High
School in Little Rock, as schools had become the main
battleground in the larger, national fight for racial justice.

Three years earlier the NAACP lawyers had argued
against segregation in the Supreme Court. On May 17,
1954, Chief Justice Earl Warren announced the unan-
imous decision in *Brown v. Board of Education* that
"separate but equal" schools were unconstitutional. Fore-
shadowing the findings of the researcher Claude Steele
almost three decades later, Warren's decision focused on
the lasting psychological damage of segregation, writing
that separating black children "from others of similar age
and qualifications solely because of their race generates a
feeling of inferiority as to their status in the community
that may affect their hearts and minds in a way unlikely

ever to be undone." As journalist Nikole Hannah-Jones argues in a ProPublica "Segregation Now" investigative feature, *Brown v. Board of Education* wasn't an argument for equitable distribution of funding among schools; it hinged on the idea that the "integration of schools was essential to the integration of black citizens into society as a whole."[4] The ruling affected 40 percent of the students in American public schools, according to author Dana Goldstein.[5] Prior to the ruling, seventeen states had laws that made integrated schools illegal. As Beals and her classmates tried to integrate Central High, Governor Orval Faubus of Arkansas called out the National Guard rather than allow African American teenagers to go to a previously all-white school. In response, President Dwight Eisenhower sent federal troops to enforce the law. Desegregation was moving slowly. A decade after the *Brown* ruling, over 90 percent of southern black students still attended segregated schools.[6]

While organizers in the South were fighting to end apartheid schooling there, civil rights organizers like the NAACP and CORE (Congress on Racial Equality) were protesting segregation of public schools in the West and Northeast, including San Francisco. While the *Brown v. Board of Education* decision made segregation illegal in the South, de facto segregation was widely practiced in the rest of the country, mostly through discriminatory housing policies. Many Progressives on the West Coast, like Spears, resisted acknowledging that segregation existed and working on solutions, sparking boycotts and lawsuits. A growing number of civil rights groups, parents, and students were also becoming increasingly critical of tracking, which they viewed as segregation in "desegregated" schools.[7]

In the Bay Area, parents of color started to organize for a more equitable distribution of resources among schools. In 1974 in San Francisco, lawyers had successfully sued on behalf of eighteen hundred Chinese American students demanding English as a Second Language programs. *Lau v. Nichols* was an important court case that, for the first time, made an argument within the context of public education that equity doesn't always mean equal distribution of resources. English learners, poor students, and students with disabilities have different, unique needs, they argued, and equity means providing extra resources and funding to respect their needs.[8] A separate 1976 court case extended these civil rights to nearly 3.7 million students with disabilities.[9]

From the walkouts in East Los Angeles to strikes in Crystal City, Texas, to Detroit, Michigan, some thirty thousand African American and Latino students went on strikes in 1968 calling for new curricula that included the intellectual contributions of Latino and African American cultures, more diversity in staff, and more humane treatment by their white teachers.[10] The new generation of organizers felt that standardization led to an idea that students of color were suffering from cultural deficits, rather than acknowledging that there might have been a mismatch between the culture of the school and the culture of communities. Students of the San Francisco State University's Black Student Union and a coalition of other student groups called Third World Liberation Front (TWLF) led America's longest student-led strike on any campus; it lasted close to five months. Activists' lists of demands called for new classes that would include the histories, philosophies, and sciences of African Americans, Latinos, American Indians, Arab and Muslim Americans, and Asian Americans. The American Federation of Teachers joined the strikers, and as a result of the prolonged standoff, San Francisco State University created the first-ever College of Ethnic Studies, in 1969.[11] Almost two decades after the founding of the College of Ethnic Studies, which created a new Black Studies Department, McKamey, Roth, and their colleagues would enroll in the seminars there that introduced a new generation of teachers to the long history of educational theory and successful practices among African American teachers, such as W. E. B. DuBois, Bob Moses, and Noma LeMoine, among others.

In 1965 President Lyndon Johnson signed the Elementary and Secondary Education Act (ESEA)—the most significant federal intervention in education in the twentieth century and a precursor to No Child Left Behind—as part of his War on Poverty, which provided significant extra funding, known as Title I, to high-poverty schools that were historically neglected by the local school boards. David Tyack writes that a great deal of that extra federal and philanthropic funding in the 1960s unfortunately went to middle-class bureaucrats to administer some new top-down approach that only intensified the same standardized strategy, like remedial classes, rather than allowing teachers to come up with instructional methods and curricula that were more rooted in the cultures and needs of their students.[12] But with this extra federal funding, enforcement, and increased oversight came a growing acceptance of a new role of Washington in state and local education matters. When federal legislators sent extra funding to local schools, they wanted some kind of assurance that this funding was reaching the students and was making a difference. Robert Kennedy was one of the chief advocates for the use of standardized achievement testing to make sure that federal funding was used to help students who were historically neglected. Cuban pins the beginning of the move toward high-stakes testing and accountability to the passage of the ESEA. Anya Kamenetz argues that the instruments that were once created to justify racist practices now became the most powerful tools used to diagnose the wrongs of racism and to fight it.[13]

Chapter 5

Pablo

It is a little past noon, and Mission High School's annual Drag Show is about to begin. The air in the school auditorium is hot, alive with loud chatter and intermittent laughter from a crowd of more than a thousand students and adults. Scattered blue, pink, and yellow lights move across the sea of teenage faces. The stage sparkles with holiday lights and glitter. The projection screen on the stage reads: "'That's so gay' is NOT okay. Celebrate gay, hooray!" A few students sitting in the front rows are reading posters near the stage. Each displays someone's "coming out testimonial": "I am coming out as Gay, because I am fabulous." "I am coming out as a poet, because everyone should express themselves honestly and creatively!" "I am coming out as straight because I love girls!"

Pablo, a senior, is standing behind a heavy, yellow velvet curtain at the back of the stage. His slender shoulders are moving up and down, as he is breathing rapidly. He can hear the voices and laughter on the other side of the curtain. The show has started. The MC on stage announces Pablo's name, and the volume of student voices in the audience goes up. His heart is racing. He wipes the sweat off his forehead with a white towel, but the drops reappear again. His tongue feels swollen and dry. Pablo asks his friends for a glass of water.

This year's Drag Show—put on by Mission High's Gay-Straight Alliance (GSA)—has already been going better than all others Pablo has been a part of since he arrived at Mission in 2009. The Drag Show is a homegrown expression created by students of Mission High, which is located near the Castro district, the historic neighborhood with one of the largest gay populations in the country. The annual show features student- and teacher-choreographed dances, student and teacher "coming out" speeches, short educational videos on LGBTQ (lesbian, gay, bisexual, transgender, and questioning) issues, and the popular "fashion show" in which teachers, administrators, security guards, and students appear dressed in drag.

Principal Eric Guthertz steps onto the stage in a white dress with a brown print on it, blond wig, and red patent leather platforms to introduce the student dance Pablo has choreographed to Nicki Minaj's song "Super Bass." As Pablo and his five friends playfully twist and turn across the stage—dressed in shorts, fishnet stockings, and white tank tops—the audience cheers. Midway through the dance, during a blaring bass solo, a few students get up and dance on their chairs.

Pablo has spent more than a year thinking about the dance moves and his interpretation of the song. He has mixed in traditional dance moves from his native Guatemala: salsa, cumbia, merengue, and tango. Other ideas came from musical artists he admires, like Boy George and

Lady Gaga. But the story is all his: he wants to convey the idea that dance, like life, is most meaningful when people are allowed to be whoever they want to be. For Pablo, it means breaking through the rigid confines of gender-based dance moves, allowing students to make up their own.

The MC announces Pablo's name again. The screaming crowd gets louder. Pablo is scheduled to be the third student speaker in the Drag Show and will share his coming out story.

"Pablo, please come out," the MC comes behind the curtain and asks him.

"I need five more minutes," Pablo replies.

What if they throw things at me while I'm talking? Pablo is thinking to himself. He starts shaking.

Someone taps his shoulder and gives him a glass of water. As Pablo drinks the water, he thinks of his friend and classmate Mario, a shy young woman who told him a year ago that she was forced to come out by her classmates before she was ready. After she came out, one young man at school threatened to hurt her. Mr. Hsu had to get involved. Pablo knows Mario is in the auditorium, counting on him to come out on the stage.

One, two, three, four, five, Pablo is now counting steps in his head, looking at his black Doc Martens, as he moves toward the stage. On *six* he raises his eyes toward the lights, standing in front of the podium. He is concentrating on the bright lights above the faces in the auditorium, imagining he is in Guatemala, standing outside, alone, in the summer night. His breathing slows down, and he lifts the black microphone toward his mouth, which is covered in bright pink lipstick.

"Hello, Mission High School," Pablo's soft voice interrupts the cheering, and the noise stills.

"Pablo, we love you!" a student cheers, and Pablo's pink lips relax into a smile. He blocks his eyes from the bright lights pointing at him on stage now and pauses to look around.

"My name is Pablo," he says in a warm, confident voice. Then he glances at his written speech on his phone one more time before he continues.

"I describe myself in a million different ways. But today, I will tell you that I am Latino and gay. Just in case you still have struggles with race, gender, and sexuality, let me tell you something. Maybe what you see, maybe the outside, it's different, but on the inside we are all the same.

"Screw 'perfect'; your imperfections, they make you. You and your flaws is what makes you beautiful. Don't ever let a single soul define you. Don't ever let a single bully, classmate or even a single teacher define you."

"Amen!" a student shouts from the audience.

"Hi, Pablo!" a senior named Carlos yells out from the balcony on the second floor.

"Hi, Carlos," Pablo says before he brings the microphone back to his lips.

"I knew I was gay before coming out. In my sophomore year, I came out to my best friend Claudia in a PE class. That morning, I felt brave, I felt free, I felt honest. Sounds easy, but I used to spend a lot of time crying, hating myself, praying to God to 'change' me.

"I told my mom the same year. 'Know that I'm not strange and that this is not just a phase. I'm trying to tell you my secret. Will you open your ears and hear my heart's voice?'

"I got rejected at home. Sometimes, it hurts. But I understand. A lot of things can't go the way you want them to, but you have to learn how to work them out.

"I told myself no matter who didn't believe in me, I would still cope because I got reasons to stand up and speak up some day. Well, I am speaking in front of y'all right now! I get strength from this and this is the strength that pushes me to make progress.

"But above everything, I still love my mom. I recognize her. She works from 7:30 a.m. till 5 p.m., Monday to Friday. Maybe she doesn't accept that little but amazing part of me, and as much as I wish she could be sitting in the front row right now, 'Mom, I love you.'

"I want to tell you that I am a crazy dreamer, but I am not alone. From Seneca Falls where the first well-known women's rights convention in the US happened, through Selma where Dr. King and other organizers led one of the protests for civil rights, to Stonewall Rebellion, the birth of the LGBTQ movement, and now here in our school, it's called progress, people, whether you like it or not."

"Hello, Mission High School," Pablo raises the microphone closer to his lips. "My name is Pablo. I can describe myself in a million ways, but for today, I will tell you that I am Latino and gay." Pablo puts down the microphone and walks off the stage, carefully and slowly stepping on his high, suede heels. A young woman in the front row jumps to her feet, applauding above her head of long, black, bouncing curls. She turns and shouts to the applauding friends next her, who rise up from their seats and join her and others in the auditorium for a roaring ovation.

∞∞∞∞∞∞∞∞∞∞∞

When Pablo was nine, he spent most afternoons lounging on his fourteen-year-old cousin Vicky's mattress, listening to her music and watching her try on different outfits. Vicky liked to pull different skirts, pants, blouses, and jackets out of her closet and put them on in various combinations until she created a new look.

"Don't ever let anyone bully you into their styles," Vicky told Pablo. "Create your own fashion."

Pablo lived with Vicky and her mother Maria in a two-room house in Las Mercedes, a small, mostly rural town about thirty minutes away from Guatemala City. Pablo's mother left to look for work in California when Pablo turned six, and she asked her sister Maria to look after him. The mirror in Vicky's room, right next to her closet, was the size of a small television screen. Vicky could only see her face and shoulders in it. As she tried on her outfits, she asked Pablo for advice.

"Yes. No. This is not a good combo. That is gorgeous," Pablo would say, sitting on Vicky's bed.

After Vicky chose her outfit, she put on mascara and brushed her hair, telling Pablo about her crushes and friends. He told her his stories and secrets. At home and at school, he felt like Vicky was the only person who didn't look at him like he had a disease. At school, Vicky wasn't considered one of the pretty or popular girls. She was more voluptuous than most other girls of her age, and some days she would complain to Pablo about the school kids who called her names. Then she would say that both of them couldn't allow the bullies to define them.

Vicky had her own sewing machine. She took cheap clothes and changed them by adding different pieces of new and old fabric: lace or illustrations with Mayan and Aztec symbols. She took her black leather jacket and sewed on images of bird feathers and trees. Her jean jacket had drawings of mythological animals on it. No one at their large, Catholic school dressed like Vicky. She stood out. And the more bullies at the school called her names, the bolder her clothes became. Pablo noticed that there was something powerful about that—Vicky's courage to be herself, to stand out. He noticed that at school some girls bullied her publicly, but their eyes showed envy when they looked at her in private. Vicky used fashion to stand up for herself. That's how Pablo wanted to be in the world too, someday, he decided back then.

Whenever anyone asked him what he wanted to be when he grew up, he replied, "a doctor" just so they would leave him alone. At school, Pablo was even less popular than Vicky. The kids at school made fun of the way he held his hands, the way he walked, and the soft tone of his voice. "You are going to die and go to hell! You should be reading the Bible more," some classmates would yell in his face, their eyes gleaming. His cousin said he danced like a girl, and that it was embarrassing his family. He stopped inviting Pablo to his parties.

"What's wrong with me?" Pablo asked his uncle's wife—who worked as a nurse at the local hospital—during a visit when he was ten.

"You have a disease," she replied. She knew of a place where Pablo could get treatment to change. But for now, Pablo would have to ask God to change him.

The teachers at Pablo's Catholic school asked him to pray too and spent a lot of time teaching him the Bible. One of two schools in his small hometown, Pablo's school was run by the Catholic Church. Except for a cross above the chalkboard, there were no adornments or windows in the classrooms. Sitting at individual desks, girls sat on one side, boys on the other. The school's fence was topped with barbed wire. Pablo didn't believe what the Bible said about God or love. It didn't make sense to him. *If God is preaching love, why do people who believe in the Bible hate me?* he often thought to himself. *Why are the people who want to kill me going to heaven and I'm not?*

When Pablo needed to hide from the bullies, he went to the safest place at school, the library. He spent many hours there and read books his school wasn't teaching. One year Pablo read everything he could find about Leonardo da Vinci. He was inspired especially by da Vinci's drive to follow his interests and learn on his own. Pablo also found books about his ancestors—the Mayans, the Aztecs—and the gods in Guatemala before the Spanish brought over Catholicism. All of these books helped him realize that other people before him had had much harder lives, but they had found ways to thrive anyway.

At home Pablo told his Aunt Maria about the books he read. Maria, like his mother, had left school in the third grade to work in the fields, but she was very curious. Sometimes Pablo told Maria about the bullies and said he wasn't going back to school. His aunt would always say the same thing, "If you go to school, you can become anything. You can do anything you want."

On particularly difficult days, Pablo liked going for long walks in the evening. He followed the sun and watched the color of the mountains change. As the stars appeared, Pablo dreamed of becoming a famous fashion designer. He would have his own parties. Everyone would be invited except for his cousin and the bullies.

◇◇◇◇◇◇◇◇◇◇◇◇◇◇◇◇◇

Mission High School had about the same number of students as Pablo's middle school in Las Mercedes, but it felt different. At Mission, no one pushed him around or punched him in the stomach. But some days the verbal banter and social isolation were overwhelming. Pablo didn't care as much about the words he heard in the hallways. He tried to walk down the halls with a friend, and the many hallways and staircases made it easy enough to escape tense situations. In some classrooms, though, there was no escape. At Mercedes, everyone had his or her own desk, and students weren't allowed to talk to each other during class. At his new school, many teachers arranged desks for group work. Now Pablo's grade often depended on his ability to get along with people, who sometimes said out loud that they didn't want him near them.

In his freshman algebra class, Pablo's teacher asked him to sit in a group of four students. Pablo sat down next to Carlos, a recent immigrant from Honduras, who wore a San Francisco Giants hat and a small cross around his neck, over his T-shirt. Pablo liked math and was good at it. Carlos was a top student in math too, and he was extremely competitive. In the first week of class, whenever Pablo solved a problem before everyone else in the group, Carlos whispered comments in Spanish. "No, you don't know this. You are dumb, because you are gay." The teacher didn't hear the comments.

A few weeks later, when Pablo was graphing a slope on the whiteboard in front of the whole class, Carlos started calling him names in Spanish out loud. The math teacher heard him this time and sent Carlos downstairs to the dean's office. But when Carlos came back, the situation was no better for Pablo. Carlos came back even more emboldened and more cruel than before.

On another occasion, Pablo's math teacher was writing out numbers on the whiteboard, and each number was painted in a different color, forming a rainbow. Carlos said in Spanish that it looked like a gay flag. Another student chimed in; she said she didn't think that gay marriage was right. At the time, Pablo hadn't come out yet—even to himself. As students joined in, he said that he didn't think that gay marriage was right either.

"Are you serious?" Carlos turned to him. "How can you turn against your own people?"

Later that day at home, Pablo was suffocating under the unbearable weight of shame. *Why am I afraid to come out? Why am I lying?* he thought. It was during this quiet, private monologue, sitting in his room alone, that Pablo came out of the closet to himself for the first time.

During his freshman year at Mission in 2009, Pablo was in classes for English learners. His teacher, Deborah Fedorchuk, had all of her students write in journals at the beginning of each class. She would write a topic on the whiteboard, set the clock for ten minutes, and encourage students to write without stopping. Whatever they wanted to say was fine, she assured them.

One day she wrote down, "Women's Rights," and Pablo surprised himself. He wrote more than ever in English: seven long paragraphs. He wrote about the men in Las Mercedes who used to say, "Oh, those feminists, they are a bunch of dykes." When women in a local grassroots feminist organization protested on the street, the men called the protesters "men-haters." He remembers writing, "Why do women have to pretend to be weak?" The women in his family were stronger than the men. Pablo's mother risked her life to come to America by herself. She worked in restaurants and sent money back home to support Pablo, her unemployed brothers and sisters, and her parents. Because she was supporting so many family members back home, it took her nine years to save up enough to have Pablo come join her in America in 2008. None of the men in Pablo's family had the courage to come to the United States first. His aunties who stayed behind worked two jobs and then took care of homes and children while the men rested after work.

Pablo wrote, and the words kept pouring out. At the end of the paper he decided that he was "for women's rights" and that he was a "feminist ally." Ms. Fedorchuk loved the essay and discussed it with Pablo at lunch. She enjoyed talking to her students about their journals. Almost every day, Pablo would come to her classroom and discuss with her various political and social issues: green economies and recycling, guns and "cholos," stereotypes, women.

"Ms. Fedorchuk was the first person at Mission who made me feel at home," Pablo recalls four years later, as a senior. "I felt mute until I met her. Her interest in my ideas made me feel alive again. I wanted to be heard so bad. I was so shy and didn't speak English. She made me talk."

Later in his freshman year, Ms. Fedorchuk told Pablo about Taica Hsu, who sponsored the school's Gay-Straight Alliance (GSA) club, in which students who shared Pablo's views on women's rights debated various social and political issues. Mr. Hsu spoke fluent Spanish and taught math—Pablo's favorite subject. Even though Mr. Hsu wasn't his math teacher, Pablo felt most comfortable asking him for help with math when he struggled in his classes and checking in about anything else that was going on in his life at the time. Pablo started going to the GSA's weekly meetings. He still struggled with his English and was painfully shy at first. But he liked the GSA's president, Michelle—a bold, openly bisexual young woman—who had ambitious ideas for events and campaigns. Eventually Pablo decided to become the vice president of the GSA.

Once a week Mr. Hsu, Michelle, and Pablo met to plan the upcoming GSA meeting. During these sessions Mr. Hsu taught Pablo and Michelle how to write agendas, keep everyone engaged, and make people feel welcome and included during meetings. That year they organized the first panel at which GSA students educated teachers on how to intervene when homophobic, sexist, or racist language is used in the classrooms. The idea came about after the group realized that most bullying was happening in the classrooms, rather than in the hallways.

The GSA invited all faculty members to come to their panel, at which students shared real examples of how teachers had intervened in a way that they thought was constructive. Pablo was one of the speakers on the panel, remembering how Ms. McKamey had responded to an African American student who made the comment "Don't be a fag" to his friend during her class. "Excuse me," Ms. McKamey had stopped the class with a visible sense of urgency and concern. "We never use that kind of language here. How would you feel if someone said, 'That's so black?'" Pablo recalled that the student had apologized, and that kind of language didn't occur in her class again. He and other panelists advised teachers to do more of that—to relate LGBTQ bullying to other forms of abuse that students at the school can identify with, such as racism or hateful language targeting undocumented immigrants. Hsu says that almost all the teachers came to the panel and later expressed their support for such discussions with students. Most teaching programs and professional development days in schools don't provide that kind of training on appropriate ways to intervene. Some teachers feel they should say something, but they don't know how to respond appropriately.

As students shared their experiences, they came to the conclusion that some teachers were better than others at stopping abusive language or establishing a classroom culture that proactively prevents bullying in the first place. They decided to share these best practices with all teachers.

The GSA panelists made many suggestions on how to address these issues, including incorporating more

LGBTQ content into the curriculum. "A small group of history teachers always included studies of the LGBTQ movements in their history classes, but many don't," Pablo says. "When they do, they show how these movements helped everyone and present gay people in a positive way."

One day during his sophomore year Pablo's best friend Claudia was telling him about her crushes during their PE class. When she was done talking, she asked, "Do you have someone you like?"

"No," Pablo said.

A week later, she asked Pablo again, while they were doing push-ups.

"You know how you tell me that you need to hug a pillow after you wake up from a nightmare?" Pablo said. "Let's pretend I'm having a nightmare right now. I need you to be there for me. There is someone I feel attracted to, and his name is Stephen."

Claudia stopped doing push-ups.

"Yes, I'm gay," Pablo said, continuing to do push-ups.

"Oh, my God!" Claudia smiled. "I knew it."

Someone overheard them talking, and the news spread quickly throughout the school.

"It didn't matter anymore," Pablo recalls during our conversation. "After I came out, I felt like I had space in the school. I felt bigger. I felt like, 'yes, I'm going to cope. I'm going to have good grades.' I used to walk down the hall, and some people blocked me. Now, when I said, 'Excuse me,' some bullies would still say, 'Fuck you,' as usual, but now they moved out of my way."

When Pablo came out to Claudia and joined the GSA, he felt physically and emotionally stronger and more confident in his abilities to cope with his new place in the world. At school, Pablo felt that people noticed him more. His grades improved, eventually landing him on the honor roll.

But at the end of his sophomore year, when school was out for the summer, life at home felt more stifling than usual. Pablo was spending more time at his house, where he lived with his mother and two uncles. His inability to be truthful with his mom weighed more heavily on his mind with each passing day.

"Are you gay?" his mother asked more frequently now, probably noticing that Pablo's clothing had become more daring. "You can't live here if you are. I'm going to send you back to Guatemala," she warned him.

"I'm not gay," Pablo responded, as usual. But lying to his own mother seemed worse than concealing the truth from anyone else.

Then on July 11, 2011, Pablo woke up, walked into the kitchen, and came out to his mother in one sentence. She slapped him across the face. He would die from AIDS, she said, and told him to get out of the house. He could come back when he "changed." She said many more things after that, but Pablo couldn't hear her anymore. As he stood in the kitchen, he thought about how, for the first time ever, his mother looked frightened and painfully frail to him.

Pablo left without taking anything with him. He walked without any destination in mind and eventually hopped on a bus. As he rode away from his neighborhood, he thought about going toward Lake Merced, across town, finding a boat, and jumping out of it in the middle of the lake. The bus took a sharp turn, and the rays of the afternoon sun hit Pablo's body, heating up his face and shoulders through the window. Pablo remembered Guatemala, his long walks in the evenings after sunset.

After the sun went down, Pablo got off near Golden Gate Park. It was cold outside, and he felt hungry. He texted Mr. Hsu. Twenty minutes later Mr. Hsu arrived in his car and took Pablo to get some dinner in a nearby café in the Haight-Ashbury district. He brought him extra sweaters, T-shirts, and jeans and asked Pablo if there was someone he could stay with. Pablo said he wanted to stay with his friend Claudia. He had met her grandmother and knew she liked him.

As Pablo ate his burger, Mr. Hsu told him that he knew a lot of people who had gone through a similar journey and that things would eventually improve. His mother would come around to accept him, but it would take a long time. But there were ways to find support and allies. Mr. Hsu drove Pablo to Claudia's house, and the next day at school he filled out a Child Protective Services form and filed a report with the government agency.

At school Mr. Hsu checked on Pablo every day. His attendance and grades plummeted, and Mr. Hsu was worried. He talked to Pablo's teachers and sent out an e-mail asking them to be more lenient with Pablo's deadlines that month. In addition, Mr. Hsu introduced Pablo to his friend Erik Martinez, who was a case manager at a local LGBTQ youth community center and educational organization called LYRIC. Pablo started going to LYRIC every two weeks. He enjoyed talking to Martinez. Pablo didn't want to sit in a small room talking to a therapist about all of the things that were horrible in his life. He wanted to be in a group of like-minded people who were dealing with similar issues. LYRIC provided that community and felt like home. Pablo's relationship with his family remained strained, but he started feeling stronger about his ability to cope with it.

"The [Drag Show] dance, my expression, the LYRIC family was my therapy back then," Pablo reflects now. "What I really needed was resilience and building my confidence and skills to speak out."

∞∞∞∞∞∞∞∞∞∞∞

In schools all over the United States, teens who identify as LGBTQ are bullied far more than others. A 2011 national survey conducted by the Gay, Lesbian & Straight Education Network found that homophobic (and sexist) remarks are more common today than racist comments. In addition, 82 percent of kids who identified as LGBTQ said they had been verbally harassed at school; 38 percent had been physically harassed, and 18 percent had been physically assaulted. These youths are more likely to skip school and have lower grades.[1]

Studies show that a gay-straight student alliance is one of the strongest buffers a school can build to reduce the bullying of gay teens. In schools with GSAs—according to journalist Emily Bazelon, author of *Sticks and Stones*—kids experience less abuse, have higher grades, and feel a greater sense of belonging.[2] Gay-Straight Student Alliance Network was founded in 1998. Although many schools still ban them, there are about thirty-five hundred clubs around the country, mostly in high schools, as well as some in middle schools, according to the GSA national network manager, Alan Ratliff.

The National Association of GSA Networks considers Mission High one of its strongest and most effective local chapters in the country. Mission High students, teachers, and administrators say that their GSA draws most of its strength from an authentic student ownership model. The work of its leadership is then reinforced by a larger, school-based approach designed to reduce stereotypes and biases, including sexism, racism, and the bullying of students with disabilities.

Most local GSAs look for guidance from the national organization, which coordinates large events for local chapters to participate in, such as National Coming Out Day. This national campaign raises awareness of the LGBTQ community, highlights commonalities among gay students and others who live with complex, multiple identities or struggle with exclusion, and gives LGBTQ students in each school the ability to express themselves publicly.

Distributing forms for the National Coming Out Day was one of the first campaigns Pablo ran when he joined the GSA, encouraging students to reveal hidden or lesser-known sides of their identity. As forms dotted the walls of Mission High, some students came out as queer; others as allies of LGBTQ friends and family; and others as poets, punk rockers, dancers, food lovers, and secret admirers. Pablo says that in his freshman year about twenty students filled out the forms. By his senior year, more than three hundred did.

During his sophomore year Pablo danced in his first Drag Show. It was the first time Mission High opened up the event to the entire school, after four years of gradual buildup. As he danced, I sat in the back of the auditorium. The vast majority of students around me clapped and cheered. A few yelled out crude jokes, and teachers had to walk several students out. When one student was reading her "coming out" testimonial, someone threw a piece of crumpled paper at her. The ball didn't make it to the podium and landed in the front rows.

Even though the reception of the first public show was not as welcoming and widespread as the one in which Pablo read his testimonial three years later, he felt a tangible change at school the next day. As he walked down the hallways, countless students approached him to express support. He also noticed that students who didn't fit in— socially isolated and bullied kids who were not LGBTQ— wanted to talk to him. Some said they wanted to dance in next year's Drag Show. Others wanted to share their own stories of social exclusion, racism, or bullying.

"Before the Drag Show I was a freak and it was a bad thing," Pablo recalls. "Now, it became a good thing. Many students still looked at us as weird, but now we were also cool. We know how to dance, how to put on the most popular party at school, and we are good at listening to different people."

When Pablo became the vice president of Mission High's GSA in his sophomore year, he proposed that the GSA put even more energy into homegrown activities designed by students. He also wanted to put on more events that celebrated queer culture; he felt that too many events focused on the ways in which LGBTQ teens were being repressed. "I didn't want Mission High to see gay students only as victims or negative statistics," he says. "I wanted everyone to see us as the most active and positive people at the school." If the GSA could put on the most popular parties at the school, Pablo reasoned, the club would attract many more allies, who would then become powerful ambassadors and disseminators of a culture of respect among students who would not otherwise connect to the GSA on their own. These student allies would also be taught to intervene and stop the spread of homophobic language.

Kim, a straight member of the GSA, is a perfect example of how Pablo's strategy worked. "I loved the dances and that's why I joined, and so many others do too," she explains. "What appealed to me is that the Drag Show was the only place at the school where the dances were modern, not traditional. I love Lady Gaga, and I wanted to dance to pop music. As we were practicing for the Drag Show, I learned about the meaning behind these dances and the Drag. But we also just hung out a lot and talked about life, and I learned about how hard it was for LGBTQ students to be out. I learned about the high number of suicides among gay teenagers.

"The Drag Show was the most powerful recruitment tool," Kim adds. "My friends saw me dance and wanted to join, and I'd say, 'Oh, I'm going to a GSA meeting today and they'd just come and hang out.' At any time, half of the kids were just hanging out there, eating pizza and seeing straight people they know support LGBTQ people."

Alejandra has been a member of GSA since 2010. She is also the president of the Awaken Dreamers Club at Mission High, a homegrown organization that represents undocumented students. Named after the DREAM Act—the proposed federal Development, Relief, and Education for Alien Minors Act—which would grant permanent residency to certain undocumented children, the club raises scholarships for undocumented students who aren't eligible for federal college aid.[3] Alejandra was taking a class with Mr. Hsu, and one day she lingered after the bell rang. Meanwhile the GSA students showed up for a meeting. Alejandra says that as she ate pizza and listened in on the meeting, she fell in love with the group's sense of commitment to a common cause and boundless inclusion. Alejandra considers Pablo one of her closest friends now. After Pablo met Alejandra, he joined the Dreamers Club. He also went to meetings at the Ole' Club, Mission High students' Latino club.

When the news broke about Trayvon Martin, a young, unarmed African American teenager who was shot and killed by a volunteer neighborhood watch in Sanford, Florida, in 2012, Pablo became the lead organizer of the National Hoodie Day at Mission, which called for the end of stereotyping of black teenage boys as public threats. Kim, who became the president of the Dreamers Club after Alejandra went to UC Berkeley, thinks that it was Pablo's genuine engagement in other student clubs as an openly gay man—who is also Latino and undocumented—that helped so many other students see him as an ally despite the fact that he had a complex, nontraditional identity.

"GSA was the only club at Mission High that was a movement," Kim emphasizes, as a senior. "It's much more than education and cultural pride. It's a movement for change that is completely run by the students. Mr. Hsu, more than other teachers I've encountered, really lets the students be in charge of the club. He really steps back, but he is also always there when we need his help with organizational skills." Students like Kim, Alejandra, and the Dreamers and Pablo's allies at the Black Student Union became key leaders of cultural change outside of the GSA by modeling a different kind of language and attitudes toward LGBTQ youth.

Pablo's third and final Drag Show was the most popular event at Mission among students that year, and because it was open to the entire school, it was probably the only event of its kind anywhere in the country. When Pablo read his testimonial to the audience, the auditorium—filled with more than nine hundred teenagers from dozens of cultural and religious backgrounds—was so quiet and respectful that I could hear Pablo's breathing in the microphone. "It feels like a mini-Utopia in here," my friend and photographer Winni Wintermeyer, who was there to document the show, whispered in my ear. Some of the loudest cheers of support came from Carlos, Pablo's biggest tormentor four years earlier. A month after the Drag Show, Pablo helped Carlos find his first job out of high school.

While the situation for LGBTQ youth remains dire in too many schools across the country, the school climate for all students at Mission visibly improved from 2010 to 2014, according to students. In a district-wide 2013 student survey, 51 percent of Mission High eleventh graders reported that other students "never" or "rarely" made harassing statements based on sexual orientation, compared to 28 percent from the same grade in other schools. Significantly higher percentages of Mission High eleventh graders also reported that "this school encourages students to understand how others think and feel" and "students here try to stop bullying when they see it happen."[4]

Until the Columbine shootings in 1999, no states had laws that clearly addressed bullying of any kind. Now forty-nine states do. Many states and school districts have instituted antibullying policies and protocols, but the results have been discouraging. A study by the US Department of Education that followed six thousand students in eighty four elementary schools over the course of three years reported in 2010 that none of the seven major, current approaches used to teach character and reduce conflict and antisocial behavior has had any significant impact. According to Scott Seider, a professor of education at Boston University and author of *Character Compass*, one of the major takeaways of this study is that "copying and pasting" outside programs doesn't work. Schools have to create their own homegrown approaches to battling biases and antisocial behavior.[5]

Hsu, Roth, McKamey, and Principal Guthertz all agree that the success of any antibullying initiative depends on the degree of student ownership of the strategies for solutions. A GSA club, the Drag Show, or any other antibullying strategy that is superimposed by adults without genuine leadership and engagement by the students will not work. Another thing that wouldn't work, Pablo adds, is expecting that one club like the GSA can by itself change the entire school culture.

Outside of classrooms, Mission supports dozens of clubs that celebrate diversity, individual difference, and inclusive leadership. But most of the important work happens in the classroom, Pablo says. Teachers who are in charge of their classrooms know how to set up classrooms that encourage positive social norms and effective group work and collaboration among students. They model behavior. They show students how to stand up for others and stop abuse effectively. And most important for Pablo, great teachers find relevant, intellectually challenging content that teaches history, fiction, grammatical conventions, and vocabulary, but at the same time pushes students to explore the meaning of courage, empathy, honesty, forgiveness, and taking responsibility for one's own actions.

◇◇◇◇◇◇◇◇◇◇◇◇◇◇◇◇

It was nine in the morning, and Pablo was late for his English class with Pirette McKamey. He was a junior, and this was going to be his first mainstream English class after two years of work in classes for English learners. Pablo didn't think his English was strong enough to be in Ms. McKamey's class. He struggled with speaking in public and with writing, especially with punctuation and grammar.

Once Pablo found his new class, he tried to open the door as quietly as he could, hoping Ms. McKamey wouldn't notice that he was late.

McKamey stopped in midsentence. "What is your name?"

"Pablo."

"Oh, I've heard a lot of great things about you!" Mc-Kamey said with a smile. "Welcome. Now, why are you late, Pablo?"

"I couldn't find the right room," Pablo apologized.

"We already got started, but please have a seat."

Pablo heaved a sigh of relief and found an empty seat in the back.

"Last semester, my English class had a few Cs," Mc-Kamey said, returning to her lesson. "Everyone else had As and Bs. I will teach you the key to get an A in my class, and it's not about memorizing. You will learn how to write. You will learn how to research and analyze. You will learn how to write about others, and this will help you learn a lot about yourself. In my class, everyone starts with an A or a B, and it will be your job to keep it from going down. We will be writing every day, thinking critically, pushing ourselves, and if you work hard, we will have a lot of happy As. By the end of this class, writing essays will feel like eating candy."

After introductions, Pablo and his classmates read a short story by Sherman Alexie, "What You Pawn I Will Redeem," in which a young man goes on a quest to repurchase his grandmother's traditional Native American regalia from a pawnshop. Once students had read and discussed the story with each other, Ms. McKamey asked everyone to write a response to it.

The next time Pablo came to Ms. McKamey's class, she had already graded and returned everyone's essays. Pablo looked at her comments; they were different from other comments he had seen on his previous essays. In the past, most of his written work had come back with a lot of red marks and feedback focused on his weaknesses. The majority of his papers got Ds or Cs and often left Pablo feeling hopeless about his ability to improve. Ms. Mc-Kamey's marks and comments focused on his strengths, and she gave him specific suggestions on what to do to improve. Instead of just saying, "Add more detail," or "not clear," his drafts were dotted with many stars next to specific sentences or paragraphs with comments like, "Oh, I like this. Can you tell me what colors, sounds, and smells you noticed?" and "This is a very interesting point. Can you tell me more about what you are thinking here? Do you see any connections between this main character and your personal life?"

Pablo still remembers what Ms. McKamey wrote at the bottom of his first essay in her class: "Pablo, you are a talented, honest writer. Excellent ideas and I see a variety of evidence in your essay that supports your argument. Please come see me at lunch or after class this week to talk some more about this essay."

When Pablo came to Ms. McKamey's office, "she said, 'I gave you a B–, but I want to give you an A. For that, you are going to work hard, you are going to add more details I've suggested, and you are going to work on your punctuation,'" Pablo recalls, three years later.

"She taught me skills to deal with my weaknesses, but she was focused on my strengths and it made me feel motivated," Pablo explains. "How teachers look at you, what they see when they look at you, makes a difference. Teachers like Ms. McKamey assume that deep down, I am a good student, I want to do my work, but something is getting in the way. She'll slip a note to me during class, or come up to me, and keep asking me to turn in the work. But she does it with a lot of understanding and willingness to help. And so I wanted to write a story that will make Ms. McKamey love it more than anything she's ever read. I started spending hours at the library rewriting my papers, and I wasn't doing it because it was all wrong, but because I wanted Ms. McKamey to love it. I didn't want her just to like it. I wanted her to love it."

Pablo and his classmates wrote in every class with Ms. McKamey, and with each essay the evidence of Pablo's identity as a writer kept mounting. He wrote about Leonardo da Vinci, the Enlightenment, and how Leonardo da Vinci's passion and commitment changed the world. He wrote about personal quests and the way Lady Gaga inspired and motivated him. As the year went on, the quizzes and the writing assignments got tougher, and Pablo and his classmates had to work harder to maintain their As and Bs. Ms. McKamey taught Pablo how to use semicolons, and his sentences grew longer and more complex.

"We analyzed a lot of stories and saw how details, precise words, and punctuation make these stories interesting. So, I started walking around the city using my eyes like a camera, noticing more details. Everything around me became a story." Pablo loved the stories, poems, and articles that Ms. McKamey selected for his class. Some days he felt as if she chose them specifically for him, as if she knew what he was struggling with in his life. When Pablo read, he felt that he got to peer into the hearts of other people. As he followed their inner voyages, Pablo felt that he gained useful insights into what to do in certain life situations of his own.

Later that year Pablo found himself on the streets for the second time. His mother didn't like his tight clothing. It looked too feminine, she said. Pablo texted Mr. Hsu again and got on the bus. Mr. Hsu drove him to Claudia's house. Pablo saved his bus ticket. He wanted something to remind him of that day. Three days later, another social worker came and drove Pablo back home.

"In Ms. McKamey's class I pushed myself academically, but I also became a better person, and that's why I loved doing the hard work," he tells me. "In this difficult time, Ms. McKamey's teaching of fiction and poetry—in particular, *Those Winter Sundays* by the poet Robert Hayden—helped me acknowledge my mother's work. I didn't just see myself in this situation. I saw her in all of this."

One late night at home, Pablo made a collage. He put the bus tickets from each day his mother had asked him to leave the house in the left corner of a drawing he made. He put four cards with the names of new people he had met because of these conflicts and disagreements on the right side.

He framed his mementos and hung them near his mirror. Each morning, as Pablo got ready for school or work, he looked at that frame near his mirror. He liked being reminded that living honestly came with a huge price, but it also opened up a whole new world he didn't even know existed. He liked thinking of all the new people he had met at Mission High, LYRIC, and San Francisco. His world seemed much bigger now, filled with more confidence, compassion, and new possibilities.

◇◇◇◇◇◇◇◇◇◇◇◇◇◇

"I'm looking for shoes, women's size 11. Do you have that?" Principal Guthertz, dressed in a suit and tie and holding a walkie-talkie in his hand, asks while walking across the room toward Pablo's friend Alejandra. On the other side of the room a young man is applying eye shadow to Mr. Hsu's eyelids. I am standing next to Mr. Hsu, helping a student named Stephen in a large, blond wig put on his green gown. Mission High School's annual Drag Show is about to begin. Dozens of students and teachers are in the backstage dressing area, rushing around the room with dresses, shoes, wigs, and lipsticks in their hands. The tables are covered in clothes, feathers, large boxes of eye shadow, and glitter.

Alejandra picks out a pair of red patent leather shoes and gives them to Guthertz. "These high heels are killing me," he comments after he puts them on. "But these wedges are so much more comfortable to walk on than my heels last year. I think I'm a wedges guy," Guthertz smiles while the walkie-talkie in his hand crackles, and Alejandra and Nicole are already putting a wig on his head.

"I like this one," he says of the dark brown, bobbed wig he has on.

Alejandra and Nicole look at each other and shake their heads in disagreement.

They put a blond wig full of large curls on Guthertz's head and take a few steps back to assess it from a distance.

"Much better," Alejandra tells Nicole, who nods in agreement.

Guthertz now picks out a green dress, puts it on, and looks at the students questioningly.

"No, definitely not," a student named Juan says. "That green dress and the red shoes don't go together at all." Juan and his friend Sebastian tell me that they are from El Salvador and have been in the country for one year. They are not a part of the GSA, but they love the Drag Show.

Pablo arrived before everyone else and got dressed a long time ago. He couldn't sleep all night and had to take a cold shower in the morning, because he felt hot all night, like he was running a fever. As everyone dashes around the dressing area joking, laughing, sharing wigs and compliments, Pablo is standing alone near the backstage entrance.

"Looking good, Mr. Guthertz!" students comment as Guthertz walks past Pablo toward the stage, dressed in a white dress with a brown print on it, a white wig, and red patent leather shoes.

The MC of the Drag Show, Mia Tu Mutch—an educator and advocate who works at LYRIC—is on the other side of the yellow velvet curtains. "This year's theme is transformation," she says into the microphone. "Can you transform your language to be supportive and inclusive of the LGBT community? When someone says, 'That's so gay.' Say, 'Hey, that's so rude.' And remember, always honor who you are. Don't look at the magazines and let them define beautiful. Be comfortable in your own skin."

Pablo is now standing near the velvet curtain, dressed in a white tank top and denim shorts. Mia Tu Mutch calls Pablo to the stage.

"Could I get a glass of water, please?" Pablo turns to his friends and wipes the sweat from his forehead.

Chapter 6

Principal Guthertz

As the head of a school at which students carry passports from more than forty countries, Eric Guthertz probably has one of the most multicultural closets of any principal in the nation. Dressed in his usual getup this morning—slim-fitted, button-down shirt, dark grey slacks, and a large, black walkie-talkie pinned on his belt—Guthertz shows off dozens of his favorite clothing items that he wears throughout the year for various cultural events. Hanging on the wall in his office that doubles as a closet, there are several guayaberas—formal men's shirts worn in Mexico, Central America, and the Caribbean—which he wears to the students' Latino Club celebrations. There is a traditional Moroccan cream-colored shirt with black buttons that a student from Morocco gave him. The Black Student Union gave him a traditional kufi hat and scarf from West Africa. His favorite piece is a dark navy, three-piece suit that students from the Chinese Club gave him five years ago.

In Guthertz's universe, hustling to find funding to keep Mission's cultural clubs and events alive is as important as improving test scores. As an educator with twenty-eight years of experience in inner-city schools, Guthertz is convinced that multicultural and student-run clubs, after-school programs, and extracurricular activities not only engage more students in the core academic subjects, they also teach crucial skills for success after high school: familiarity with different cultures and worldviews, experience working through cultural misunderstandings with respect and common sense, and the ability to see diversity as an asset of a community. Emphasizing such social, emotional, and ethical skills also contributes to a positive school culture in which all students can thrive, Guthertz argues. "GSA is a huge part of this proactive work, but we also have dozens of other clubs—the Multicultural Club, Chinese, Filipino, Black, and Latino student assemblies. Our Youth Leadership Council helps us decide what clubs and after-school programs we should be running. We are teaching students how to be effective teaching assistants in special education classes, which demonstrates responsibility. There is the Best Buddies program where students hang out with students with disabilities. We have Mentoring Circles that help students learn self-advocacy skills. And there is the Student Advisory Council of thirty diverse students who help me make budgeting decisions."

Guthertz's convictions come at a price. The continuity of school funding—and with that the job security of teachers and staff who run many of these programs—depends on the school's ability to show consistent growth in standardized test scores. In 2009 Guthertz almost lost his job to secure SIG (School Improvement Grant) funding for the school, as part of President Obama's Race to the Top initiative. The $4 billion education funding package awarded competitive grants to states that agreed to meet a set of principles, such as using standardized test scores in teacher evaluations, easing restrictions on the number of charter schools, and restructuring or closing low-performing schools (as measured by test scores).[1] During the economic recession Race to the Top offered hard-to-resist financial "carrots" to low-performing schools like Mission in exchange for "sticks." Mission High had to choose between firing a principal, firing half of the teachers, closing the school, or replacing it with a charter school. The district found a loophole to avoid all of these scenarios. Guthertz had been a principal for less than two years and could be listed as a recently "replaced" principal. In 2012 the school's score on the Academic Progress Index (API) dropped by one point (out of the total of one thousand maximum points any school in California can receive on the API, which is calculated primarily based on standardized test scores), and the school faced the loss of close to $1 million, about 12 percent of its annual budget.[2] The district appealed the decision and requested recalculation of the scores, which came back with a one-point gain, saving the jobs of at least seven teachers, Guthertz says.

Despite these external pressures to prioritize test scores in math and English, Guthertz refuses to tell educators at Mission to "teach to the test" at the expense of giving up rich curriculum or hands-on projects, field trips, and music and art classes, or of closing student clubs and elective courses. He is convinced that such a pedagogical stance pays off, and he has data about his school to prove it. College enrollment went up from 55 percent in

2007 to 74 percent in 2013. While the API index fluctu-
ates from year to year, there has been an overall gain of 86
points since 2009. School attendance has been rising. The
graduation rate went from the lowest in the district, at 60
percent in 2008, to 82 percent in 2013, on a par with the
district average. The graduation rate for African American
students was 20 percent higher at Mission than the district
average in 2013. While the rest of the country is embroiled
in a debate over how to reduce suspensions, Mission High
has reduced its suspensions, from 28 percent in 2008 to
3.4 percent in 2014.[3] In the yearly student and parent satisfaction survey of 2013, close to 90 percent said they like
the school and would recommend it to others.[4]

As part of the proactive effort to build a positive school
culture, Mission High is using restorative practices, a
research-based intervention strategy that uses conflict or
misbehavior as an opportunity to teach students to take
responsibility for their actions. In May 2014 I spent a
day in the "referrals" room with two restorative practices
coaches, Cat Reyes and Juan Garcia, as well as Assistant Principal Valerie Forero, observing this program in
action. As pairs of students were sent out of classrooms
for disruptions, disrespectful language, and status rival-
ries, Forero, Garcia, and Reyes led them through a series
of questions to help name their own actions and discuss
alternative behaviors that would prevent conflict or misbehavior in the first place, such as not reacting to instiga-
tions and asking a teacher to be moved to another seat. In
too many schools across the country, Guthertz says, students who are kicked out of class spend time alone or do
chores, without an opportunity to reflect on why they were

removed from the classroom. The cycle continues, eventually contributing to the growing suspensions and expulsions epidemic of Latino and African American students in the United States.[5] The key assumption underlying this restorative work is that students already have good values and intentions, and the school staff can help students develop habits, skills, and a common language to turn negative incidents into positive learning experiences.

While Guthertz and his team spend at least half of their time building a healthy and inclusive school culture outside of the classrooms, most of the work that helps students develop as mature and compassionate adults happens in the classrooms, Guthertz says, echoing Pablo's view. That's why teacher-leaders and the administrative team regularly observe classrooms and comb through reams of data, paying particular attention to the number of referrals and suspensions, as well as the number of Fs and Ds desegregated by ethnicity and race, to see which students and teachers need extra support. When teachers struggle, Mission High provides one-on-one coaching by successful and experienced educators, such as McKamey and Roth. Teachers meet regularly to plan units together and analyze student work collectively. As a result, unlike most inner-city schools, Mission High has very low attrition among teachers—by district and national standards. Mission High is the only school in the district that teaches high numbers of African American, Latino, and low-income students and is no longer considered a "hard-to-staff" school, according to the San Francisco Unified School District's chief communications officer, Gentle Blythe. "Mission High is famous at the district because it is known as a learning community and good, supportive place to work," Dayna Soares, who has now been teaching math for two years, tells me. "It's hard to get a job here."

◇◇◇◇◇◇◇◇◇◇◇◇◇◇◇◇◇

Mission High School's museum maintains a deep archive of historic photographs of the school and its people, athletic trophies, and articles, as well as newspaper clippings featuring alums. There are portraits of Maya Angelou, Grammy-winning Carlos Santana, and the award-winning chef Charles Phan. The museum is full of multigenerational stories, like the sister and brother security guards, Iz (or "Izzy" as the staff call her) and Ed Fructuoso, who both graduated from Mission High and still work here. Ed's daughter, Reign, recently graduated from Mission High. Principal Guthertz's daughter, Eva-Grace, started at Mission in 2014.

Almost every week a former graduate or a family member of a former graduate comes to Mission High to look at the graduation photos dotting the hallways and other memorabilia the school has been archiving in the museum, Guthertz tells me one morning in May 2014, as we walk down the hallway toward Mission High's school museum. Just last week Veronica Gomez—the granddaughter of Mission alumnus Ronald Gaggero—came to see the school her late grandfather used to talk about when she was a little girl. Gomez told Guthertz that her grandfather dropped out of school in 1960 to enter the workforce just two months before he graduated. His girlfriend—who became his wife of forty-four years—had gotten pregnant.

Gaggero became a successful owner of several small businesses in San Francisco and raised three children with his
wife, but he always told his granddaughter that his biggest
regret was not getting his diploma. Guthertz and his team
invited Gomez to attend the graduation of Mission High's
class of 2014 and presented her with an honorary high
school diploma for her late grandfather.

Mission High serves an often overlooked but vital role
in the community. It is a central meeting ground and celebration space for the predominantly working-class parents
whose children go there, as well as a repository of its collective memories and community pride. The yearly choir
and Latino Club performances bring out hundreds of parents. When in December 2014 the deaths of Eric Garner
and Michael Brown—unarmed black men killed by police
officers who were not indicted—sparked national protests
across the country, Mission High's Black Student Union
organized a community event for students and parents in
the city. The Gay-Straight Alliance, as well as Teachers
for Social Justice, hold their national gatherings at Mission High.

Before No Child Left Behind was passed in 2002, districts rarely closed schools based primarily on their performance on test scores,[6] but NCLB identified closings
as one of the remedies to low achievement and provided
financial incentives to shut down many of them. Studies
that looked at the impact of such interventions in Chicago, Washington, D.C., and New York show that large-
scale closings rarely increased student test scores, and in
some instances had long-term negative effects.[7] If we want
to look at schools as factories whose main mission is to

produce productive workers to fuel the economy, and we believe that high test scores produce such workers, then closure may not seem like a big deal, Guthertz comments. But if we think of schools as extensions of our communities, a major piece of a social safety net and the cultural ecosystem of a community, then closures and other radical disruptions cause more harm than good, in his opinion.

Guthertz loves giving personal tours, including stops at the museum, to any outsiders who come to Mission, because he can show all of the qualitative and quantitative factors besides test scores, which he believes tell a more accurate story about the place that he has called home for fourteen years—first as an English teacher and now as an administrator. "We sent more African American students to college this year than the district," he says as we enter Mission High's school museum. "Our achievement gap in grades is significantly lower than the district average, thanks to the hard work of our teachers."

"Sorry, I talk too much," Guthertz stops himself midsentence. "My father was a PR man," he adds. "I probably get it from him, but we have such amazing students and teachers here. The best in the city, in my opinion."

The museum holds a piece of Guthertz's family history, also, which dates back to the Gold Rush years of San Francisco, he says, pointing to a small drawing depicting Mission High sometime around the 1906 earthquake. The earthquake wiped out about a quarter of San Francisco's buildings, including Guthertz's great-grandparents' house. His grandmother Selma was three years old at the time. She remembered living in a tent city in Dolores Park next to Mission High School with her parents and sixteen hundred other homeless families.

Selma's parents were Jewish immigrants from Austria, who came to San Francisco in the late nineteenth century and sold jeans, picks, and sundries to the young migrants from all over the world seeking gold and freedom. They were able to buy their own home in San Francisco. "I grew up with these stories of my grandmother coming in here, to Mission High, to wash up and get food," Guthertz says now, pointing to the only illustration his family has from that time. "She was my favorite adult when I was growing up, so I have really positive associations with San Francisco and Mission High, which provided refuge and comfort to my great-grandparents." Guthertz's grandmother was ninety-seven when he came to work at Mission High as an English teacher in 2001. By then he had been a teacher for fourteen years. "She was really proud of me," he recalls.

When Guthertz was a student, he never imagined that he would some day work as a teacher or patrol the halls of a school as an administrator. As a student, he often found himself at the principal's office for cutting class. Until he made it to college, he never felt that he belonged in an academic setting. "Many of my teachers were really good, but I didn't come across anyone who made me feel like they saw me, believed in me, or were trying to push me," he tells me. At the age of twelve he was diagnosed with what would now be called an attention deficit disorder, but his mother refused to put him on Ritalin, giving him coffee instead, as a natural stimulant.

In high school Guthertz worked as a teaching assistant for students with special needs. "This is when I first realized that I love working with students, especially those who don't always feel at home in a school. I had my own struggles and I could relate to them." At the time he dreamed of becoming a musician and living in a big city. He was accepted to UCLA, where he majored in English and music. After college he worked various odd jobs in Los Angeles: doing marketing for a car rental company, as a factory worker in an airplane plant, as a paralegal, and then as a kindergarten teacher in a local Jewish community center. Working in the kindergarten reminded him that he loved working with kids, and that's when he decided to get his teaching credential.

After graduation from UCLA with a master's degree in education in 1987, Guthertz started a job as an English teacher in Belvedere Junior High School in the East Los Angeles neighborhood of Boyle Heights. "I really enjoyed working there," he recalls. "That's where some of my greatest mentorship came from. I had so many people to learn from about assessment, curriculum design, high expectations, classroom management, and just a way of being in the world. Most teachers were Latino, from the neighborhood. Administrators were former teachers, also from the community, and they were really supportive of the students and new teachers like me. It was a struggling neighborhood, with police helicopters hovering over homes and newspapers in some of the windows instead of glass, but the school was such a proud and celebratory place." The first year was the hardest for Guthertz, but he felt that he could see some successes early on and was happy teaching.

"Two things are always happening when you are starting out," he says. "You are beating yourself up all of the time. But you also feel success. I saw students who used to tell me that they hated school become stronger writers, willing to take risks with what they chose to read and write, speak out more in class."

Two years later Guthertz found himself involved in one of the largest teacher strikes in American history. More than twenty thousand teachers were deadlocked with the Los Angeles school district for months, as United Teachers Los Angeles (UTLA) made one of its strongest pushes ever to gain broader powers at the school level for its teachers. Los Angeles teachers asked for more voice on school management issues and increased pay. The union wanted to create school councils to make many decisions that traditionally have been the sole province of the principal, such as budget allocations, class scheduling, and choices of curriculum and tests. "In East Los Angeles, we had no serious professional development," Guthertz says. "There was one district day of professional development, but there was nothing in-house: no sharing of student work, planning together, making decisions around courses, no training on teaching reading, writing, or working with English learners. We wanted a voice in our professional development."[8]

Today teachers at Mission High choose curriculum, design their own assessments, interview and train new colleagues, and are a part of leadership structures that make major decisions. But such autonomy was rare in most schools two decades ago. In 1989 UTLA argued that teachers had the least power at schools, yet were held most accountable by parents, the public, and administrators when academic goals were not met. Guthertz was a union representative at his school, as union members called for "teacher empowerment" and "shared decision making" as the keystones of improving schools.

This was a deeply formative experience in Guthertz's evolution as a teacher, an administrator, and a longtime teachers' union member. The union served as a major platform to help teachers gain more power and become more effective at their jobs. He vividly recalls gathering with more than twenty thousand other Los Angeles teachers at the sports coliseum to ratify a vote on the negotiated proposals. "That was a very powerful time. Suddenly, teachers were called to the decision-making table. We were fighting not just to decide what goes on in individual classrooms, but what goes on in the entire school."

The union won the right for teachers to design their own district-wide tests as accountability tools to measure the quality of schools. Guthertz and his colleagues in the district started meeting on a regular basis to develop what educators refer to as "performance assessments": open-ended tasks—without multiple-choice questions— designed by teachers and meant to measure a broader range of intellectual skills more authentically through writing, research projects, oral presentations, and participation in group projects. "In English, we used different modalities—oral piece, written piece," he recalls. "In math, there was a section that looked at the whole process of solving something, not just the final answer, and there was a group portion of the test as well. It was very powerful and well embraced in Los Angeles as an authentic assessment. Unfortunately, it was viewed as more expensive and time consuming than the multiple-choice tests, which you can just feed through a machine and don't need a teacher to grade them." The standardized testing option was considered faster and cheaper, Guthertz explains. But he is not so sure that is the case when considering all of the indirect costs associated with preparation for these tests, such as time spent "teaching to the test" and spending limited funds on testing materials, testing equipment, or test-oriented curriculum rather than using those funds and time to allow teachers to design intellectually engaging lessons and classroom tests that are more in tune with the individual learning trajectories of each student.

When I ask Guthertz what he thinks about *Vergara v. California*—the 2014 court decision that made teacher tenure illegal in California and is now being copied in other states—he says that he is disheartened by the anti-union stance and how much of school reform energy and resources are devoted to finding ways to fire a small number of highly ineffective teachers. States that use evaluation systems based in part on standardized test scores have found that only a very small percentage of teachers are rated as highly ineffectual.[9] The process for dismissing a single ineffective tenured teacher involves many steps and takes too long, Guthertz says. Most teachers agree that tenure should be granted after a longer period of time than two years, but throwing out tenure completely would cause more harm than good, Guthertz believes. "Stability and continuity is key to successful education," he says. "There can be situations, based on what kind of political wind is blowing or pressures to raise test scores, that without tenure, you could get rid of lots of people. It's also significantly cheaper to have new, young teachers. What would stop some principals from getting rid of veteran teachers every two years as a way to balance the budget?"

Dismissing ineffective teachers won't be enough to reduce our achievement gaps, Guthertz argues, because it doesn't improve teaching in a significant way. The vast majority of American teachers are somewhere in the middle, he says, and are struggling to get better and actively looking for opportunities to grow. "You don't want to make decisions on firing or promotion based on a few observations and test scores," Guthertz says. "It's a highly complex intellectual endeavor that requires attentive investigation."

Guthertz says he is "100 percent pro-union and pro-tenure." Teachers' unions historically and today are among the few formidable forces that have fought the top-down pressures of teaching to the test, he emphasizes. But he is also clear-eyed about some of their shortcomings. The seniority clause—or "last-in, first-out" staff placement mechanism—is broken and hurts teacher diversity. Recruitment of diverse staff is a huge priority for Guthertz, because he views it as a crucial piece of the larger puzzle in solving racial gaps in achievement. Conversations about race are much more constructive and effective when there is a critical mass of teachers of color in the room. Nationally, the teaching force is 82 percent white, while students of color make up close to half of the public school population, according to a 2014 study by the Center for American Progress.[10] With forty-three out of seventy teachers identifying as people of color, Mission High is outperforming the national average, but it is still far from mirroring its student body.

The San Francisco Teacher Residency is a great model for having constructive, pro-union conversations while addressing diversity issues in the profession, Guthertz says. It's a partnership of the district, the local teachers' union, Stanford University, and the University of San Francisco to bring in a more diverse pool of teachers. Mission High was the first pilot for the partnership and added two math teachers of color to its cadre, including Dayna Soares, whose professional development is embedded in the school like a medical residency program.

"There should be more constructive, respectful conversations like these all over the country, rather than using courts to settle such complex issues," Guthertz says. "Most teachers want to be effective. They came into this profession because they want to be strong, positive forces for children. Systemic opportunities for self-reflection by teachers, peer supports, collaboration, and coaching improve teaching. That's where we should be putting most of our energy, rather than finding easier ways to fire a very small percentage of ineffective teachers in our classrooms."

In 1991 Guthertz moved to Mountain View in Northern California. He got a job as an English teacher in an alternative high school in the juvenile justice hall in San Jose. Soon after he moved, he visited his high school friend Don Kinsella, who lived on the corner of Haight and Fillmore in San Francisco. Don introduced Guthertz to his roommate, Jennifer, who turned out to be a new English teacher as well. Standing in the doorway, the two launched into an in-depth, hour-long conversation about the importance of having students write in journals every day as a way to settle into the class, practice literacy, make connections with the content, and build a sense of community in the classroom.

A year later Guthertz and his future wife moved in together. Jennifer worked at the Piedmont High School in Oakland, where she had been a student herself. Meanwhile, Guthertz got tapped to start a new school for homeless teens. The San Jose–based Bill Wilson Center already provided a variety of services for homeless children and young adults, such as emergency shelter, counseling, and job training. Now the nonprofit wanted to create a school. The opportunity sounded enticing. "I always wanted to be in urban schools," Guthertz recalls. "I loved being around kids who are not necessarily following a straight, comfortable line. And I knew I would learn a lot by creating a school from scratch."

Initially the new school Guthertz opened operated in the drop-in center of the shelter. On any day, twenty-five to sixty kids of all ages would come into the shelter. They were either receiving social services at the center or lived in a juvenile group home. If it rained—or a band like the Grateful Dead were going through San Jose—more kids would flood the shelter. The students could access any services they wanted, as long as they agreed to go to school.

Working with kids of all ages helped Guthertz learn how to teach students individually and provide "scaffolding" (personalized academic supports) to help all students with diverse skills learn at high levels. He had to learn how to build relationships with students who didn't believe they belonged in an academic setting. And as someone who moved between classrooms and counselors every day as a student, Guthertz appreciated how crucial social and health services were for students with no social safety nets. The shelter is also where he learned most of his skills as an administrator. He was the only teacher and the only administrator so he had to plan lessons and budgets, buy supplies, and deal with all of the organizational issues and paperwork that come with running a school. "I realized that I like thinking of education in terms of very different things—lesson planning, budgets, discipline," Guthertz recalls.

Eventually the school rented its own space in an old auto body shop of a former high school near Santa Clara University and developed a great collaboration. Professors would come in to teach classes, college students came in as tutors, and Guthertz and his students had access to performance spaces at the university where students could stage their plays in front of a large audience. He ended up spending "nine happy years" running and teaching at the Bill Wilson Center School, which was one of the best and most difficult experiences in his life, he says. He still has dreams about it.

When Guthertz's first child, Asher, was born, he started to feel that he was spending too much time away from his son. He left the house at 6:00 each morning and usually didn't come back until 9:00 p.m. As George Bush Sr. came to power, funding for the center was drying up as the federal government pushed for the funneling of social services through churches and private institutions instead of government and nonprofit shelters. But the straw that broke the camel's back for Guthertz was seeing one of his longtime students come to school with a huge crack in his skull that was patched back together with a row of bloody, metal staples. The male student, who had been coming to school for years, was working as a prostitute and got into a fight with a client, who kicked him in the head. He said he went to the hospital, where the doctors used a stapler and just let him go. "My heart sank and something broke that day," he recalls. "After nine years, I decided that it's time for a change."

◇◇◇◇◇◇◇◇◇◇◇◇◇◇◇◇◇

When Guthertz was hired as an English teacher by Mission High in 2001, the school had been coming to terms with the disappointing outcomes of a radical "reconstitution" plan implemented in 1996–1997, calling for tougher accountability: the district removed the principal and fired all teachers, as a solution to low standardized test scores. The plan didn't work. By the time the new principal Kevin Truitt came on board in 2001, the school had the lowest test scores and attendance rates among all city high schools, suspensions were up and more teachers were leaving Mission than any other school in the district. With Truitt on board, the school was looking for alternative ways to address its low performance and persistent achievement gaps in grades, attendance, and graduation rates. Like most schools across the country, despite endless new state and district initiatives, "more rigorous" curriculum, and "tougher" accountability measures, the dial wasn't moving.

The cash-strapped California school had also just received some money from the Gates Foundation and the district, a grant designed to fund the creation of smaller high schools and implement school improvement recommendations based primarily on the research of Linda Darling-Hammond, professor of education at the Stanford Graduate School of Education. Darling-Hammond is a highly respected researcher among teachers, and the school was enthusiastic about implementing her suggestions. One of her recommendations included increasing paid time for teachers to plan lessons together and discuss outcomes to see if their methods worked. Because Guthertz had experience planning lessons collectively and sharing student work from his job in East Los Angeles, Principal Truitt asked him and eight other teachers to lead this new experiment at Mission.

"Back then, there were only a few groups of teachers who met informally to plan lessons together, but for the most part teachers worked in isolation," Guthertz recalls. "There were some people who said they didn't want to collaborate and very few teachers were willing to share student work with each other." Guthertz and his teacher-leader allies started working to spread new norms throughout the school: encouraging teachers to discuss their students collectively, share best practices, and plan lessons cooperatively. When it came to looking at student work together, there was more resistance, but Guthertz took the initiative and started meeting with two colleagues in the English department to grade and discuss student writing together.

Around this time, in 2002, the school administration worked on implementing another teaching approach, which Darling-Hammond calls "Multicultural and Anti-racist Teaching." This research-based pedagogical approach argues that many students of color have negative experiences in schools—and society—that undermine their own conception of their ability to succeed academically. Darling-Hammond, like other education researchers such as Lisa Delpit and Claude Steele, argues that schools need to be set up as intentional communities to combat these "stereotype threats." This research demonstrates that integrated classes, personalized teaching that engages student intellect, culturally relevant curriculum, and a school culture that doesn't force students to reject their home cultures have shown increases in achievement.[11]

To implement these changes, the school initially followed a more typical, top-down strategy of reform: the state sent in a consultant to implement changes. "It was an outsider who came in and talked about the civil rights movement and did touchy feely group discussions," Guthertz recalls. "Someone else came in and for one day taught behavior management strategies that focused on controlling and penalizing students versus making changes in teaching practices that would engage and support them. That blew up at the school. The administration got rid of that program." The issues that come with this kind of approach to school reform—"do what the district, state, or consultants say"—have been a recurring theme in the long careers of Guthertz, Roth, and McKamey. "It comes off as an attempt to hijack the effort by the teachers to think about education," McKamey comments. "It's the deepest disrespect. The teacher has been teaching for ten years and someone is going to come in and say, 'I'm going to show you something.' Most of these people have never taught in the classroom."

In 2005 Principal Truitt called together a small group of teachers, including McKamey (who had joined Mission High a year earlier as an English teacher) and Guthertz (Roth wasn't working at Mission High yet), and asked them to come up with their own solutions for incorporating "anti-racist teaching" and reducing racial gaps at the school. "We started very slowly, getting to know each other," Guthertz says. "What would a school focused on equity look like? We talked about curriculum, pedagogy, and affect: what you teach, how you teach, and your relationship with the students." Because African American students had the highest dropout rates and received the largest proportion of Fs and Ds at the school, administrators and teachers at Mission High agreed to focus on this subgroup first, extending their work to Latino students the following year.

McKamey insisted on starting out by making a video of interviews with African American students describing their experiences at Mission. "What interests and inspires teachers? Students," McKamey says, explaining why she wanted to start with the voices of students. "The following year, we did a panel with Latino students with the same intent." McKamey insisted that teachers interview students who were "in the middle": succeeding in some classes and struggling in others. Educators have a tendency to focus on the most underachieving African American students, McKamey says. This typically shifts the conversation to the personal challenges students bring to school, rather than forcing teachers to notice and discuss strategies that work.

As African American students discussed the kind of classrooms that helped them succeed and motivated them

to come to school (teachers' names were not used), similar
themes and patterns emerged. Students said they learned
best when teachers broke down the content and skills for
them, saw and heard them as individuals, understood the
particular strengths of their students, paid attention to
their goals, and gave them specific tools to achieve their
ambitions. Students also noted what didn't work: teachers
who seemed rigid or downright mean. They talked about
teachers who noticed what they *weren't* doing right—coming to class late, not turning in an assignment—rather
than everything they *were* doing correctly: coming to class
despite challenges at home, working hard in the classroom,
participating in discussions. The students also talked
about getting bad grades but not fully understanding why.

"At the center of what the students said was that how
the teachers saw them elicited a feeling," McKamey recalls
of those interviews. "They said they could tell how the
teacher felt about them by the way the teacher looked at
them or talked to them. So, they read the teacher's response
to their work, behavior, and oral contributions in class as a
response to them as human beings. Why did one teacher
understand what they were trying to accomplish with their
writing and another think it was just a paper of problems to
solve? Why did one teacher praise a student's comments in
class, even if they were spoken out of turn, while another
did not even bother to acknowledge that a student had spoken? The sense the students made of all this was that some
teachers wanted to work with them and others just didn't.
This played out in terms of a student's uneven performance;
for teachers who cared and supported them, no matter how
inexpertly, they gave great effort, often exceeding their own

expectations. For the others, those teachers that did not express care, they languished."

McKamey and her colleagues then made another video in which they interviewed Mission High staff about teachers who had made a difference in their lives. "Our work was always about trying to touch that place of joy and meaningfulness, help teachers reconnect with what we are doing, what we are about, in the middle of all the sweat and hard work and frustrations," she says.

The teachers played the videos at a school-wide faculty meeting that was followed by a discussion. The videos were well received. Shortly afterward a committee of about fifteen teacher-leaders and several administrators started to meet to investigate specific areas of concern and design solutions. "We were always looking at and trying to understand different kinds of data, including anecdotal," McKamey tells me. "Then we would settle on something we needed to concentrate on each year." They voted to call their working group the Anti-racist Teaching Committee. "Some people were upset about the name, but we talked about it openly," Guthertz says. "The idea behind it is to signal explicitly the idea that if you don't keep the conversation about racial achievement gaps at the forefront, institutionally and systemically—like how you structure your Advanced Placement and honors classes or how you engage or scaffold students individually—the structures can fall back to the status quo again really quick."

The following year Guthertz decided to accept the job of assistant principal. He felt he would have more impact implementing systemic changes across the school, including the expansion of teacher-driven professional development.

McKamey was given the position of instructional reform facilitator. The committee now started looking systemically at the achievement gaps in grades of African American and Latino students, attendance, referrals, and graduation rates. History teacher Amadis Velez became the go-to person to translate raw data into accessible charts and graphs for other teachers. The committee leaders were constantly walking through classrooms and talking with other teachers and students to gather more qualitative data.

In 2008 Principal Truitt took a leadership position in the district, and Guthertz took the job of principal. The next three years were a time of visible improvements in a broad range of qualitative and quantitative measures. Suspensions and dropouts went down. Attendance and college acceptances went up. The achievement gap in grades went down. When Guthertz and I met for the first time in his office in 2010, he was quick to point out that although the media often credit him with all of the improvements, these changes were a result of the foundation that Principal Truitt laid with the teachers and the work of current administrative leaders and teacher-leaders like Roth and McKamey. Journalists and studies also often connect shifts in yearly test scores to one-dimensional, recent changes, he says, while overlooking years of work and multiple, overlapping initiatives that improve teaching. Americans love "big changes" in one year, but school reform is incremental, slow, and messy, and the results often don't show up for five years or more, he notes.

In his role as principal Guthertz always seeks to promote the kind of work that helped him grow as a teacher by building an open and trusting environment in which teachers are empowered to investigate issues and design their own solutions. School reform has to originate from the base of your school, Guthertz and Roth argue. It has to come from and be owned by staff. It can't be parachuted in from the district or state. Guthertz is disheartened by the national conversation that focuses most of its energy and dollars on a "deficit-based" model of sorting and tracking teachers just like we do with students. Instead of asking, "How can we measure and fire 'bad teachers' faster?" Mission High chooses to focus on how to help teachers become better. Most of our country's 3 million teachers are dedicated professionals and need sustained opportunities to improve, Guthertz says. The go-to approach to building a better teacher—occasional common planning of lessons and using test scores and sporadic observations to evaluate educators—doesn't help teachers improve their practice in meaningful and systematic ways. Teachers need daily opportunities to plan lessons together, analyze student outcomes, and receive thoughtful, one-on-one coaching.

Student engagement is not possible without teacher engagement, McKamey says. When teachers are treated with respect as professionals, they are intrinsically motivated and engaged in their job. Teachers can't teach for twenty-five years and stay engaged in their work if they are not constantly challenging themselves and given a voice in their growth process.

As a part of the alternative, teacher-led school reform strategy at Mission, Guthertz empowers the two co-chairs of each department to come up with their own ideas on how to improve the quality of student work and instruction in their departments. One year, for example, the social sciences department prioritized concentrating on teaching analysis and then detecting, grading, and commenting on those outcomes in student writing. The same year, the members of the math department focused on planning lessons together, thinking about sequencing different concepts that are aligned to state standards, and calibrating their grading rubrics.

One of the strengths of the teacher-driven community strategy is that it doesn't follow a top-down, rigid model, Guthertz tells me. It shifts and evolves organically, from the inside out, depending on the needs that teachers detect in the data. Meanwhile, the Anti-racist Teaching Committee, led by McKamey, is making sure that the racial disparities in achievement are not moved to the back burner, as often happens when teachers dive into the complexities of building new structures and making changes in their classrooms.

Guthertz says that today, almost all teachers participate in collaborative curriculum planning and meet to discuss support for students they share. Most are open to observation, coaching, and observing others. There are daily conversations throughout the school about data, and staff members are constantly tinkering with existing programs in an effort to make them more effective, as the student body and school dynamics change. After years of building trust, many teachers analyze student work together now, although this process still lacks systemic consistency and could be more productive, Guthertz admits.

Most of this teacher-driven work of improving learning for all students wasn't in place when Guthertz first started working at Mission. He believes it has become more embedded throughout every part of the school as a result of the teachers' leadership. But that doesn't mean there aren't challenges, he says. College enrollment among Latino students has gone down slightly. The numbers of African American and Latino students in AP math and science classes don't fully mirror the larger student body of the school. The passing rates for African American and Latino students on the California High School Exit Exam went down in 2013 and 2014. The work continues.

Teachers have varying opinions about the reasons for the achievement gaps at Mission High and how Principal Guthertz is leading the school to make changes. Even though his evaluations by teachers are among the best in the district, as in every organization, opinions differ. Some teachers say that he pushes for radical changes too often. Although the majority of teachers are comfortable with his changes, a few have become vocal opponents. Some have told me that they want to see Guthertz more in the classrooms, pushing improvements in the quality of teaching. But there is clear agreement among most teachers that Mission High is a good place to work because Guthertz is one of those rare principals who deeply respects teachers and is supportive of their craft.

"The devotion level among teachers has gone up in the past ten years," science teacher Rebecca Fulop, who has worked at Mission High for a decade, tells me. "No one here does 7:45 to 3:10 and then calls it quits. That by itself doesn't necessarily make teachers effective, but the dedication here is extraordinarily high. The joyfulness of learning has increased. Most kids want to come to school. Respect of students toward teachers and students toward other students has increased."

"I love working at Mission," security guard Iz Fructu-oso, who has worked at the school for eight years, tells me. "We have a real community here." As someone who has worked in inner-city schools for twenty-two years, Fructuoso says that one of the most important things for a healthy school climate is stability. She says that when she worked at the Luther Burbank Middle School with Roth and McKamey before it closed in 2006, it felt like the school had a new principal every year. "A new man would come in and change all of the rules around, again," she recalls. "This makes kids feel like adults are not in charge. Students need consistency and clear structures."

Guthertz knows that some teachers are critical of his decisions. He admits that the more democratic, "shared leadership" that he fought for as a teacher in Los Angeles in 1989 is not an easy process. "Our teachers have a voice in the budget, a voice in the class offerings, a voice in the master schedule, a voice in discipline policies, curriculum, pedagogical approaches. Yet teachers still sometimes say in surveys that they don't feel like they are being heard. We may have a shared vision, but two priorities could be at odds sometimes. So, sometimes I have to make decisions and get used to not being popular. It's not my strength. I don't like being mean. I prefer being kind, but confrontation is critical sometimes."

◇◇◇◇◇◇◇◇◇◇◇◇◇◇◇

One spring afternoon in 2012 seven male freshmen trickle into Guthertz's office for the weekly Monday Mentoring Circle he co-leads with Assistant Principal Brian Fox.

Every student in the room entered Mission with a red flag raised by the district: a combination of a cumulative GPA below 2.0 and a low attendance record. The district encourages each school to provide extra support for these students. Since Mission High's administration doesn't believe in tracking—separating high- and underachieving students into different classes—all students in this room are taking challenging, mixed classes. The Mentoring Circle acts as an additional way to provide extra support. In this group, students help each other, do homework together, and learn how to talk to teachers and advocate for themselves.

Joaquin, a student who is also in Hsu's math class this year, is wearing his signature Golden State Warriors hat. He explains to me that at the start of the year, the students, Principal Guthertz, and Mr. Fox made a deal: if the entire group could get their GPA above 2.0 by the end of their freshmen year, they would all go to the House of Air, an indoor trampoline park located in San Francisco's Crissy Field. In addition, whenever the group improves their GPA on a weekly basis, they get to go to the Bi-Rite Creamery next door for free ice cream.

Rasheed, another freshman in Hsu's class, is facilitating today's meeting and is already halfway through the check-ins.

"How was your weekend, Joaquin?"

"I worked all weekend. On my homework," Joaquin says.

"Nice! How are your grades right now?" Rasheed asks.

"I only got one F, but I improved my grades in every class though," he replies.

"Where is your F?"

"Spanish."

"Do you know why?" Rasheed asks.

Joaquin shakes his head. Guthertz moves over to his computer to look at notes from the teacher. "It says some essays are missing," he reports back to the group.

"What do you need to do now?" Rasheed asks.

"Talk to the teacher," Joaquin replies. "And work on getting those assignments to him."

Guthertz decided to create Mentoring Circle after he and his colleagues surveyed students who had appeared in the 2007 videos, asking them to define what makes them want to come to Mission and what makes a "good" school. What jumped out was that the vast majority of students said that they wanted to feel there is at least one adult at the school who deeply cares about them, notices them, believes in them. Mentoring Circles became one of many ways to make sure each student feels he or she has an advocate in school. They also provide important qualitative data for Guthertz and his administrative team. Hearing struggling students speak about their challenges and successes in the classrooms every week allows his team to see what works and make better decisions on how to prioritize their limited funds.

When I asked Rasheed a year later to name an adult at the school that he felt he could turn to for anything, he mentioned three: Fox, Hsu, and his basketball coach, Arnold Zelaya. Joaquin mentioned Guthertz and Hsu. Many students said that they had never met or talked to their principals in previous schools, but most students I interviewed at Mission knew Principal Guthertz by name, had participated in some academic and social activities with him, and generally felt they could seek help in his office if they needed it.

As Rasheed continues to facilitate today's circle, the voice of the school's dean and basketball coach, Zelaya, comes over the loudspeaker. It's announcements hour at Mission, and Zelaya reminds students that this is the week of the standardized tests. In the past few weeks leading up to the tests, teachers have been helping students look at their individual scores and work in groups to support each other. The staff provided free pizza. Most students at Mission High don't care that much about the state standardized tests. They know that college admissions judges and people who give out financial aid will look at their grades, essays, and community engagement. So each year Guthertz strikes a bargain with the students: if standardized test scores go up, students get to choose their reward.

In one corner of Guthertz's office there is a green composting box full of live worms. He almost had to eat one during student assembly last week, because this year he offered two alternative prizes for higher test scores: rent a boat for a dance party or watch him eat live worms during an assembly. Luckily for Guthertz, most students voted for the boat party, but he had the worms on hand just in case. When he first became a principal, he promised to have the school mascot tattooed on his shoulder—and later proudly delivered. The following year, in 2009, Sam Mogannam, the owner of the next-door gourmet grocery store, Bi-Rite Market, rallied five famous chefs from top restaurants in San Francisco—including Delfina, Frances, and the Slanted Door—to serve gourmet meals to the nine hundred students at lunch as a reward.

"I know that some students say that standardized test scores don't matter, but they do," Guthertz says now. "Some colleges look at them. Teachers really look at them to decide how you are doing. And they really matter to our school. We don't spend too much time talking about this throughout the year, but this is the time when we really need you to do your best."

After Guthertz and Fox go over a few test-taking strategies, everyone leaves the Monday Mentoring Circle to enjoy this week's reward for improving their grades: a trip to the ice cream shop. "Everyone raise your cones in the air," Guthertz exclaims as they leave the store, sugar cones in their hands. "Congratulations on working on your grades, let's keep pushing until the end of the school year!"

THE STANDARDS AND
ACCOUNTABILITY MOVEMENT

(1980–Present)

In April 1994 Mission High freshman Jose Luis Pavon, along with about 150 of his classmates and the school's Latino Club, staged a walkout. Jose was disappointed by the lack of intellectual challenge and rigor in his classes, even though he was enrolled in several honors courses, he told Kathy Emory in 2001. Emory was writing her dissertation at the University of California at Davis on the politics of school reforms. The students also demanded more content that celebrated the contributions of the Latino, African American, and Asian American communities, which together constituted roughly 95 percent of Mission High's student body.[1]

Responding to the continued protests by the students, San Francisco's school superintendent, Bill Rojas, appointed a new principal in 1994, Lupe Arabolos. She started out at Mission as a teacher in 1985 and believed in the ideals of the "community schools." Before she became a principal, she partnered with San Francisco State University to create a Step-to-College program meant to "demystify college" for Mission High students, offering academic instruction by professors, counseling, and new classes that counted as college credits at state universities. Like Principal Guthertz and his leadership team almost a decade later, Arabolos developed partnerships with dozens of community-based organizations to bring in health and mental services for the low-income students who didn't receive sufficient city services in their neighborhoods. And like Mission High today, Arabolos insisted on including the voices of teachers, parents, and students in the conversations about school reforms. Emory reports that as a result of such community-based changes, the dropout rates at Mission decreased by 93 percent from 1993 to 1995, and students reported feeling more challenged and welcome at the school.[2]

Despite these gains, Rojas fired Arabolos two years after he appointed her, as well as two other popular administrators, citing insufficient growth in standardized test scores. Like most of today's school reformers, Rojas believed that test scores were the most important bottom line for measuring "student performance." The dismissal of Arabolos sparked huge protests by students, staff, and community organizations. In May 1996, about two hundred students walked to City Hall to meet with Mayor Willie Brown, demanding his support for Mission High. Brown later organized a meeting between student representatives and the school board. Emory reports that a student representative said he was disappointed to hear Superintendant Rojas state that "a school is like a business." "Mission is more than a business," the student replied to Rojas. "We're a community."[3]

The tumultuous relationship among Arabolos, the Mission High community, and the controversial superintendent Rojas neatly summarizes how the top-down, business-inspired model of schooling—started by the Administrative Progressives at the turn of the century—was playing out on the ground all over the country, often at odds with the wishes of parents and students. In the late 1980s, a new coalition of political and business leaders was working to push through a new era of "tougher" and more "rigorous" top-down reforms. They brought a new movement called "standards and accountability" to national prominence by critiquing public schoolteachers as incompetent and responsible for mediocre international test scores and achievement gaps.

In 1983 President Ronald Reagan commissioned a group of corporate, political, and education leaders to produce a report, which was titled *A Nation at Risk: The Imperative for Educational Reform*. It became a major influential federal document, summing up the growing unease with public schooling among the business community, and in part blamed mediocre student performance on international tests for the decline of the American gross domestic product (GDP) in the late 1970s and early 1980s. The report went beyond the measures of the Administrative Progressives by calling for more standardized testing, numbers-driven teacher evaluations, and pay based on data-driven teacher performance (merit pay).[4]

The very same assumptions and ideals that are espoused in *Nation at Risk* informed later reform efforts, such as the No Child Left Behind (NCLB) Act (2002), Race to the Top (2009), and the more recent Common Core State Standards Initiative. Common Core created the first-ever national benchmarks for knowledge and skills, as well as new, computer-based standardized tests. And while the new school reformers—including the founders of the charter school movement and Teach for America—advocated closing the achievement gap, most of them rejected other goals of the desegregation era, such as racial integration, culturally relevant curriculum (some calling it "voodoo education"), and encouraging parents of color to be in charge of neighborhood schools.

In the two decades following the release of *Nation at Risk*, state after state mandated higher curriculum standards and new tests, with the aim of holding students, teachers, and principals accountable. The new reformers assumed that test scores in reading and math alone can roughly predict how future adults will perform in the workplace and in life. Under the George W. Bush administration, Congress passed NCLB with bipartisan support and declared that by 2014, 100 percent of students would be "proficient" in reading and math, as measured by standardized test scores. Schools that didn't bring all students to proficiency, like Mission High, would be publicly shamed, might lose their federal funding, or might be closed.[5]

In the years after NCLB became law in 2002, many schools adopted scripted curriculum and standardized lessons, and sometimes even prescribed day-to-day schedules for teachers to follow. In many high-poverty classrooms that didn't perform well on the tests, multiple-choice questions became a major part of the daily curriculum. Numerous researchers observed that teachers started paying attention to students in the middle, those right beneath the "proficiency" level, often ignoring low-achieving and high-achieving ones. Now "learning" and "student outcomes" became synonymous with high test scores in math and reading.[6] Policy makers started using these scores to evaluate the quality of teaching. Bill Gates, who had been frustrated by the lackluster results of his earlier efforts to put computers in the classroom and break up high schools into smaller establishments, offered grants to districts that agreed to use test scores in teacher evaluations. President Barack Obama embraced these ideas and provided over $4 billion in competitive grants through the Race to the Top initiative to states that agreed to focus on evaluating teachers based on test scores and other "measures that are rigorous and comparable across classrooms."[7]

By 2008 schools like KIPP, a celebrated charter school chain in America—which practice "no excuses" discipline tactics—were held up by the media, philanthropists, and political leaders as the best way to educate underachieving students of color and a model that should be scaled up. The "no excuses" stance prioritizes top-down teaching strategies, such as strict discipline, a focus on eye contact and student posture, school uniforms, and silent hallways.[8] While the federal government and major philanthropists intensified standardization, a growing number of education advocates and parents said they hadn't realized how much high-stakes testing would change instruction for the worse. The overwhelming emphasis on testing led some schools and districts to cheat. Some schools cranked up discipline and school-based arrests, leading struggling students to drop out—and thus improving scores.

As parent and student protests against testing and cheating scandals grew, President Obama called for states to find alternatives to multiple-choice testing in 2009. The federal government awarded $330 million to two multi-state consortia—PARCC and SMARTER—to develop better national standards and tests that could measure learning more effectively consistent with the new Common Core requirements.[9] Many teachers say that the new curriculum standards are an improvement. They articulate skills that need to be mastered, rather than dictate specific content areas as previous standards did. Common Core tests are being piloted and will be used in various states, as this book goes to print, but they will continue to include computer-based multiple-choice tests—even though test makers promise there will be fewer of them and many more opportunities for students to write and "perform tasks," such as composing research papers or engaging in a scientific investigation. While most states have adopted the new national standards, many are dropping out of two national consortiums that are writing the new Common Core tests and are deciding to create their own state assessments.[10]

The supporters of higher-quality curriculum standards and tests believe that Common Core could help reduce the achievement gap. This logic assumes that the quality of tests and curriculum can significantly impact teaching. But many education experts—and teachers across the country—are skeptical. A 2011 Brookings Institution study found no correlation between high curriculum standards and high student achievement.[11] California has long been considered to have some of the best standards in the nation, but the state has some of the worst student outcomes on test scores. Developing systems that would support teachers to plan lessons together, analyze outcomes, receive peer support, and create their own, hyperlocal "research and action" school reform committees, like those at Mission, requires significant funding. It is difficult to imagine funds being available for this after all of the required computers, new Common Core textbooks, and online curriculum designed to beat the new tests have been purchased.

Nationally, historian Larry Cuban notes, the once-flourishing alternative and progressive classrooms organized around the individual needs of students, like those at Mission High School today, have been almost entirely replaced with a single model of "good teaching" and "good schools"—a utopian factory model that Administrative Progressives envisioned nearly a century ago. Yet there is very little evidence, Cuban writes, that higher test scores lead to better job performance or "cause" better economic performance nationally. Meanwhile, all of the other important historical purposes of schooling—preparing literate and active citizens, independent and creative thinkers, and community leaders—have been pushed out of most schools at the expense of creating "human capital" for the economy.[12]

Chapter 7

Ms. McKamey

"I want to say something important about writing," Pirette McKamey tells her English class one Tuesday afternoon in October 2012. "Writing is very, very hard, and it's never finished. I've re-read some of my essays twenty times and I still go, 'I can't believe I made this mistake or that mistake.' So, this is a long, difficult process." Dressed in white cotton pants, a patterned shirt, and black leather loafers, she is standing in front of twenty-five seniors.

"I'm going to read Jamal's essay as a model today," says McKamey, who reads students' work at the beginning of each class as a way to honor their craft and effort. "I like his essay because of the heft of its content. It also feels real. It was written with real engagement and honesty. That makes it worth reading." In his essay Jamal has compared his life ambitions with the goals of two other people he has chosen from the many real and fictional people the students have studied in a five-week-long "Quests" unit in which students considered the deeper meaning behind different types of individual journeys while developing their reading and writing skills. Jamal has picked Jackson Jackson, the main character from Sherman Alexie's short story, "What You Pawn I Will Redeem," and Haiti's former president, Jean-Bertrand Aristide. A month later Jamal uses this essay as a foundation to develop a ten-page research paper entitled "Black on Black Violence," which examines the root causes of homicides in his community.

"'A successful quest requires support, yearning, and perseverance,'" McKamey begins, reading Jamal's words. "'Everyone experiences some kind of a quest in their lifetime. Some take longer than others, some are more important than others, and some are not even intentional, but are a part of our everyday life. Some quests are very internal and personal. Others are external, rooted in collective memories and yearnings.'" As she reaches the end, five minutes later, she looks up from the paper and asks, "What did you like about the essay?"

"I love how Jamal brought three parts and three very different people together," Alex jumps in.

"I liked that a lot too," McKamey responds. "What else?"

"His connections and transitions from one person to the next were really good," says Ana a little more hesitantly, glancing at the teacher for affirmation.

"That's true," McKamey replies.

"I felt passion and enthusiasm in his essay," Juan comments. "Passion that fuels a bigger purpose is the theme that drives the essay—in making music, in searching for your past, in wanting more freedom for your country."

"Exactly," she responds. "That's a really good observation."

As the discussion winds down, Max Anders—the student teacher McKamey is coaching this year—passes out a handout titled "Punctuating Titles: Underlines or Quotation Marks?" Meanwhile, McKamey explains to me that when she and Anders graded everyone's essays yesterday, they noticed one common mistake: despite previous practice, students still weren't always sure which titles needed to be underlined, italicized, or put in quotation marks. Anders has created a short guide using real examples from student work and a worksheet for students to practice some of these skills.

Students then get to work while both teachers walk around to answer questions.

After a brief punctuation lesson from McKamey, Anders steps up to the front of the room. "Last class we learned about the Vietnam War, and we focused on Vietnamese history," he says. "Today we will continue by reading Tim O'Brien's *The Things They Carried*, the American perspective." The students read a chapter titled "The Man I Killed." When they're done, Anders asks them to pick out a quote they found intriguing, to be analyzed collectively.

"Let me remind you what analysis is," McKamey says, standing in front of the class. "When I was little, I remember I used a hammer and screwdriver to crack a golf ball open. I really wanted to see what was inside. As I cracked that glossy plastic open, I saw rubber bands. And I went, 'Ha! I didn't know there were rubber bands in golf balls. I wonder what's inside other balls?' It made me curious about the world. So, we are doing the same thing. We'll analyze the author's words to dig in deeper. That will allow us to engage with the text on the author's terms."

David raises his hand. He reads a line from the chapter:

He was a slim dead, almost dainty young man of about
twenty. He lay with one leg bent beneath him, his jaw
in his throat, his face neither expressive nor inexpres-
sive. One eye was shut. The other was a star-shaped
hole.

"What do you notice in this passage?" McKamey
probes.

"The man the narrator killed is the same age as him,"
Roberto comments.

"Exactly," she replies. "Now you are one step deeper.
What do I feel inside when I think of that?"

"Guilt, regret," Ajanee jumps in.

"That's right," McKamey comments. "I personally
would use the word *compassion*. But what you said is 100
percent correct. It's just that all of us will use different
words to analyze this. And what does that do when we
realize that this man is the same age as us?"

"It makes me think that he's young, likes girls, probably doesn't want to fight in a war," Robert says.

"Exactly. Now, take that even deeper."

"It's like he is killing himself?" Juan asks.

"Perfect! Now you made a connection," McKamey
says, excitement in her voice. "That's what this quote is
really about. Now, why is O'Brien saying 'star-shaped
hole'? Why not 'peanut-shaped hole'?"

"That's very unusual," Irving comments.

McKamey nods. She remains quiet for a minute, looking around the class.

Ajanee raises her hand and offers an answer, "The image in his mind is burned."

"Exactly!" McKamey replies. "O'Brien wants us to keep that same image in mind that he had as a young soldier in his mind. It's the kind of image you never forget. That's what writing is really about."

∞∞∞∞∞∞∞∞∞∞∞∞∞

When Pirette McKamey was a teenager, she composed most of her writing in her head before committing it to paper. Riding on the school bus, she looked out the window, and as familiar houses and people glided by, she carefully constructed each sentence, arranged each paragraph, selected quotes, and then added her own musings. Some stories were essays or book reports for her middle school assignments. Others were fiction she wrote as a way to work something out: a recent conversation or an event that needed unfolding, a yearning or frustration waiting to be untangled. When she got home, she would write down everything she had composed in her head. On the page it was usually pretty close to how she had visualized it on the bus. Years later, as a teacher, she would often tell her students that writing allows us to get to know ourselves, our thinking, and the world around us in a way no other form of communication can.

McKamey grew up in Levittown, a suburb of Philadelphia, in a neighborhood of mostly white families. At her public middle school, she was usually one of two or three African American students placed in the higher-tracked classes. Most African American students lived in the projects and were put in lower-tracked classrooms. In seventh and eighth grades McKamey wrote stories almost every day, but she wasn't considered a good student. She often came to school angry, cut classes, and made a name for herself socially. Her straight As from elementary school plummeted, and she had to make up failed classes in summer school.

Whenever McKamey tried to reengage—to buckle down and do the work—her teachers didn't seem to notice her effort. They didn't call on her and didn't push her further. She felt that they had made up their minds about who the good students were and who wasn't worthy of second chances. But despite her dropping grades, McKamey's parents continued to believe in her. Her mother and father often told her that she was smart and a strong writer. When she finished middle school, her parents sent her to a private Quaker boarding school in Newtown, Pennsylvania, about twenty minutes from their home. McKamey's mother was born and raised in Germany as a Catholic, but joined the Quakers after she moved to Pennsylvania, following her husband to the United States after World War II. Her father was African American. He was an atheist, but he supported his wife's religion. He said that Quakers were a positive force in their family, their community, and the world.

George High School had more teachers and smaller classes than the public school, and McKamey felt noticed there. Her grades improved, yet her work and engagement were still uneven. She came to classes that she viewed as intellectually engaging, but if she was bored, she cut school. It didn't help that when her teachers praised her in public, their feedback usually centered on her personality rather than her ideas or her coursework. Her economics teacher, Fran Bradley, was the biggest exception. Whenever McKamey asked a question or made a comment in her economics class, Bradley would engage in a lengthy and enthusiastic discussion about the substance of what McKamey was saying. Sometimes he would read passages from McKamey's work in front of the class. At the end of the semester, when Bradley returned one of her papers, he told her that she should study economics in college.

Almost thirty years later, McKamey still often remembers her former teacher and recently sent him a thank-you letter when she heard that he had retired: "I have had a teaching career for twenty-five years myself now, some of it spent mentoring novice teachers, so I know how rare what you did is," she wrote. "Fran, you always made me feel smart." McKamey's parents also said that she was intelligent, but Bradley was the first teacher who had the skills to provide evidence: his comments in class about the substance of her ideas, his feedback on her writing, the enthusiasm in his voice when he discussed her thinking. Over the course of a year, that proof solidified into a confidence that couldn't be easily shaken anymore. It was that pride in her intellect that gave her the fortitude and resilience to cut through many racial stereotypes and negative myths as she made her way through high school and then Boston University.

Some students gather enough confidence from their teachers, family, mentors, and peers to succeed in spite of subtle and overt social cues that signal the perceived intellectual inferiority of black people. But too many African

American students that McKamey encounters fall off the cliff. They internalize the damaging feeling of inferiority that young adults pick up even from the most casual encounters in and out of the classroom. Some are explicit demands for silence directed at black students. Others are more subtle rejections: averted gazes, hesitations, and pauses.

Jesmyn first met McKamey four years ago, when she walked into a night class to fix an F she had received in English. The first thing Jesmyn declared—with much conviction—was that she wasn't good at school. The second statement she made was that she was a bad writer. Her teacher listened patiently, she recalls, and looked at her differently than any other teacher before. "Ms. McKamey was able to see the good in me through the worst of my times," Jesmyn recalls now. "When I came to Mission, I was going through a lot of challenges in my life and I was a mess. I had a huge attitude. But Ms. McKamey continued to remind me that I was a wise and beautiful young lady every chance she got. If I didn't feel like reading or writing and I gave her attitude, she'd give it right back to me, but then there was a compliment about my work right after."

She got an A– in that night class with McKamey. "I worked my butt off learning grammar and writing," she says. "When I heard my grade, I thought they made a mistake." A year earlier, she had transferred to Mission High with a GPA of 1.1.

In too many schools across the country, African American students are more likely to have lower grades than other students, be placed in lower-tracked classes, be diagnosed with special needs, and be suspended for "willful defiance."[1] But despite the depressing statistics and the prejudices that perpetuate them, most schools have always had some educators who succeed in reducing or erasing these patterns in their classrooms.

After years of teaching, studying her subject and the craft of teaching, and learning from her students and her colleagues, McKamey is one such teacher today. She has succeeded by forging alliances with like-minded colleagues such as Robert Roth and Taica Hsu and working with her peers to personally mentor at-risk students like Jesmyn. Teaching is a very complex, highly intellectual endeavor, McKamey tells me. Teachers need to know their subject deeply as well as how students think about and learn the subject. They need to have the skills to see what students know and where they are in their learning trajectory. Teachers need to practice using their judgment to decide which method to deploy and when. And they need to work on their affect by practicing specialized skills to build positive relationships with students from different cultures.

For McKamey, the most important value driving her teaching and coaching is her conviction that being a good teacher means hearing, seeing, and succeeding with all students—regardless of how far a student is from the teacher's preconceived notions of what it means to be ready to learn. When teachers are driven by a belief that all of their students can learn, they are able to respond to the complexity of their students' needs and to adjust if something is not working for a particular individual or group of students. "I'm not just a delivery person, delivering content," McKamey explains. "Students learn through their own channels, their own brains. And all student work and actions in the classroom are valuable information. The students are always telling you something."

In every school where McKamey worked until she arrived at Mission, there was always a small group of teachers who would sit in the lounge and say negative things about African American students. Some would call them lazy and apathetic. Others would say that students who live amid poverty, violence in the community, and single-parent households could not be expected to do as much work as students from a more stable, middle-class, two-parent home. The vast majority of teachers don't say things like that, yet too many don't connect their self-esteem as professionals to how their African American students are doing. When most of their African American students are failing, they don't view it as a crisis, but as the natural state of things. That's why McKamey and a group of her colleagues keep an eye on grades, attendance, and referrals categorized by race, ethnicity, income, and special needs. They devote most of their resources to helping fellow teachers learn how to monitor their qualitative and quantitative data for all students and make personalized adjustments to bolster students' daily classroom work. In this hyperlocal model of education, the voices and needs of students are the main driving force for making changes in the classroom, and by extension, the entire school. The impetus for change radiates from the inside out, rather than being imposed by bureaucrats and politicians who don't have direct contact with students or knowledge of their intellectual and emotional development.

The best way to improve teaching and reduce the achievement gaps, McKamey argues, is to allow teachers to act as school-based researchers and leaders, justifying classroom reforms based on the broad range of performance markers of their students: daily grades, the quality of student work and the rate of its production, engagement, effort, attendance, and student comments. That means planning units together and then spending a lot of time analyzing the iterative work the students produce. This process teaches educators to recognize that there are no standard individuals, and there are as many learning trajectories as there are people. When teachers share student work together, they train their eyes and minds to see and hear everything their students are thinking and experiencing and can choose the best tools to help students. This method also allows teachers to develop skills and a discipline for their own process of self-reflection and how to comment and grade for improvement—not just sorting and tracking. "At the center of growth as a teacher is self-reflection," McKamey says. "It means developing habits of mind and specialized skills to look at student work every day and ask: What did I intend to do today? What did my students do? Did it work? If not, how can I change to improve?"

McKamey's twenty-six years of successful teaching tell her that thoughtful, collective analysis of student work—when implemented well and bolstered by effective one-on-one coaching—allows for useful professional development and real accountability from respected and trusted colleagues. There is a strong element of peer pressure in these collective reviews of student outcomes, and they are much more likely to tap into the intrinsic motivation of a teacher than the bonuses and evaluations based on

test scores favored by bureaucrats and many philanthropists today. "I have never heard teachers talk about evaluations or bonuses as something that motivates them to
improve," McKamey notes. "What teachers talk about is
the feedback they get from students, parents, and peers
they respect."

Many teachers I have spoken with, both beginners
and veterans, support this observation. Having just finished her second year of teaching high school math, Dayna
Soares believes that opportunities to plan lessons together
and review daily classroom work with her colleagues help
her more than any other kind of professional development.
"Looking at one student's piece of work for an hour is so
valuable," Soares tells me. "You are training yourself to pay
close attention: What was I trying to teach, and what is
the outcome? What worked and what didn't? I elicit information from this one piece of student work and then can
translate it to all other students."

Nationwide, such collaboration is still rare. A 2009
MetLife survey of over one thousand teachers found that
just one-quarter had at least three hours each week allot-
ted for collaboration.[2] But more schools have started pur-
suing this goal in the past decade. In education parlance,
it is often referred to as "professional learning communities."[3] This is significant progress, but not all collaborative
meetings among teachers are equally effective. The presence of a specific lesson plan or student work is key. Without precise context, Soares says, conversations tend to veer
off into housekeeping issues, which can be discussed via
e-mail, or highly speculative areas, often rooted in emotionally invasive discussions of a student's personality or

home life. As teachers review student work together, staying focused on successes in the classroom is essential as well, McKamey says. The default in too many collaborative meetings is to focus on underachieving students and to complain about what students are not doing—often blaming the students, parents, or other teachers. This doesn't help teachers to improve.

In order to help teachers focus on what is working, McKamey encourages them to choose a piece of work by a middle-achieving student who made a recent shift: went from chronic Cs to a B+, or persevered through a challenging assignment despite past difficulties, or analyzed something more deeply, or showed intellectual engagement instead of just trying to get a good grade. When teachers identify middle-achieving students rather than just failing ones, they can enumerate effective strategies and extend them to other students, such as daily "research journals" with status reports and questions for students who are developing a complex research paper for the first time.

Learning to pay attention to the smallest, most subtle strategies can create huge changes in the classroom, McKamey says. The teacher's affect in the classroom is extremely important. Many people often assume that a teacher's personality is most responsible for creating positive relationships, whereas it is actually a set of teaching practices and skills. "Early in my career, students told me that I frown too much when I read their work during class," McKamey says. "They thought I hated their writing while I read it. I had to learn to smile or laugh more when I read their work in public." Focusing on successful strategies also changes the tone of the faculty meetings,

McKamey says. It makes teachers hopeful about their ability to improve and willing to try different tools.

Facilitation by respected teacher-leaders is also important. "Pirette is highly respected at school," says Soares. "And to be honest, she's slightly feared, which is a good thing because it forces you to bring your best self to these meetings. We are not just chatting and making each other feel good. It's serious work, which means pushing each other sometimes. I've been at some meetings that are not facilitated by effective leaders like Pirette. Sometimes, one negative person is allowed to derail the whole thing, so you spend the whole meeting managing that person, which takes away time from learning."

How can schools identify their teacher-leaders? McKamey and her colleagues look at a variety of quantitative and qualitative measures: grades and attendance data disaggregated by race, ethnicity, and income status; student feedback about teachers; observations of many classes in a row to understand the intentions and sequencing of lessons; observations of the degree of work production in the classroom and student engagement with that work; detailed review of student work produced in the class; and extensive interviews with students and teachers. Though difficult to implement, these criteria are far more informative than standard measures used by state bureaucracies, such as yearly test scores and occasional observation by administrators.

Yet teacher-leaders readily admit that even the most competently run faculty meetings can only achieve so much on their own. "Teachers will often say in collective gatherings that they plan to implement some new tool, but then struggle," Roth observes. "What helps people to keep going with this experiment, even if they don't love it, is effective, one-on-one coaching." Most districts across the country, including San Francisco Unified, where Mission High is located, typically send in outside consultants as coaches—usually former teachers from the area—to support and mentor their peers. While this is occasionally necessary in small schools that don't have their own capacity for coaching, McKamey believes that schools should rely primarily on their in-house teacher-leaders to do this work whenever possible. School-based coaches come with huge advantages: they are able to model what they are trying to teach to other educators in their classrooms every day, they are typically respected by their peers, they have deep relationships with the colleagues they are coaching, and they know students intimately.

Alison White, a second-year English teacher, worked at another high school before coming to Mission in 2014. At her previous school, she had a district-assigned, drop-in coach for a year. His lesson planning, classroom management, and grading recommendations were helpful, but they didn't always work. Now, when McKamey recommends a strategy, White can usually see tangible changes in her classroom the next day. She believes McKamey's coaching is more effective because she can see White's teaching as a whole. This past year, she has been meeting with McKamey to plan curriculum, design meaningful assignments, analyze her students' work, and discuss how to teach individual students.

Max Anders, now in his second year of teaching by himself, says that for him the biggest problem with coaches who don't teach at the school is they don't know his students. He had been working with a district-assigned coach sent in from the outside and also with McKamey. The district coach spent time helping him figure out a way to distinguish "low-achievers" from "high-achievers," whereas McKamey spent two years working with Anders to disrupt this two-tiered system and teach individually. "My understanding before was you give work for the middle," explains Anders, who was teaching Plato's "The Allegory of the Cave" for the first time to his English seniors in 2014. "But the best is to give rigorous work that challenges everyone, and all students are in that uncomfortable place and rise to the occasion. You can't do it unless you are preparing all students, particularly lower-skilled students, to get there. Working with Pirette helped me become more deliberate about whom I check in first when I give the assignment, how I group kids together, and whom I work with outside of class." Anders reflects on the effectiveness of these strategies. "It's about creating opportunities for less confident students to share their thinking. I've seen situations where a student shares something and the rest of the class changes their perception of how they view and see that student. 'Whoa, I didn't know that student was that intelligent.' And it upsets this two-tiered system."

Mac Esters, a biology student teacher at Mission, observes that many strategies that he learned from McKamey—don't expect success, work toward it; try and retry things; failure isn't an option—are oft-repeated phrases that come off as clichés, unless you are watching someone like McKamey live them as she does, every day. "Watching these practices in action is jarring and refreshing and a daily challenge to all other educators at the school. I know that her ever-present loving kindness, mixed with high expectations of both herself and her students, can be cultivated, and deepened, and strengthened, and I hope to find that in myself too some day."

"Even just hearing how effective teachers like Pirette talk about students has made a huge impact on my practice," veteran teacher Rebecca Fulop observes. "When Pirette talks about a student like Jesmyn, whom I also taught, she calls her 'dignified' and 'beautiful.' I see how she talks to her students in the hallway and I see the impact it has on students and how much stronger of a relationship it creates. The biggest change I've made in my teaching as a result of these observations and collective sharing of student work is the least quantifiable, but has had the biggest impact. I learned to be more empathic toward students, to go out of my way to show them that I believe in them. It comes out in small ways, like standing outside of my classroom to have a quick conversation with my kids as they come in. It creates a feeling of safety, that they are going to be respected, and that translates into a willingness on their part to put in the intellectual and academic effort. This change didn't even add that much time to my schedule and has made some of the biggest impact."

<hr />

McKamey, Fulop, Soares, and five other teachers are seated around a table in an empty classroom, one late autumn morning in 2013. Light November rain is drumming against the windows as an English teacher named

Shideh Etaat passes around roasted almonds and Soares talks about her Thanksgiving plans. The teachers have convened for one of their four weekly common planning time hours—or "CPT" as they call it. Most teachers use this time to plan lessons together and to discuss the needs of the students they share. This group sets aside one hour each week to focus exclusively on deep, hour-long, collective case studies of individual students' work. Since most of the teachers in this group teach different subjects, the student work varies from week to week. The teachers compare notes about the teaching approaches that work for specific teens, and they can also mentor one another.

Today Dayna Soares has brought in a math worksheet from a recent test on which students were required to supplement their solutions with written justifications. "Jenny is a freshman and has a good foundation, lots of skills," says Soares by way of introduction. "Sometimes, she gets confused on steps. Sometimes, she will boycott the work because she doesn't see the reason to do it. I also had them do a mini-reflection the day before the test. And Jenny wrote, 'I need to work more on my distribution.'"

Teachers take five minutes to review the work and the supporting documentation for the assignment—or "scaffolding" as they call it—which is meant to help students learn a specific sequence of steps to complete a complex task. Last week Etaat, for example, brought handouts she had given to students with directions for creating a poem, including which questions to consider to develop a character for the poem, some sample starter stanzas, and a poem she wrote herself based on her assignment a week before.

Such "scaffolding" is crucial in learning, because it helps students develop mental blueprints of how to execute specific tasks on their own in the future.

Fall wind whistles through the antique window frames as teachers read in silence. "We'll start with what you think the student did well," says Mac Esters, the student teacher running this week's meeting. "Then, we'll discuss evidence of teaching, what Dayna could do better, and what we can take away for our practice."

"She understands 'like terms,'" Etaat, a first-year English teacher, comments. "Students have a hard time combining positive and negative terms. She is doing a really good job with it and not slipping."

"What I see is a high level of engagement," McKamey notes. "She attacks each problem until she is done with her knowledge. Her own assessments look accurate."

"There are a lot of systems in place, and I can see that she is using them," says Fulop. "She puts boxes around the answers, as you taught her. She clearly knows how you want her to do the problems."

"What I also see is Jenny praising teachers and table mates who are helping her, but not herself," Fulop continues. "We should help her see her own abilities more. She does distribution really well, but she says in her self-reflection that she doesn't."

"Jenny has understood the process of how you learn in this class and how you collaborate with table mates and teachers to complete problems," McKamey comments. "But math is always teetering between the abstract and concrete. It's really hard. Students always need more practice. They need evidence that they can succeed. When they're told, right, right, right, OK, got that, let's move on to the next thing—that's what builds perseverance."

"I sometimes call it 'persisting through confusion,'" Fulop observes. "I do a lot of individual, one-on-one work. 'Take a guess. Even if it's not correct, I want to hear your ideas.' Academic self-confidence is a big issue in our school. What I see is students who are intellectually capable, but don't believe that they are. They defeat themselves before they even give themselves a chance to try. Half of my students struggle with that."

"I would be very interested in talking about modeling those tools of persistence," Soares says. "Are there common questions a student can ask that will trigger their self-knowledge before they call over their teacher?"

"I don't think it's primarily about the box of tools or questions," McKamey jumps in. "It's more than that. Students persevere because they are strong. Opportunities to persevere prove that they can stick with it. They are willing to stick with it even in hardship: to stick with it for the teacher, because she or he really cares. To stick with it for the assignment, because it's so meaningful and enriching. Intellectual engagement, not just fun or doing it for the grade. There's got to be a reason to pull out that tool kit."

"I see a perfectionist, too," Fulop continues. "If Jenny doesn't know how to answer something, she won't put her guesses on the paper. I encourage people to put all of their ideas out there."

"Exactly," McKamey says. "This is flexibility, as opposed to perseverance. Another skill. She has holes in her knowledge. And you mentioned absences. Math knowledge is so fragile and delicate. When I observe math classes, if I miss a class, I come back and I'm lost. When I miss English or history, it doesn't happen as much."

"I'm curious, what happens in an English or history class that's different, where people don't get lost as much?" Soares asks.

"Pacing and the rhythm of the class matters a lot," McKamey replies. "Some classes have a little direct instruction for fifteen minutes, practice for twenty minutes, then some group work, and then back to direct instruction. In other classes, there is a long lecture in the beginning and then a lot of practice. So if you walked in late, there is nothing you can do."

"I agree, and another thing is review," Fulop suggests. "We have a lot of absenteeism, so we have to review more often."

"What do I do with a kid who is absent a lot?" Soares asks, noting that Jenny doesn't always show up for class. "Do I give them something different to work on? Or insist that they work on the same stuff?"

"This is when I work with students during lunch," McKamey replies.

"If they show up," Etaat says. "I've observed you. I see the urgency that students feel about turning in their work when they are in your class. I see the strategies that you use to instill that sense of urgency. But I struggle with that. I invite students to come to lunch. But a lot of them, they push me away. How do I get them to come?"

"There's a million strategies," McKamey replies. "I'm constantly responding to what I see in front of me. I collect work: three pieces of paper each day. They'll get it back the next day. I'm telling them it's all about the work, and I'm also giving them evidence that it's true. I'm planning from the beginning of the year. I start lighter, and then give them a lot of careful, positive feedback. I'm getting them addicted to that feeling. Training them to persevere. Then things get harder. And I tell them, it's going to be so, so hard. That French Revolution test will be so hard. But that's OK. If they get a C on that, that's OK, because they have so many other grades, and so many other positive experiences with me. So, they keep going. Everything is about the work, and there is daily evidence that it's all about the work. And in the beginning of the class, I tell them, everyone here starts with an A or a B. All you have to do is keep it up."

"You return their work the next day, every time?" Fulop inquires.

"That's what I try to do. I can't stress the importance of that enough," McKamey says.

"What if the kid chooses not to come and isn't excused?" Etaat asks. "But then shows up two weeks before the project is due and is kind of interested. If I excuse things, the message is that showing up in class doesn't matter."

"That's a great question," McKamey replies. "I know exactly what you mean. I have a separate grade for the research paper, for example, and for things that they do submit. So, that grade where they had to do things on time will be a D. But if it's a decent research paper, I'm not going to fail her. As she shows up and does the work, I'll bend over backward to show successes. I'm really showing off her work with every opportunity I have—privately and in public."

"I want to say one more thing about how you keep students," McKamey adds as the rain starts falling harder. "Every time a student does an assignment, they are communicating something about their thinking. And even if it's far away from what you thought they'd do or hoped they do, they are still communicating the ways they are putting the pieces together. There are so many opportunities to miss certain students and not see them, not hear them, shut them down. It's easy to do, and it takes a lot of skill, experience, and patience not to do that. Despite years and years of teaching, sometimes I still have to give myself a lot of room to catch up. There are times when the student is communicating something to me and I can't hear their thinking at the moment, but I can't ruin it," she says. "I have to keep it alive."

◇◇◇◇◇◇◇◇◇◇◇◇◇◇◇

"It worked, it really made a difference," Alison White, an English teacher, reports back to her coach McKamey one afternoon in December 2014. They're meeting in McKamey's office, a small, sun-lit room near the school entrance filled with thick binders for various units McKamey has built up over the past twenty-six years: Chinua Achebe's *Things Fall Apart*, Shakespeare's *Macbeth*, Gabriel García Márquez's *Chronicle of a Death Foretold*, and units on "Quests" and "Courage." As White's first semester at Mission High comes to an end, she wants her coach to know that she has just experienced one of the best student discussions of the year in her class. The students were enthralled by the ideas they had been exploring through reading Toni Morrison's *Sula*, White tells Mc-Kamey: thoughtful in their comments, respectful with each other, and able to make sophisticated connections between the text and contemporary events.

White did not feel this way about her teaching at the beginning of her first year at Mission, four months earlier. When McKamey first observed White in the classroom, she was spending more time dealing with student behavior management than teaching content and skills. That day, White had introduced her seniors to a short story by Jack London called "To Build a Fire," in which an overly confident man decides to hike the Yukon Trail in Alaska. Accompanied only by a husky, "the man," as the protagonist is called, is unprepared for the extremely cold weather and dies along the way. After students read the story, White asked them to answer questions about the text in writing and then facilitated a brief discussion. The lesson didn't go as well as White had hoped. Students looked bored with one of White's favorite short stories: several had their heads on their desks, a few kept looking at their phones, and some were chatting out loud with their friends.

When the teachers debriefed, White expected Mc-Kamey to spend much of her time discussing alternative "classroom management" strategies. While McKamey suggested several tactics for setting up more structure and stricter boundaries in the class, she spent most of the time discussing White's lesson plan. "You will get them with your content, Ali," she said. "The solutions to academic problems are academic." Discipline problems typically arise when there are issues with content and teaching approaches. McKamey suggested increasing engagement and rigor by adding "even more content and context" and "direct instruction" (explicit teaching of content or skills, modeled by a teacher and followed by student practice). "Students need to visualize what this character is facing in that story," McKamey explained. "How about adding a few mini-lectures in the next few weeks on the weather patterns in Alaska, the geography and history of the Yukon Trail, and something about the huskies? Your students are eager to learn something every day," McKamey said. "They want to take something concrete home with them."

"I never thought I would be teaching geography and history in an English class," White reported back to McKamey a few weeks later. "The students were so much more engaged. It makes sense. The PowerPoint lessons about the weather in Alaska and the Yukon Trail and the huskies in Greenland are connected to real life. The story becomes more interesting when it's not just a vehicle to teach the definition of a 'metaphor.'"

McKamey's suggestion to add more direct instruction puzzled White at first. When White was getting her teaching credential at San Francisco State University, direct instruction was most often used as an example of "bad teaching." White's professors of education were enthusiastic proponents of the new Common Core Standards, which aim to promote more challenging content. Much to McKamey's chagrin, higher expectations are often mistakenly interpreted as a need for the complete elimination of direct instruction. Successful teachers don't use one tool to the exclusion of others, McKamey argues. They use their professional judgment to make wise choices about the most effective tools based on the needs and challenges they see in front of them.

This is White's favorite part about working with Mc-Kamey. When White asks for help, her coach offers a variety of tools that she can try, but what works for McKamey won't necessarily work for White. Teachers—like students—have unique talents and skills, and they need to practice using their own judgment. "Ms. McKamey is not telling me 'do it exactly like that,'" White explains to me. "Her suggestions come more like questions: 'How come you do this and not that?' And at first I took those questions as instructions, but then I realized that she is training me to pay attention to the intent behind everything I do. There are many ways to get to the same place, but the most important thing is to figure out the bigger goal and the best way to get there in each unique situation."

In October of that year, McKamey and White delved into teaching strategies to facilitate more spirited and authentic student discussions. When McKamey observed White during that month, she noticed that whenever a student made a comment, White would rephrase it in her own words and then repeat it to the whole class. Mc-Kamey felt that this was cumbersome and disruptive, but most important, it sent a subtle message to students: their own ideas only had value when they were articulated in a different way by the teacher. "To ask students to define something in your specific way is the opposite of rigor," McKamey told White. "Everyone interprets texts differently. Rigor means asking students to really untie the knots of their own thinking. They have to figure out how to interpret the text and then they have to figure out how they connect their viewpoint to the text or prove it through the text."

White had another question, which came up a few weeks after she introduced Toni Morrison's novel *Sula*, based on the lives of African American characters. "I'm scared to talk about race," White confessed. "I'm very aware that I'm a white woman teaching this text by an African American author to a classroom comprised primarily of students of color. And I am very uncomfortable that I'm avoiding these conversations because I'm afraid of them. It feels like complacency; like a white person who only aims to be comfortable. At the same time, I don't want me teaching this book to come off as if I understand the black experience. How do I navigate the discussions about race?"

"First of all, the fact that you are thinking about these issues is everything," McKamey replied. "I bring my limitations to everything I teach, and you bring yours. I'm scared to talk about race, too. It is hard for all human beings. But there are teaching strategies you can use to get better at this."

Throughout November, McKamey and White discussed various parts of the novel and shared their interpretations with each other. At some point, McKamey suggested that White bring in other authors. "*Sula* is a beautiful novel, but it's a very sad book about the tragedies of African American life," McKamey said. "Let's bring in some counter voices that turn racism on its head, like bell hooks or Chris Rock."

In the next week, while White was doing research online, she discovered a video of spoken word artist Neiel

Israel reading her poem, "When a Black Man Walks." The poem moved White, and she asked McKamey if she could use it instead of hooks and Rock. "Of course, Ali," McKamey replied after watching the video. "You have to use it."

When White met with McKamey the following day, her coach suggested another strategy for navigating classroom discussions. It had to do with allowing young people of color to be the driving voices in discussions about race, with White there as a teacher creating a safe space for everyone, especially her few African American students who might feel more vulnerable in a conversation about racism against black people. "Let's ask them to write their responses to the poem individually first," McKamey said. "You walk around the class and see what the students are writing. Then, let's divide people into pairs and ask them to discuss their writing. Then you pick a few students first and encourage them to share their reflections with the rest of the class."

The following week, the twenty-two seniors in the classroom watched the video of "When a Black Man Walks." Earlier that week, on December 10, a grand jury had made the decision not to indict the police officers who choked an African American man named Eric Garner to death in Staten Island, New York. The Facebook and Twitter feeds of Mission High students were full of posts about the "Black Lives Matter" protests and outrage over the series of recent killings of unarmed black men by police officers.

"Think about our readings of *Sula* this semester and what Sula and Jude have been saying," White said, turning to her students after they finished watching the video of

Israel's poem. "Think about this poem. Think about Eric Garner, Ferguson, and the events that are unfolding in our country. And tell me what you think is the point of this poem, thinking back and making connections to everything we learned and discussed so far."

Students hunched over their notebooks and the sound of moving pens and pencils took over the classroom.

As students wrote, White walked around the classroom and looked at the students' writing: "Black men instill both desire and fear in the same people. The power of black men is that they live every day like it could be their last." "Skin color should not be the cause of violence. We have come a long way to end racism, but we have a longer way to go." "Black men change our future when they speak up, when they become a role model, and when they die."

"The students were so thoughtful in their discussion of *Sula*, the poem, and everything we'd been reading, and how it connects to our current issues of race and police brutality and these protests," White says at the end of the year to McKamey in her office. "I was deeply moved and overwhelmed," she adds. "They were being their true, best selves."

Chapter 8

Jesmyn

The high-pitched buzzing of a chainsaw woke Jesmyn up. She squinted at the amber light in the window. A piece of wood creaked outside, and a pile of boards fell on the ground. Her pit bull, Lady, let out a wailing yawn. Jesmyn checked the time on her cell phone. She wanted to make it to school early today, in time to review her research paper before presenting it in front of her classmates. She got out of bed, shuffled to the bathroom, got dressed, and ran out the door. Out in the courtyard of her apartment complex, a construction worker blocked her. "We need to get you a hardhat. Wait here," he said. She stood still, as strangers in hardhats removed panels off her grandmother's apartment building, gutted windows in her aunt's home, and unhinged doors at the place where Jesmyn's childhood friend used to live.

When she was eight, Jesmyn and her friend would find empty cardboard boxes, flatten them into sleds, race up the hill near their apartment complex, and slide down the dirt on the cardboard, spinning around, laughing until their stomachs hurt. One day at the bottom of the hill

Jesmyn and her friend noticed a short, black object sticking out of the ground. Her friend pulled it out. It was a handgun. Jesmyn went home and told her mother about it. Jesmyn's mother ran outside, screaming, and took the gun away from her friend.

For many years after that day, Jesmyn thought that guns grew out of the ground, like flowers. Whenever she walked outside, she watched the ground beneath her feet. She thought guns were growing all over her neighborhood. She stopped playing with her friends outside for a while and spent more time alone in her room, where she could relax and feel calm. She didn't want to bother her mother with her fears of getting shot by the guns popping out of the ground. Her mother was raising Jesmyn by herself and working two jobs. She had enough worries on her mind already. That's when Jesmyn learned to keep all of her fears to herself, something she would have to unlearn in high school.

The construction worker came back with a hardhat and walked Jesmyn across the courtyard toward the bus stop. She had missed the first bus. She knew she'd be late to school, again. Mr. Roth had talked to Jesmyn twice last week about being late for his classes, and so had Ms. Stewart, Mission High's attendance liaison. Getting to school on time has always been a struggle. She gets distracted easily, she says, and gets pulled into the lives of other people too much on her way to school. But her attendance had been improving every year since she transferred to Mission in 2008. This week she slipped again, because of the demolition work at her public housing complex.

Another bus came. Jesmyn found a seat in the back and went over the bullet points in her head to prepare for her presentation. On her lap she held her purple purse containing a ten-page, single-spaced paper titled "Race and Education in America." The previous night Jesmyn had finished her research paper, which explored why schools were failing so many African American students. She had spent her entire Sunday revising her final paper with her English teacher and mentor, Ms. McKamey. The two sat at a dark walnut office desk in the sunny living room of Ms. McKamey's home in Oakland as Jesmyn struggled to organize her words and ideas.

The paper includes summaries of academic articles that describe different takes on why racial gaps in education persist. Jesmyn also quoted Claude Steele from *Whistling Vivaldi: How Stereotypes Affect Us and What We Can Do*, and included interviews with Mission High students about their experiences in different classrooms. She also added a short essay about the experiences of her classmate, Devon, in a juvenile detention center. When Jesmyn was investigating issues about school suspensions for this paper, the news about the killing of Trayvon Martin in 2012 had just broken. When Mr. Roth, the teacher of her honors ethnic studies class, for which she was writing this paper, had called Jesmyn to check on how she was doing with her writing, she had asked him if she could add the case of Trayvon Martin to her essay. "Of course," he had said.

Before Jesmyn arrived at Ms. McKamey's house, she read everything she could find about Martin's case. She read the reactions of her friends on Facebook. She combed Twitter posts. She watched TV. She ignored her friends' texts and invitations to go to the movies in order to work on incorporating the case in her paper.

Jesmyn had a strong first draft in which she attempted to weave everything together, but some elements were still missing. She wanted to add her own knowledge and talk about the daily weight of what she referred to as "the stares and the sighs" black people deal with every day: the suspicious gazes of the store clerks who assume she has walked in to steal something, the white people who cross the street when they see a black person ahead, the sighs of some teachers when she asks for one more explanation of the task, and the shushing by others when she wants to make a comment. Jesmyn wanted to explain how these quiet stares and impatient sighs accumulated over time and on some days made her feel frustrated and distracted when she came to school. She felt that this was an important angle people needed to understand about achievement gaps, but she needed her teacher's advice on how to include her own experiences in a research paper without compromising its integrity as an objective exploration.

When Jesmyn struggled with something—academically or in her personal life—she often went to Ms. Mc-Kamey's office. She loved that Ms. McKamey didn't tell her what to do. She just listened and helped her analyze her situation to the point where Jesmyn could come up with her own conclusions. When she met Ms. McKamey, it was the lowest point in her life, she says. Even though Jesmyn's mother thought her middle school in the more affluent, Marina district of San Francisco was a better school than the ones in their own neighborhood, Jesmyn received mostly Fs and Ds there. Her attendance was inconsistent. The school district flagged her as a student at risk of dropping out before she transferred to Mission High.

By her senior year at Mission in 2012, things were looking up. She had three Bs and one C. If she could get her only failing grade up by the end of the semester, her average would be high enough to apply to state universities and community college. She really needed that. She'd be the first member of her family to go to college. But more than a college degree or a good job, Jesmyn wanted the knowledge, skills, and patience to come back to her neighborhood and help lift the spirits of her community. She dreamed of returning as a social worker who could help people in need feel heard and valued.

Local newspapers and TV people usually talked about her neighborhood as one of the poorest and most violent in San Francisco, but Jesmyn loved it. She was born and raised here, and every area in these apartments reflected her favorite memories: playing outside with her friends, barbeques, little cousins' birthdays, meeting her boyfriend Travis. He brought her Lady as a present a year ago—a small fur ball with legs too thin for her bulging, pink belly. One time Lady saved the life of Jesmyn's mother, who has no sense of smell. She didn't detect a gas leak in their apartment building. Lady howled and paced around until Jesmyn's mother realized what was happening.

Jesmyn's bus wasn't moving fast enough. She was still hoping she could make it to class on time. She wanted to review her paper one more time before her presentation, but she was having trouble focusing on it. Lady was weighing heavily on her mind. In two weeks, when construction workers would be taking out Jesmyn's windows, she would have to move to a temporary apartment building across town. The new housing did not allow dogs.

◇◇◇◇◇◇◇◇◇◇◇◇◇◇◇◇

"Mr. Roth, how come you never pick up my calls any-more?" a student named Alvin asks jokingly at the end of the "Do Now" assignment one morning.

"When I do, you know what happens?" Roth, standing next to a projector, replies. "I pick up. 'Hi. It's me. How are you doing?' That's what I get from you. When Jesmyn calls, it's a serious academic discussion. She is not calling just to say hi."

As students laugh, Jesmyn puts her "Do Now" on Roth's desk.

"All kidding aside," Roth is now standing in the middle of the room. "Last week you picked your own partners. But this week, I'll pick a partner for you. Together, you will cre-ate a 1930s poster," he announces. "This will be one of five pieces that we will put in the magazine you've been work-ing on about the thirties." He reminds students about the project, which includes student-created news stories, edi-torials, and ads for products of the 1930s like Coca Cola, refrigerators, and Ford's Model A. "This poster has to be written in first person, about the hardships of the Depres-sion. You can be a photographer, filmmaker, or a writer from that time. You have to write it like you are feeling it, in character, including the content we've been studying."

After Roth assigns partners, Catharine moves over to Jesmyn and the two pick out markers. Catharine is draw-ing "1930" in bloc letters.

"Can I do a rap?" Rosa asks.

"Yes, you can. But I suggest that you do a draft first and then put it on the poster."

Roth takes a step back to read what Juan has written: "In the last two days I only had two customers in my store. I had to lay off all of my employees. There is a long line of people by the bank. Everyone is trying to get their money out of it, but the banks don't have any cash."

Jesmyn hasn't added anything yet to her poster. Instead, she takes everything out of her schoolbag and stacks it on the desk: binders, papers, and folders. "I put seven pencils in my bag this morning and I can't find a single one," she grumbles out loud. "I don't feel like doing this right now," she snaps, pulling out a form for a field trip and filling it out.

"Jesmyn," Roth pleads. "You can't be doing this right now!"

"I don't remember anything about the New Deal or the Bonus Army or any of this," Jesmyn says, continuing to fill out the form.

"You have a lot of notes on this, Jesmyn. Take your notes out," Roth walks over to her desk. Jesmyn ignores his request, turns over her form, and keeps writing on it.

"You are going to have to fight with me today!" he raises both arms in the air. "You don't want to fail what you started, you have to stay focused." Roth and Jesmyn walk out of the class for a minute. After they return, she sits down and starts reading what her partner Catharine has written so far. She picks up a Sharpie and adds a few sentences.

After class, Jesmyn tells me that earlier that week, she had taken Lady to San Francisco's animal shelter to give her up for adoption. It was one of the hardest things she has ever had to do. The shelter worker gave her some forms to fill out. She wrote that Lady was "sweet" and "jumpy." A young woman came and took Lady's leash out of Jesmyn's hand. Lady wagged her tail and pressed her ears down along the sides of her black-and-white head as she followed the worker down the hall, through a glass door, toward the metal cages.

◇◇◇◇◇◇◇◇◇◇◇◇◇◇◇◇◇

Claire Lilienthal, the middle school Jesmyn attended, sits at the northeastern tip of San Francisco, where the city's more affluent residents live. The neighborhood is dotted with luxury stores and yachts and has a clear view of the Golden Gate Bridge. The school has much higher test scores than Mission High. Most of Jesmyn's classmates were white or Asian American. She quickly became friends with the few African American students at the school, but she never felt accepted by them. "I was always yearning for their respect, but it wasn't fully there," Jesmyn tells me as we go out for lunch one day in 2010. "They were black kids from my neighborhood, but I was the only one going back home to the projects. Their parents had cars, cell phones, steady jobs. Their grades were better than mine. Maybe we didn't connect as much because I was more discreet with my personal information. I didn't feel that they would understand."

On the bus rides home, Jesmyn often sat alone, closer to the front, away from the bullies and the popular kids. The rides were long. Her neighborhood is tucked away in San Francisco's southeast corner, a postindustrial area with sparse storefronts, liquor stores, and empty warehouses.

Jesmyn remembers climbing the steps of the yellow school bus one hot spring day after school. She found an empty seat, curled over her knees, and pressed them against her chin. The school bus usually passed through the Presidio of San Francisco, a park in the Marina, to get to Jesmyn's neighborhood, leaving bright green lawns and lush parks behind. There were more birds in the park that day than usual, jumping from one tree branch to another, chirping. The afternoon sunlight was barely touching the treetops. Jesmyn looked at the sage-colored leaves of eucalyptus trees gently swaying in the wind. She forgot all about the bus and the students. She felt relaxed, alone, as quiet as a tree.

"I'm not a nature girl, but when I watched those treetops in the sun, I felt so calm and at peace," she recalls when I ask her to describe her happiest memories from her middle school years. "All I could see was the beauty of nature. I wasn't worried about doing bad in class. I wasn't worried about my bad grades. I wasn't worried about being the tallest girl with the darkest skin in school. I wasn't concerned about not having someone strong to lean on. This is the biggest thing I struggle with in my life: being calm, being at peace, and enjoying myself. Every day I work hard to find places where I can feel this way."

"When I'm in school, when I get real work done there and feel like I'm learning, I feel like that," Jesmyn continues. "I don't want my teachers to pretend that they can understand what's going on in my neighborhood. I'll deal with my personal issues after school. I'll go to the Wellness Center and see my counselor, Chandra, I'll talk to Ms. McKamey and my friends. When I'm in class, I want to work on my skills and gain knowledge. I need my teacher to get my butt to work. When I work hard, when I'm learning, I feel like I'm going toward a better place. That's when I feel at peace."

As San Francisco's afternoon fog creeps in quietly through the open windows of our lunch café, Jesmyn zips up her 1980s-inspired black leather jacket and adjusts the ivory scarf over her neck. She takes a sip from her strawberry-banana smoothie. Then she notices a small fly underneath the clear plastic lid. "Oh, I'm so sorry, hun!" she says to the dead fly while lifting the plastic lid. "I didn't see you there. You were just chillin' and bam. At least you went out with a bang, high on sugar."

"One of my first teachers in the ninth grade always gave me a lot of encouraging words in my personal life," Jesmyn recalls as we talk about different educators in her life. "She was very sweet and supportive when I struggled outside of school. She wanted to talk to me about my personal life, but she wasn't encouraging me in the schoolwork. Her feedback on my work was rare and mostly negative. It felt like she didn't see me as a capable student. I got Fs in her classes and then had to fix them in night school."

"I can tell if teachers really believe in me—if they really expect a lot from me—by looking at the grades they give me and the feedback on my work. I'm one of those students where you have to push me to do something," Jesmyn says, placing her hand on her chest. "My motivation is far from perfect. If I have an F in your class, I know that I didn't do my work. But you probably didn't do your work either since you let it go like that. The teacher is a half of a circle here. I'm not saying that everybody is going to be easy to push, and it takes a lot of energy to coach and guide someone. But that is what teaching is all about.

"When I have a B in Ms. McKamey's class, she is going to let me know. Some other teachers won't. Teachers like Ms. McKamey and Mr. Roth are not waiting until it's too late to fix the grade. They are fixing it every day. Some teachers will say, 'Jesmyn, why do you have an F?' And then ask an Asian American student why she has a C. Why don't you ask me that when I have a C? Why wait until an F?"

"I had a teacher that often talked about having very high expectations for us, but then left me hanging," she adds. "Those kinds of teachers don't believe in you unless you believe in yourself. It only works for students who are already confident in their work, or get help at home. My mom didn't go to college and can't help me with school-work. I often need extra help after classes, I often need one more explanation in the class, or one more question answered. I have to learn how to build grammar skills. I have to learn how to build that work ethic where I just sit down and do it. It's a long process."

At some point during her time at Mission, Jesmyn realized that sometimes it was the most verbally encouraging teachers who unconsciously stigmatized black students. "Some teachers hover over African American students more than others in a classroom setting. 'Is everything OK? Do you need help?' When I am looking for support, I am not looking for pity," she stresses. "I'm looking for a lot of understanding."

As we walk toward the bus stop, Jesmyn says that some teachers need to get extra education on how to communicate and work with students of different cultures, especially African American students. "I talk a lot, ask questions more. My personality is more dominant. But it's viewed as acting out instead of showing engagement. Some teachers become more standoffish and ignore you. Some send you out of class. Others give you a good grade that you didn't deserve. And instead of telling me directly what the problem is, 'Jesmyn, sit down. Jesmyn, you are talking over me and it's rude,' the respect level just drops to the ultimate low."

"There are a lot of days when I walk in upset," she adds. "Some mornings my mom and I have an argument. Some days people will look at me the wrong way on my way to school. Mr. Roth will say, 'Look at you kiddo! Showed up even though you were mad!' How can you be mad at that? He knows. He can tell by my face. Not trying to get into my business too much, but showing his recognition to the whole class: 'I see you. I know you are not having a good day. I'm thanking you for showing up. Now, get your butt to work.' I love that."

◇◇◇◇◇◇◇◇◇◇◇◇◇◇◇◇

It's 8:10 a.m. and Jesmyn rushes into class, research paper in hand. She puts a metal can of iced tea and a pack of Skittles on her desk. A student named Yessenia is sitting in Mr. Roth's chair, her eyes glued to a computer screen as she re-reads her paper on the health conditions of women in US prisons one more time before printing it out.

"Yessenia, you have been sitting in that chair for three days. I think you are ready to print!" Roth takes a break from taking attendance. "I know," Yessenia laughs.

Jesmyn is eating an apple at her desk while reviewing the bullet points for her presentation. She is in her senior year, a month before graduation, and her GPA is 2.7. She has already passed the placement tests for the City College of San Francisco, which she plans to attend in September. She wants to get two part-time jobs over the summer, one at Payless Shoes and another with Aim High, a nonprofit that she attended herself while at Mission High, which helps low-income students of color choose high schools and plan their college path.

The bell rings, and Roth calls on Jesmyn. She nods and pulls a hood over her head. Her dark blue sweatshirt reads "Claire Lilienthal Track." She brings out her notes and puts a can of AriZona watermelon-flavored drink and a pack of Skittles on a stool in front of the blackboard.

"My paper is about race, education, and the case of Trayvon Martin," she begins. "Before I get started, how many of you have heard about Trayvon?" This is a few weeks after the shooting, and half of the class raise their hands.

"In that case, I will start by summarizing the known facts of the Martin case," Jesmyn says. "It's important to establish what we know happened. On the evening of February 26, 2012, Trayvon Martin—an unarmed seventeen-year-old African American student—was walking back home from the store. He was wearing a hoodie and carried Skittles and iced tea in his hands. George Zimmerman, a volunteer security guard, followed him, then confronted, shot, and killed Trayvon. Zimmerman has not been charged with a crime."

"I am wearing a hoodie," Jesmyn notes after she finishes the summary of the case. "Do I look like I'm going to kill you?" Students shake their heads.

"What if I have my hand in my pocket? Do I look like I'm going to pull out a gun?" she asks.

"No," Maria says out loud.

"Well, I want to tell you that when I'm in the world, that is not the response I get," Jesmyn continues. "When I'm in the world, I am always a suspect. When I walk into a store, salespeople always run up to me and ask me if they can help me. Then they follow me as I walk up and down the aisles, but they don't follow other, light-skinned customers. When I walk down the streets in white neighborhoods, I get these looks like I came to slash car tires. I just wanted you to know that," she says.

Jesmyn catches her voice rising and sits down on a chair. She takes a few deep breaths and a sip of the iced tea and looks over her bullet points again. "I'm sorry. His case really hit home with me," she says. "This has been the hardest project for me. But back to the facts." She stands up again.

"If you listen to the recordings of the conversations between Zimmerman and the police, it's clear that Zimmerman is on edge. He says that the person in a hoodie is on drugs or looking to get in trouble. He talks about how there have been all of these break-ins in the community. That's racial profiling," Jesmyn says. "In our schools in America, African American boys are three times more likely to be suspended," she continues. "Instead of having a conversation with us, some teachers just choose to send us downstairs and have the police deal with us. It shows that they don't believe in us.

"Last year I was recommended to be a part of this nonprofit program that was looking into the achievement gap.

They were trying to solve it in San Francisco, but I was the only black girl in that task force. A few times I missed their meetings, because I was behind on my school papers and wanted to finish them. They put me on probation. Then they kicked me out. So they were making recommendations on how to close the achievement gap without any African American students present.

"President Obama said that if he had a son, he'd look like Trayvon. What these words showed is that even though Mr. Obama is our first black president, things haven't changed enough. In this country, if you are a black person like me and you are wearing a hoodie, you are a suspect, every day.

"There are teachers out there who think racism is not a big issue anymore. People say we live in a postracial society. Trayvon Martin's case shows that it's not that way yet.

"Last week there was a national Million Hoodie March in New York. It was devastating watching Trayvon's parents speak. It inspired us to organize a Hoodie Day at our school. I hope you all can come.

"All I ask of you, let's talk about race. Let's not make it a taboo topic. We haven't forgotten how far we have come from and how much we have grown, but we have to remember that the fight is not over yet."

"Trayvon is dead. Trayvon doesn't have a voice anymore," Jesmyn says, wiping away tears from behind her glasses. "I am going to speak for him now." As she sits back down on the chair, the sound of the tires of commuter cars breaks the heavy silence of the room.

"I could honestly see you making a speech in a few years and moving a whole bunch of people," Yessenia says. "You should do a speech during our graduation," she adds.

"Yes!" several students in the class raise their hands in support.

∞∞∞∞∞∞∞∞∞∞∞∞

Jesmyn did make a speech during her graduation, in May 2012. And so did George. Jesmyn had a good summer after she received her diploma. She worked part-time at Aim High and eventually became a teacher, talking to middle school students who would be the first to go to college in their families about "college skills." Her classmate Maria's little brother, Sergio, was in Jesmyn's class at Aim High.

In her Aim High classrooms, Jesmyn spoke with confidence and a sense of authority, but she also wasn't afraid to use her sense of humor and present her point of view. She paid attention to her students' questions and the level of energy in the class. She was good at getting students back on track when they got distracted. As students read articles about choosing colleges or high schools, she told them, "Always think for yourself. All opinions on schools are not always right. Go to the school, visit it by yourself, talk to students there. Make your own decisions in life."

After Jesmyn got off work at Aim High, we drove over to Office Max together. She liked my appointment calendar and wanted to get one before she started classes at City College of San Francisco in September. She had an interview with Payless Shoes the next week. We brainstormed about the best attire and how to highlight her strengths on her resume. We agreed to meet in the fall on the campus of City College. But on the day of our meeting, Jesmyn didn't come. She wasn't responding to my text messages, either. Weeks went by without a response, which was unusual.

Then one day I got a call from Roth. He said Jesmyn's boyfriend Travis had been shot in the face and died on the spot. Jesmyn wasn't responding to his calls or texts either, but she did pick up a call from Ms. McKamey.

She wasn't doing well, McKamey reported. Her voice sounded disembodied.

Jesmyn had been dating Travis for four years. He was her closest friend, and she spent a lot of time at the home of his grandmother, Edna Tobie. She felt comfortable there. This news came just a little under a year after Jesmyn lost her father, who had recently been released from jail and died in a car accident. That same year Jesmyn had been forced to move to another government housing complex and give up her dog, Lady. "It's relentless," Roth told me on the phone. "Too much for any child to handle. There is no time to recover."

"You are a survivor," Ms. McKamey told Jesmyn at the end of their call.

"I'm a survivor," Jesmyn repeated. "I'm a survivor, Ms. McKamey."

Epilogue

Prudence L. Carter, a professor in the School of Education at Stanford University, evokes a powerful metaphor to describe what she views as the moral injustice behind our country's standardized education system. Carter describes public schools as a system that provides three distinct pathways to social mobility. Our affluent students are moving through a system in a luxury, high-speed elevator supported by skilled, highly paid teachers, intellectually challenging classes, and private tutors. Our middle-class children are riding behind in an escalator. Their parents struggle to keep up, but ultimately they find sufficient ways to help their children be prepared for college. And then there are our country's low-income students—smart, resilient, talented young people like Maria, Darrell, Jesmyn, and Pablo—who are trying to catch up by running up a staircase that is missing steps, has no handrails, and is covered with broken glass.

Students from low-income families represent roughly half of all children in our public schools, and nearly two-thirds of black and Latino youth under the age of eighteen live in poverty.[1] Their schools are much more likely to have less-qualified teachers; substandard college preparatory classes, books, and school supplies; and underfunded arts and sports programs. In most states there is roughly a three-to-one ratio between spending on students in rich and poor districts.[2] Disparities also exist within districts and between states, with New York spending $17,326 per student in 2015 and California just $8,308.[3] When low-income students don't make it to the arbitrary "proficiency" benchmarks set by psychometricians each year, politicians of all political stripes label students, their teachers, and their schools as "failing." Many schools respond by pushing low-income students into remedial classes and away from the intellectually challenging ones that most students I interviewed told me motivate them to come to school more than any other variable.

Carter and a growing number of our country's leading education scholars and leaders—including Linda Darling-Hammond, Gloria Ladson-Billings, Patricia Gandara, and Yong Zhao—argue that this is exactly the wrong response.[4] What is still missing, a century after the Administrative Progressive education reform movement began, is sufficient supports, capacity, and resources to close the educational opportunity gaps. These scholars, along with a growing coalition of civil rights groups and teachers' unions, are calling for a new system of "reciprocal accountability," one in which politicians are kept accountable for the appropriate "inputs" to reach the "outcomes" they demand. These scholars are joined by growing numbers of students and parents across the country, who don't want standardized tests to be the most important "outcome" in how we measure the quality of education.[5]

The experience of the last ten years clearly shows that when we grade schools primarily based on state test scores, they become more segregated and overly standardized. The United States now tests its students more than any other industrialized nation.[6] But that is not how countries with high-performing students, such as in Finland, Singapore, and Australia, are raising achievement. These nations use a very different accountability system, in which national, standardized tests—which are administered a lot less frequently than in the United States—are used for guidance, as a red flag that tells the education officials which schools are struggling and need extra support. These countries use a combination of infrequent national assessments and real student work, graded by teachers, to achieve school accountability.[7]

There is a growing consensus among scholars who study schools and education policy that our country should move in a similar direction.[8] Linda Darling-Hammond, as well as Gene Willhoit and Linda Pittenger of the National Center for Innovation in Education, believe we should have a similar accountability system. They have put together a thoughtful testing reform plan in their 2014 report, "Accountability for College and Career Readiness: Developing a New Paradigm." These scholars call for a reduced number of state standardized tests and increased capacity at the local and state levels to develop "performance assessments," like those Guthertz and his fellow teachers in Los Angeles briefly worked on in 1989, and which included student work like essays, group projects, individual presentations, and science projects. Teachers can be trained to grade such work together and to detect a broader range of important skills, such as ability to synthesize and analyze complex ideas, communicate effectively in front of classmates, debate thoughtfully, and learn from mistakes. Instead of spending most of the time prepping students for the big Common Core test in April—or computerized district-mandated mini-versions of it throughout the year—teachers would be incentivized to teach their students how to produce work and demonstrate skills that reflect what is done by various professionals in the real world every day.[9]

California is one of the few states taking the first steps in the nation toward such reform.[10] The budget for 2013 included a provision for "local control funding formula," which rewards local districts for designing more holistic school accountability systems and—in the spirit of "reciprocal accountability"—for the first time gives them additional funds based on the number of "high-needs" students their schools are serving.[11] The San Francisco Unified School District has reduced standardized test scores to 30 percent of the overall school grade in high schools and is experimenting with including other quantitative and qualitative measures, such as student and parent surveys and social and emotional skills.[12] This is a hugely important step in the right direction, but it's not sufficient for raising the quality of education. Reducing the number of tests and adding "multiple measures" to our system of grading schools won't automatically translate into better teaching and learning.

After spending four years at Mission High and immersing myself in the history of the education reforms of the past century as well as countless studies on teaching and learning, I now strongly believe that the most effective policy changes to improve the quality of public education and reduce achievement gaps would prioritize building up the capacity of classroom teachers to be in charge of school reforms and accountability. Teachers in all schools—and in high-poverty schools like Mission High especially— need more time, resources, and support to plan lessons and reflect on outcomes, comb through qualitative and quantitative data to justify classroom and school-wide changes, keep themselves and their peers accountable, and receive training from respected peers when they are struggling. When teachers are given sustained opportunities to improve their craft, they can develop skills to provide intellectually challenging education in personalized, diverse classrooms.

At the student level such moves toward more integrated, student-centered classrooms would look very much like Jesmyn's experience in the classroom of Ms. McKamey or Rasheed's experience in Mr. Hsu's class. Despite the fact that Jesmyn came to Mission with a low GPA and a sense of alienation from the public school system, she found herself in a learning environment in which she felt valued, inspired, and pushed. When Jesmyn talked about teachers who motivated her to learn, like all students I interviewed, she talked about teachers who saw her individual strengths, intellect, personal interests, and effort. Jesmyn wanted opportunities to work hard, feel challenged, and produce meaningful work that would provide evidence of her own intellect and skills. She wanted to know why the material she studied mattered, how it connected to other things in the past and other disciplines, and how it will connect to her future career. A seat in an integrated, diverse classroom taught Jesmyn and her classmates to get along with people from different backgrounds and viewpoints, take criticism, ask questions, and solve problems collectively—skills that reduce conflict and teach students the value of intercultural communication and collaboration, which most employers now demand.

Increased support for teachers to prepare rigorous lesson plans and design engaging assignments would allow educators to set up such effective, intellectually challenging classroom experiences. Students would be able to learn mainstream content that the standards require and be allowed to explore their interests, including the heritage of their own culture. Such an approach allows students to have a voice in and ownership of their learning and increases academic engagement and confidence. Instead of cramming for short versions of standardized tests throughout the year, sitting in remedial classes, and rushing through content to catch up, students from all backgrounds would have opportunities to apply their knowledge in a variety of formats, which neuroscientists tell us physically alters our brain and contributes to long-term learning. Teachers would have more time for constructive feedback and one-on-one discussions with students, which all students I interviewed told me helped them learn and strengthened their relationships with teachers.

Educators need to study their craft and improve in the course of their entire careers—a working condition that most teachers at Mission High placed above increased pay, even though teachers in America are underpaid and most at Mission can't afford to live in San Francisco. As science teacher Rebecca Fulop put it, "I signed up for reduced pay in my life to make a difference in students' lives. And the worst thing that I deal with is this daily frustration that I can't be there for all of my students they way I want to, because I don't have enough time, resources, and capacity to do it."

Increased investment in teacher development and trust in their professional judgment would also allow more educators to create their own research and action groups to solve school-based problems—like the "Anti-racist Teaching Committee" McKamey cofounded with her colleagues, which disaggregates local data and coaches individual teachers. Such peer-led groups much more effectively address complex root causes behind educational disparities than one-size-fits-all interventions from the district or state level. According to the 2013 MetLife Survey of the American Teacher, more than half of teachers were interested in "hybrid roles" that combined classroom teaching with a leadership role at the school, district, or state level.[13]

Shifting most of our education reform focus from standardized tests to improving the skills of teachers doesn't mean that we have to give up the most valuable part of NCLB: our national commitment to paying attention to how all students are doing in every school. The history of public schools in the United States is marked by persistent racism and neglect of students of color, low-income students, and students with disabilities. As McKamey explained, there are some educators who don't attach their self-esteem as professionals to how African American students are doing. NCLB insisted that we disaggregate data based on ethnicity and race, socioeconomic status, and special needs. There are many different ways to design accountability systems in which no student would fall through the cracks. Darling-Hammond suggests that reducing the number of sit-down, standardized state tests and increasing yearly "performance assessments" graded by trained teacher peer groups at the state, district, or school level could be one way to create additional checks and balances.[14]

Mission High teachers never complained to me about being overworked, but that toll is obvious to any visitor who spends significant time with them in and out of school. Every teacher I met frequently worked more hours than anyone I have met in the white-collar world—journalism, tech, law, corporate, and nonprofit. For more than a decade, McKamey woke up at 5:00 a.m., got to school by 6:30 a.m., left school at 4:30 p.m. for a dance class, then worked almost every evening and every Sunday. Every teacher I knew often met with his or her colleagues to plan lessons on Saturdays or Sundays, unpaid, because they didn't always have enough time to do it during the workweek, when they teach five classes, need to read and grade hundreds of assignments each week, and must plan the next lesson. Many teachers met with students after school and on the weekends, unpaid. The most effective educators, like Roth and McKamey, had twenty-five years of teaching under their belts, but how can we expect a new generation of teachers to work such hours and stay in the profession for decades? No wonder close to half of teachers leave the profession before they acquire five years of experience.[15]

American teachers have heavier teaching loads than educators in other OECD countries and have less time for planning, support, and leadership responsibilities outside of classrooms. Teachers across the country have told me that too often when government dollars go toward teacher capacity building, they end up funding another layer of new administrators and consultants, rather than trusting classroom teachers to develop their own, school-based professional development and accountability. Too many philanthropic dollars today seem to be focused on perfecting different data collection methods, gathering bullet-pointed lists of ingredients in effective schools, or funding charter schools, which are more likely to be staffed primarily by inexperienced teachers.[16] This doesn't seem like a wise investment strategy. A sound, diversified portfolio would mean supporting our country's novice teachers as well as veterans, like McKamey and Roth, to make sure that we are documenting and promoting a variety of pedagogical approaches.

I would be more cynical about the prospects for such change, but it's hard not to be optimistic after years at Mission High. After all, it's a school that has survived hundreds of top-down educational reform fads and different experts telling teachers what to teach and how to teach. While its future remains uncertain, Mission has survived and continues to transform the lives of thousands of students. As I write this final part of the book, and the country is embroiled in a bitter debate over educational reforms, Mission High School students and teachers have quietly made history again, and on their own terms.

Twenty years after Jose Luis Pavon and his classmates walked out of Mission demanding more culturally relevant curriculum with local emphasis, and intellectual rigor, the students and teachers of Mission helped pass a resolution that will allow every high school student in the city to enroll in an ethnic studies class by school year 2015–2016. Carter writes that an analysis of mainstream school curriculum today tells us a great deal about the consequences of constructing "one best system" and "one curriculum" for all students. A 2001 report found that of the ninety-six Americans who were named for study in the course descriptions for California, 77 percent were white, 18 percent African American, 4 percent Native American, 1 percent Latino, and none Asian American.[17] Ethnic studies classes fill that gap and will now be extended to every high school in a city where young people of color constitute 90 percent of students in the district.[18] As teachers often say—and students demand—curriculum should be both a window into the broader world and a mirror of a student's home culture.

On December 9, 2014, a Mission High senior named Alejandra testified in front of the San Francisco Unified School District's Board of Education, while her teachers Aimee Riechel, Anette Norona, and Roth sat behind her. "When I went into history class, I could find nothing about myself," Alejandra explained. "I could find nothing about my culture. But thanks to Ethnic Studies, I found the Filipinos. I found the Mexicans. And every other culture that was blacked out of the history books. So, my question is why? What did we do wrong not to deserve to be put in these pages? Why are we set aside under the Anglo point of view? Why are we always pushed and pushed and pushed until we are silenced. . . . If you take Ethnic Studies away, you will be removing everything that people of color have been working for. You will say, 'No, that doesn't matter.' And I say, black lives matter. All lives matter. And I think that Ethnic Studies is a change that can teach the world that."[19]

Alejandra's testimony reminded me of another, less tangible, but important lesson of Mission High: who is making decisions in our public schools, where and how they make them matters a great deal in a democracy. Democracy can't survive without strong public schools, but public schools don't work very well without a sustained democratic decision-making process for their students, parents, and teachers, either. The story of Mission High School is an illustration of how democratic, student-centered, and teacher-driven educational reform works when it is coming from the inside out, when it is informed by the real needs of a community. While there are essential ingredients that shape every effective school, the most important solutions live in the process of decision-making at every level.

I am convinced that finding the solution to quality education is not about perfecting our quantitative measurements and standardized tests, scaling up one best system for all students, or parachuting in a bulleted list of answers. We are not going to gain global economic advantages by copying and pasting school systems from other countries. Diversity breeds innovation, and our biggest, unrealized economic and political advantages lie in our commitment to move toward personalized education, integration of students in every possible way, and more equitable distribution of resources to make it happen. Rather than tinkering with the top-down factory model system that the Administrative Progressives designed a hundred years ago, such a bottom-up reform approach would be a fundamental, twenty-first-century update, giving our overlooked students and future leaders—like Maria, Darrell, George, Rasheed, Pablo, and Jesmyn—a sustained voice in our debate over the future of American education.

Author's Note

In creating this book from 2010 to 2014, I wanted students to drive the main themes in a conversation about good schools and great teachers. As I spent time at Mission High, I tried to ask all students: What motivates you to learn? When do you feel like you are learning? What kind of teaching helps you succeed and overcome challenges? What is your definition of a good school?

When I asked students who their favorite teachers at Mission High were, the names Robert Roth, Taica Hsu, and Pirette McKamey came up a great deal, along with many other names that I was unable to include here. Because I wanted to explore several themes deeply through individual stories, I could only cover a small slice of a large high school. Since students were raising similar themes, but had different interests and talents, I eventually decided to explore these ideas through diverse subjects, settling on the social sciences, math, English, school climate, and bullying.

In 2010 I started sitting in on the classrooms of Robert Roth, the first teacher I picked, observing him and his interactions with students. I spent about two years coming regularly to Roth's classes, sometimes going to every class for weeks. Then I spent one year, on and off, in Hsu's class and about six months, on and off, in McKamey's and Anders's classes. The classes were so intellectually engaging—more than most of the courses I took as an undergrad at UC Berkeley—that I often had to remind myself that I'm not a student. I also spent a great deal of time in at least thirty other classrooms at Mission and other schools, observing various teachers and different pedagogical approaches.

In every class I observed, I tried to walk around the room when students were working and offer help, when appropriate. This was an extremely helpful recommendation that McKamey made when we first met. In this way I got to know a lot of students through their classroom work and develop deeper relationships. Because we talked about their work, I got to know them through their ideas and learning processes. I was also consciously choosing students who would represent the broader demographics at the school in which Latino, African American, and Chinese students form the largest minorities. Because Latino and African American students face the greatest challenges in American public school systems, I wanted to focus on these subgroups more than others. Because this book is about young adults, most under the age of eighteen, I changed the first names of most of the students in this book and omitted all last names to protect their identity and privacy.

In the classrooms, I took handwritten notes of every exchange and at the end of the day transcribed parts that I felt were significant. I also took lots of photographs of student work in the classrooms with my phone: their essays, art posters, quizzes, and poems. Students were proud of their work and rarely denied me permission to take photos of their assignments. If we worked on a longer research paper together, I would ask students to e-mail me their drafts and finished papers. I asked those students whom I followed more intensely to share with me their classroom work from other classes that was really formative, compelling, or significant to them.

At some point Roth recommended that I check in with the teacher or students after the class to get their take on what they thought about the class: what worked, what didn't, what stood out to them. Over time these exchanges helped me become a sharper observer and better understand the intention behind each activity, see how different forms of engagement manifested, and look more closely at the work students were doing in the classroom.

After a year at Mission I realized that looking at how an entire unit unfolds in the classroom over the course of three to five weeks—the agenda of every lesson, different activities, the pace, and student work—gave me even deeper insights into many of the invisible parts of teaching. It helped me understand what McKamey meant when she told me about the depth of teaching, how after eight years of teaching, she began to see it as a three-dimensional model, with all of the different parts moving at the same time and reinforcing each other. Of course I am not a teacher and can't see or understand all of the parts, but this process helped me visualize how teaching works and think of it in new ways.

Over the course of four years at Mission, I spent most of my time hanging out with the students, in and out of the classroom. Outside school we ate lunch and dinner at nearby cafés and went for walks or drives together. Sometimes I went over to their homes and met their families or helped students with homework. I recorded most of my interviews outside of classrooms, and many others I transcribed from my handwritten notes. Because this book is about young adults, many younger than eighteen, I made sure that I reviewed the drafts of my writing with them several times to make sure they were accurate, as well as that students felt comfortable with me including information about their lives that was at times private and sensitive.

I personally observed all of the classroom scenes set at Mission, except for those in the math and English classrooms in Pablo's chapter, which took place before I met him during one of the Gay-Straight Alliance student meetings. All scenes that I personally observed are written in the present tense. Everything I describe from the students' and teachers' memories is in the past tense. Whenever possible, I tried to corroborate what the students and teachers told me with at least one other person. Whenever I described students' thoughts, I asked them to return to the location of the event and walk me through that moment, as I did in the case of Maria taking a test in a silent classroom that I observed or Pablo's thoughts before he came out on stage to read his coming-out testimonial in front of the school.

In addition to classrooms, I also went to various school events, student-run clubs, and teachers' meetings and spent a lot of time hanging out in the hallways. As students and teachers were raising different themes—the difficulties of teaching writing, math, the nature of different tests—I read everything I could find on the topic. This information helped me pick the scenes as I was outlining my chapters and place what I saw in the larger context of school policy, educational theory, or history.

Ultimately I learned the most when I kept quiet and just watched things unfold or listened to people talk. My questions were never as good as the themes that the students, teachers, and school staff raised and discussed among themselves. The most important things about education I learned by listening to teachers and students talk to each other and then having them explain things to me later. And when it came to explaining, even at the end of their longest and hardest days, their wells of generosity and patience were always full.

Acknowledgments

The first and biggest thank-you goes to the more than two hundred students, teachers, and staff of Mission High School who generously opened up their lives to me to share their stories and insights over the course of four years. I was extremely fortunate to meet Jesmyn on my first day at Mission High. My reporting of every chapter was informed by Jesmyn's brilliance, wisdom, keen observational skills, and clarity in areas that would have been invisible to me without our friendship. Pablo was particularly generous with his time and trust in me. I continue to be inspired by his courage, resilience, and commitment to social justice and inclusion every day. Maria was the first student who helped me understand the subtle and profound difference between a standardized test and one created by her teachers. My friendship with Darrell helped me see the roles intellectual pride and freedom to think play in authentic learning. Since I learned math in a very procedural way in my school in the former Soviet Union, I could not have written the section about math without the patience and help of Rasheed, George, and Rocio.

Hundreds of other students generously contributed their time and insights about the sources of their motivation to learn, but I want to thank in particular Ajanee,

Jhonae, Brianna, Darius, Jaime, Sharon, Nicole, Irvin, Destiny, Christian, Latrelle, Ishmail, Rosa, Gretty, Alvin, Catharine, Josh, Fola, Yessenia, Patrick, Jackie, Jose, Mandy, Borrell, Robert, Juan, Grace, Alex, Lenny, Jennifer, June, Carry, Vivian, Tiko, Lorraine, Micky, Davina, Brandon, Tony, LaKenya, Alex, Stephanie, Maurice, Alia, Carlos, Noe, Ana, Tyre, Marvin, Anthony, Audrey, Armani, Pepe, Connor, Dejon, Megan, Solange, Conrad, Roxy, XiuYing, David, Josselyn, Xochi, and Anna.

As I note in my conclusion, teachers work longer hours than anyone I have encountered in my reporting career or personal connections. Despite this reality, all teachers I met were extremely generous with their time and insights, often seeing me on the weekends and after school to patiently answer all of my inane questions. I am especially grateful to Robert Roth and Pirette McKamey, who—more than anyone—gave so much of their limited personal time to this project. I learned the most important things about teaching from these two, the finest educators I have ever encountered, and their wisdom will continue to inspire my work for years to come. Some day I hope to live my life with the same degree of generosity, empathy, purpose, and dedication.

As many teachers told me, Amadis Velez's ability to inspire students to view themselves as college material is legendary, and his long hours and dedication to helping all students, especially undocumented immigrants, to access college deserve a book of their own. As someone who never liked math at school, I couldn't have sat through dozens of algebra and statistics classes without the craft and enthusiasm of Taica Hsu. Eric Guthertz opened the doors to Mission High School for me and made me feel at home there every time I came. He then responded to all of my e-mails and meeting and data requests within a day and with the same patience and generosity every time. Mission High's former choir director, Steven Hankle was the first teacher—and a good friend—I met at Mission High, whose dedication to and knowledge of individual students and love of music helped me get to know the broader community of the school. Many other teachers and staff members contributed their time to this project, but I want to thank, especially, for four years of consistent help, Jenn Bowman, Aimee Riechel, Tadd Scott, Betty Lee, Blair Groefsema, Henry Arguedas, Anette Norona, Max Anders, Rebecca Fulop, Shideh Etaat, Dayna Soares, Alison White, Nancy Rodriguez, Kimberly Gossin, Ed and Izzy Fructuoso, Kyra Bajeera, Valerie Forero, Arnold Zelaya, Brian Fox, Wendy He, Nadine Yee, Joe Alberty, Robert Milton, and Joel Johnson.

Safir Ahmed and Diane Stair laid the groundwork for this book with their early enthusiasm, encouragement, patience for my half-baked ideas, and brilliant insights into the craft of storytelling. Safir's infinite wisdom and unconditional kindness, as always, helped me get through some of the most trying days in this long process. My friend and mentor, the author Jeff Chang, patiently read my early, fuzzy book proposal drafts. Jeff's intellect, ability to inspire, and encyclopedic knowledge of American politics and culture boosted the confidence of this immigrant kid enough to write the first draft of a book proposal. The author Jonathon Keats, my friend and one of the funniest and most original conceptual artists I know, read the first drafts of all of my chapters. Like the best teachers, Jonathon didn't edit to highlight only what's wrong with my work. He was honest when something wasn't strong enough, but he spent more of his time highlighting the strengths of my early attempts that I often didn't see and gave me tools to make the next draft better. His feedback helped me grow as a writer more than all of my journalism and writing classes combined. The questions and enthusiasm of Silvia Pareschi, the gifted writer, blogger, and translator, helped me think of new ways to write about schools and students.

A huge thank-you to former Nation Books editor Carl Bromley (now with The New Press) for inspiring me to do what I didn't think was possible and taking a chance on me, even though I don't have an impressive following on Twitter. I wouldn't have met Carl if it wasn't for the support and mentorship of Katrina vanden Heuvel, the editor and publisher of *The Nation*. Carl and Marissa Colóne-Margolies improved the structure of my book and guided me through all of the challenges of the early writing process. I thank my Nation Books editor Daniel LoPreto for embracing this project with great care and enthusiasm, guiding me through every step of the editorial process, championing this project, and bringing it into the world. Deeply felt appreciation goes to my agent, Jill Marr, who took on a first-time author and helped me through every part of the process. I thank Winni Wintermeyer and Chris Woodcock, two of our country's best photographers, who documented this project in ways that I can't do with words alone. The wonderful crew of the Perseus Book Group, including Melissa Raymond, Rachel King, Sharon Langworthy, Lindsay Fradkoff, Jaime Leifer, Jack Lenzo, and Julie Ford, provided crucial help at the end of this project. I am deeply grateful to Michelle Wasserman, Micaela Gardner, and Onnesha Roychoudhuri for saving me at the last minute with research and fact-checking help.

My editor at *Mother Jones*, Monika Bauerlein, gave me the most meaningful reporting assignment of my career, which eventually morphed into this book. She knew that I love spending time with teenagers and encouraged me to approach reporting through the voices of students. The vision of Monika and her fierce, brilliant coeditor, Clara Jeffery, and their commitment to deep reporting built the foundation for this project. The enthusiasm and mad editorial, reporting, and research skills of Laura McClure, Titania Kumeh, Dave Gilson, Mark Murrmann, Kiera Butler, Maddie Oatman, and Erika Eichelberger helped make an editorial beat at *Mother Jones* a reality. *Mother Jones* publisher Steve Katz and president and CEO Madeleine Buckingham made me feel like the most important person in the office every day.

Throughout the process of writing, I also benefited in immeasurable ways from the wisdom of education historian Larry Cuban. He made himself available every time I asked and discussed different themes that students and teachers were raising. Professor Cuban helped me place the smallest classroom interactions in the broader context of history and current debates in education. He even observed several classrooms at Mission High, which helped us discuss what we both noticed in the context of other schools he has visited in his forty years as an educator, researcher, and historian.

This project started during one of the many conversations, meetings, lunches, and drinks with the staff and extended family of *WireTap*, a political magazine for young adults, which we published together from 2005 to 2010. The friendship, political commitment, and personal stories of Jamilah King, Tomas Palermo, Dani McClain, Gavin DeVore Leonard, Adrienne Maree Brown, Tanzila Ahmed, Samhita Mukhopadhyay, Twilight Greenaway, Onnesha Roychoudhuri, Jessamyn Sabbag, Samantha Liapes, and Billy Wimsatt inspired me to pursue my passions and helped make countless impossible things possible. Wire-Tap Think Tank, which we formed in 2010 after the magazine folded, has been there for me through every struggle and triumph since, professionally and personally. They were the first readers of the entire manuscript, and their feedback was invaluable.

Anna Lefer, Jee Kim, Grant Garrison, and Benjamin Shute opened the most important doors for us in the philanthropic world to make *WireTap* a reality, and I am especially grateful for their generous mentorship and guidance. Don Hazen, the executive director of AlterNet and founder of *WireTap*, opened the first and most important door into journalism for me, even though I had no relevant experience on my résumé or any powerful connections.

My Re:Baltica family in Latvia—Inga Springe, Sanita Jemberga, Arta Ģiga, Aaron Eglitis, Peter Folkins, Kaspars Goba, and Ieva Goba—inspired me and helped me put everything in a global perspective. My Notto sister, Mary Roach, took me to lunches and bought me martinis on the toughest days. Her sense of humor and practical guidance were invaluable during revisions and after. A big hug to chef and writer Samin Nosrat for introducing me to all of my Notto sisters and brothers. And to Jon Funabiki,

Valerie Bush, LynNell Hancock, Prudence L. Carter, and everyone involved in the Equity Reporting Project developed by Renaissance Journalism, for opening up a huge, new world of research and data to me.

I would not be in journalism if I hadn't met my high school Latvian language and literature teacher, Zinta Bāliņa, who provided personalized teaching in a very standardized school and went the extra mile to get to know the intellects and strengths of all her students. To this day, I remember the sound of her voice and the kind words she said to me about my writing. My Diablo Valley Community College professor of history, Manuel G. Gonzales, made me fall in love with history and was the first person in my life who made me feel like an intellectual every time I was in his classes. He continued to support and guide me after college, and I am deeply grateful for his friendship.

I reserve the warmest and deepest gratitude for my family, who were there for me during all of the highs and lows during this long project: my mother, Fruma Rizga; the world's best sister, Sabina Hentz; Everett and Joseph Hentz; Yvette and Gerry Stern; Charlotte Stern; Dayala Levenson; Danny Stern; Anita Horn; Māris and Gunta Rizga; Igor Bulayev; Pēteris and Metta Rizga; Džeina Ezera; Fira and Shaya Polskaya; David Polsky; Fred Polsky; and Larisa Rizga. My nephew Boris Bulayev read my first book draft over his short vacation and provided indispensable feedback. Sarah Firman's expertise in education improved my drafts.

I am deeply grateful to Kaspars Pavārs, Parul Vora-Weber, Jeff Weber, Sarah Coleman, Akim Aginsky, Jake and Jaia Aginsky, Carrie and Yasha Aginsky, Sara Gruen,

Jonathan Gaynor, Robo Gerson, Valerie LeClair, Christi Azevedo, Lourdes Chang, Justin and Cynthia Maxwell, Andrew and Andrea Smith, Aya Brackett, Corey Creasey, Lauren Pincus, Jonathan Har-Even, Amy and Itamar Har-Even, Gina Basso, Brad Steinberg, Charmagne and Andrew Kringstein, Seeta Peña Gangadharan, Seth Horowitz, Eric Garland, Robin Kraft, Arthur Hough, Chris Bazar, Velma Dean, Jeff Perlstein, Judith Mirkinson, Irēna and Edijs Sarma, Ilze Sarma, Valdis Novikovs, Rinalds Immertreijs, Ringla Rutkovska, and Susan Gardner for their support and mini-celebrations at critical junctures.

And the last, most important, and biggest thank-you goes to my husband, best friend, and biggest supporter, Mike Stern. He walked every step of this deeply personal journey with me, listening to my musings about every new person I met and every education book or study I read, helping me articulate my initial intuitions and think through difficult knots. He helped me overcome every challenge, made me laugh, sang for me, danced with me, and took me on vacations. I hope some day I get to be there for him in all of the ways that he has been there for me.

Notes

PREFACE

1. Lisa Delpit, *"Multiplication Is for White People": Raising Expectations for Other People's Children* (New York: The New Press, 2012), 5.

2. For an excellent, succinct review of the different dimensions of the achievement gap, see A. Wade Boykin and Pedro Noguera, *Creating the Opportunity to Learn* (Alexandria, VA: ASCD, 2011), chs. 1–2.

3. Public school enrollment figures for the 2011–2012 school year can be found at the National Center for Educational Statistics, http://nces.ed.gov/programs/coe/indicator_cga.asp.

4. National Center for Education Statistics, http://nces.ed.gov/pubs2013/2014098/findings.asp.

5. School Accountability Report Card for Mission High, http://www.sfusd.edu/assets/sfusd-staff/rpa/sarcs2/sarc-725.pdf.

6. US Department of Education, "Programs: School Improvement Grants," http://www2.ed.gov/programs/sif/index.html.

7. San Francisco Unified School District Student Survey, 2010, 105, 107.

8. Ana Tintocalis, "Mission High Counselor on a Mission to Make College Dreams Come True," *KQED News*, May 30, 2014, http://ww2.kqed.org/news/2014/05/30/mission-high-counselor-on-a-mission-to-make-college-dreams-come-true.

9. Michael J. Petrilli, "All Together Now? Educating High and Low Achievers in the Same Classrooms," *Education Next* 11, no. 1 (Winter 2011), http://educationnext.org/all-together-now/.

10. Brandon H. Busteed, executive director of Gallup Education Commentary, "Make a Difference: Show Students You Care,"

Education Week, September 30, 2014, http://www.edweek.org/ew /articles/2014/10/01/06busteed.h34.html.

11. Paul Tough, *How Children Succeed: Grit, Curiosity, and the Hidden Power of Character* (New York: Houghton Mifflin Harcourt, 2012), xiii–xxiv.

12. C. A. Farrington, M. Roderick, E. Allensworth, J. Nagaoka, T. S. Keyes, D. W. Johnson, and N. O. Beechum, *Teaching Adolescents to Become Learners: The Role of Noncognitive Factors in Shaping School Performance; A Critical Literature Review* (Chicago: University of Chicago Consortium on Chicago School Research, 2012), http://ccsr.uchicago .edu/sites/default/files/publications/Noncognitive%20Report.pdf.

13. Sarah Carr, *Hope Against Hope: Three Schools, One City, and the Struggle to Educate America's Children* (New York: Bloomsbury Press, 2013), 6–7; Diane Ravitch, *The Death and Life of the Great American School System* (New York: Basic Books, 2010), 199–221.

CHAPTER 1: MARIA

1. Richard Fry, "Hispanics, High School Drop Outs and the GED," Pew Research Center: Hispanic Trends, May 13, 2010, http://www.pew hispanic.org/2010/05/13/hispanics-high-school-dropouts-and-the-ged/.

2. New America Foundation, Federal Education Budget Project, "No Child Left Behind—Overview," April 24, 2014, http://febp .newamerica.net/background-analysis/no-child-left-behind-overview.

3. California Department of Education, "Persistently Lowest Achieving Schools," http://www.cde.ca.gov/ta/ac/pl/tier2.asp.

4. Clare Ribando Seelke, "Gangs in Central America," Congressional Research Service, February 20, 2014, http://fas.org/sgp/crs/row /RL34112.pdf.

5. National Conference of State Legislatures, "In-state Tuition and Unauthorized Immigrant Students," February 19, 2014, http://www .ncsl.org/research/immigration/in-state-tuition-and-unauthorized -immigrants.aspx.

6. California Department of Education, "2010 STAR Test Results: Mission High School," http://star.cde.ca.gov/star2010/ViewReport .asp?ps=true&lstTestYear=2010&lstTestType=C&lstCounty=38& lstDistrict=68478–000&lstSchool=3834082&lstGroup=5&lstSub Group=78.

7. California Department of Education, "2010 STAR Test Results: State of California, Hispanic or Latino—California Standards Test Scores," http://star.cde.ca.gov/star2010/ViewReport.asp?ps=true&lst TestYear=2010&lstTestType=C&lstCounty=&lstDistrict=&lst School=&lstGroup=5&lstSubGroup=78.

8. US Government Accountability Office, "No Child Left Behind Act [Review]," September 2009, http://www.motherjones.com /documents/406650-gao-nclb-report.

9. Edward Haertel and Joan Herman, "A Historical Perspective on Validity Arguments for Accountability Testing," Stanford University/UCLA, June 2005, http://www.motherjones.com /documents/406652-history-of-testing.

10. Larry Cuban, interview with author, June 2, 2012.

11. Jesse H. Rhodes, *An Education in Politics: The Origins and Evolution of No Child Left Behind* (New York: Cornell University, 2012), 169.

12. Kenji Hakuta, Yuko Goto Butler, and Daria Witt, "How Long Does It Take English Learners to Attain Proficiency?" Stanford University, January 2000, http://www.stanford.edu/~hakuta/Publications /(2000)%20-%20HOW%20LONG%20DOES%20IT%20TAKE%20 ENGLISH%20LEARNERS%20TO%20ATTAIN%20PR.pdf.

13. Will Kane, "Latino Kids Now Majority in State's Public Schools," *The San Francisco Chronicle*, November 13, 2010, http:// www.sfgate.com/education/article/Latino-kids-now-majority-in-state -s-public-schools-3166843.php.

14. Linda Darling-Hammond and Frank Adamson, *Beyond the Bubble Test: How Performance Assessments Support 21st-Century Learning* (San Francisco: Jossey-Bass, 2014), 18–20. See also C. A. Farrington, M. Roderick, E. Allensworth, J. Nagaoka, T. S. Keyes, D. W. Johnson, and N. O. Beechum, *Teaching Adolescents to Become Learners: The Role of Noncognitive Factors in Shaping School Performance; A Critical Literature Review* (Chicago: University of Chicago Consortium on Chicago School Research, 2012), http://ccsr.uchicago .edu/sites/default/files/publications/Noncognitive%20Report.pdf.

15. Paul Tough, *How Children Succeed: Grit, Curiosity, and the Hidden Power of Character* (New York: Houghton Mifflin Harcourt Publishing, 2012), xiii–xxiv.

16. L. Darling-Hammond, G. Wilhoit, and L. Pittenger, "Accountability for College and Career Readiness: Developing a New Paradigm" (Stanford Center for Opportunity Policy in Education, 2014). See also Farrington et al., "Teaching Adolescents to Become Learners."

17. Paul Black and Dylan William, "Inside the Black Box: Raising Standards Through Classroom Assessment," *Phi Delta Kappan* 80, no. 2 (October 1998): 139–148, https://datacenter.spps.org/uploads/Data_InsideBlackBox.pdf

18. Paul Vitello, "Robert Glaser, Who Shaped the Science of Student Testing, Dies at 91," *New York Times*, February 15, 2012, http://www.nytimes.com/2012/02/16/us/robert-glaser-cognitive-psychologist-and-expert-on-student-testing-dies-at-91.html.

CHAPTER 2: MR. ROTH

1. Larry Cuban, *Hugging the Middle: How Teachers Teach in an Era of Testing and Accountability* (New York: Teachers College Press, 2009), 21, 29.

2. Eric R. Kandel, *In Search of Memory: The Emergence of a New Science of Mind* (New York: W. W. Norton, 2006), 210. See also Claudia Dreifus, "A Conversation with Eric R. Kandel: A Quest to Understand How Memory Works," *New York Times*, March 5, 2012, http://www.nytimes.com/2012/03/06/science/a-quest-to-understand-how-memory-works.html?pagewanted=all&_r=0.

3. Peter C. Brown, Henry L. Roediger III, and Mark A. McDaniel, "Ditch the 10,000 Hour Rule! Why Malcolm Gladwell's Famous Advice Falls Short," *Salon*, April 20, 2014, http://www.salon.com/2014/04/20/ditch_the_10000_hour_rule_why_malcolm_gladwells_famous_advice_falls_short/.

4. Jeremy Peter Varon, *Bringing the War Home: The Weather Underground, the Red Army Faction, and Revolutionary Violence in the Sixties and Seventies* (Berkeley: University of California Press, 2004), 26.

5. Ronald G. Tharp and Ronald Gallimore, *Rousing Minds to Life* (Cambridge, UK: Cambridge University Press, 1988), 30.

6. Samuel E. Abrams, "The Mismeasure of Teaching Time" (Center for Benefit-Cost Studies of Education, Teachers College, Columbia

University, January 2015), 15, http://cbcse.org/wordpress/wp-content
/uploads/2015/01/The-MismeasureofTeachingTime-SA-1.14.15.pdf
?utm_source=Announcement%3A+The+Mismeasure+of+Teaching+
Time&utm_campaign=The+Mismeasure+of+Teaching+Time&utm
_medium=email.

7. Theresa Perry, Claude Steele, and Asa Hilliard III, *Young, Gifted, and Black: Promoting High Achievement Among African-American Students* (Boston: Beacon Press, 2003), 1–87.

8. Dr. Noma LeMoine, interviewed by Richard Corpus, "Dr. Noma LeMoine Interview—CABE 2014," YouTube, posted by Velazquez-Press, May 1, 2014, https://www.youtube.com/watch?v=Uq1Cbc4YPIc.

9. National Writing Project and Carl Nagin, *Because Writing Matters: Improving Student Writing in Our Schools,* rev. ed. (San Francisco: Jossey-Bass, 2006), 19–20.

10. NWP and Nagin, *Because Writing Matters,* 21–22.

11. "Before Coming Out, a Hard Time Growing Up," *New York Times,* February 11, 2014, http://www.nytimes.com/2014/02/12
/sports/football/for-nfl-prospect-michael-sam-upbringing-was-bigger
-challenge-than-coming-out-as-gay.html?hp&_r=1.

THE PROGRESSIVES (1890–1950)

1. The Educational Policy Institute, "The Landscape of Public Education: A Statistical Portrait Through the Years," http://www
.educationalpolicy.org/publications/EPI%20Center/EPICenter_K-12
.pdf, 3.

2. Sheila Curran Bernard and Sarah Mondale, *School: The Story of American Public Education* (Boston: Beacon Press, 2001), 64.

3. David B. Tyack, *The One Best System: A History of American Urban Education* (Cambridge, MA: Harvard University Press, 1974), 28–29.

4. Tyack, *One Best System,* 177–179.

5. Dana Goldstein, *The Teacher Wars: A History of America's Most Embattled Profession* (New York: Doubleday, 2014), 81–83.

6. James W. Stigler and James Hiebert, *The Teaching Gap: Best Ideas from the World's Teachers for Improving Education in the Classroom* (New York: Free Press, 1999), 173–174.

7. Tyack, *One Best System,* 239–240.

8. Theresa Perry, Claude Steele, and Asa Hilliard III, *Young, Gifted, and Black: Promoting High Achievement Among African-American Students* (Boston: Beacon Press, 2003), 1–87.

9. Perry, Steele, and Hilliard, *Young, Gifted, and Black*, 26.

10. Goldstein, *Teacher Wars*, 62.

11. Goldstein, *Teacher Wars*, 59, 64.

12. Stigler and Hiebert, *Teaching Gap*, 173.

13. David F. Labaree, *Someone Has to Fail: The Zero-Sum Game of Public Schooling* (Cambridge, MA: Harvard University Press, 2010), 92–94, 122.

14. Larry Cuban, *How Teachers Taught: Constancy and Change in American Classrooms, 1880–1990* (New York: Teachers College Press, 1993), 1–45.

15. Labaree, *Someone Has to Fail*, 118–122.

16. Labaree, *Someone Has to Fail*, 83.

17. Bernard and Mondale, *School*, 101.

18. Anya Kamenetz, *The Test: Why Our Schools Are Obsessed with Standardized Testing—But You Don't Have to Be* (New York: PublicAffairs, 2015), 51.

19. Kamenetz, *Test*, 47–49.

20. Bernard and Mondale, *School*, 104.

21. Tyack, *One Best System*, 257–258.

CHAPTER 3: GEORGE

1. Manuela Zoninsein, "China's SAT: If the SAT Lasted Two Days, Covered Everything You'd Ever Studied, and Decided Your Future," *Slate*, June 4, 2008, http://www.slate.com/articles/news _and_politics/dispatches/2008/06/chinas_sat.html.

2. Didi Tang, "Chinese Teens Seek Freedom and a Competitive Edge at U.S. High Schools," *The Japan Times*, August 14, 2014, http:// www.japantimes.co.jp/news/2014/08/14/asia-pacific/social-issues-asia -pacific/chinese-teens-seek-freedom-and-a-competitive-edge-at-u-s -high-schools/#.U-0E_1YYGlI.

3. Asia Society, Business Roundtable, Council of Chief State School Officers, *Education in China: Lessons for U.S. Educators* (New York: Asia Society, 2005), 18, http://asiasociety.org/files/EdinChina2005.pdf.

4. For example, see Marc S. Tucker, ed., *Surpassing Shanghai: An Agenda for American Education Built on the World's Leading*

Systems (Cambridge, MA: Harvard Education Press, 2011), http://hepg
.org/hep-home/books/surpassing-shanghai.

5. Robert A. Compton, Adam Raney, and Chad Heeter,
"Two Million Minutes: A Global Examination," *Harvard Educational Review* 78, no. 4 (2008), http://hepg.org/her-home/issues
/harvard-educational-review-volume-78-issue-4/herbooknote/two
-million-minutes-a-global-examination_338.

6. Yong Zhao, *Catching Up or Leading the Way: American Education in the Age of Globalization* (Alexandria, VA: ASCD, 2009),
ch. 7, 8, 9; Thomas L. Friedman, "Need a Job? Invent It," *New York
Times,* March 30, 2013, http://www.nytimes.com/2013/03/31/opinion
/sunday/friedman-need-a-job-invent-it.html?_r=1&; Lisa Delpit, *"Multiplication Is for White People": Raising Expectations for Other People's
Children* (New York: New Press, 2012), ch. 7, 9.

7. Zhao, *Catching Up or Leading the Way,* x, 41–59.

8. Zhao, *Catching Up or Leading the Way,* vii.

9. Zhao, *Catching Up or Leading the Way,* 81–84.

10. Zhao, *Catching Up or Leading the Way,* 60–63.

11. Tang, "Chinese Teens Seek Freedom and a Competitive Edge
at U.S. High Schools."

12. Tang, "Chinese Teens Seek Freedom and a Competitive Edge
at U.S. High Schools."

13. Tony Wagner, *Creating Innovators: The Making of Young
People Who Will Change the World* (New York: Scribner, 2012), 12,
24–30, 52–59, 141–142, 149–152.

14. Thomas L. Friedman, "Need a Job? Invent It."

15. Joan Boaler, *What's Math Got to Do with It? How Parents and
Teachers Can Help Children Learn to Love Their Least Favorite Subject* (New York: Penguin, 2008), 19, 25, 30.

16. Salman Khan, *The One World Schoolhouse* (New York:
Hachette Book Group, 2012), 81–99.

CHAPTER 4: MR. HSU

1. Nikole Hannah-Jones, "Segregation Now: The Resegrega-
tion of America's Schools," ProPublica, April 16, 2014. http://www
.propublica.org/article/segregation-now-full-text.

2. Dana Goldstein, *The Teacher Wars: The History of America's
Most Embattled Profession* (New York: Doubleday, 2014), 181.

3. Jo Boaler, *What's Math Got to Do with It? How Parents and Teachers Can Help Children Learn to Love Their Least Favorite Subject* (New York: Penguin Books, 2008), 40–56.

4. Elizabeth Green, "Why Do Americans Stink at Math?" *New York Times Magazine*, July 23, 2014, http://www.nytimes .com/2014/07/27/magazine/why-do-americans-stink-at-math.html.

5. Boaler, *What's Math Got to Do with It?*, 5.

6. Carol S. Dweck, *Mindset: The New Psychology of Success* (New York: Ballantine Books, 2006), 6–7, 26–27.

7. Dweck, *Mindset*, 206–212.

8. Lisa Delpit, *"Multiplication Is for White People": Raising Expectations for Other People's Children* (New York: The New Press, 2012), 14.

9. Claude M. Steele, *Whistling Vivaldi: How Stereotypes Affect Us and What We Can Do* (New York: W. W. Norton, 2010), 118–121.

10. "Program for Complex Instruction," Stanford University, http://cgi.stanford.edu/group/pci/cgi-bin/site.cgi.

11. Tom Loveless, "How Well Are American Students Learning?," March 2013, Brookings Institution, http://www.brookings.edu /research/reports/2013/03/18-tracking-ability-grouping-loveless.

12. Claude M. Steele, "Race and the Schooling of Black Americans," *The Atlantic*, April 1, 1992. http://www.theatlantic.com/magazine /archive/1992/04/race-and-the-schooling-of-black-americans/306073/.

13. Theresa Perry, Claude Steele, and Asa Hilliard III, *Young, Gifted, and Black: Promoting High Achievement Among African-American Students* (Boston: Beacon Press, 2003), 123–134.

14. Boaler, *What's Math Got to Do with It?*, 113–114.

15. Association of American Colleges and Universities and Hart Research Associates, "It Takes More Than a Major: Employer Priorities for College Learning and Student Success," Washington, DC, 2013, https://www.aacu.org/leap/presidentstrust/compact /2013SurveySummary.

16. Steele, "Race and the Schooling of Black Americans."

17. Michael J. Petrilli, "All Together Now? Educating Low and High Achievers in the Same Classroom," *Education Next* 11, no. 1 (Winter 2011), http://educationnext.org/all-together-now/.

18. Chester E. Finn Jr., "Is Differentiated Instruction a Hollow Promise?" *Flypaper* (blog), May 1, 2014, http://edexcellence

.net/commentary/education-gadfly-daily/flypaper/is-differentiated
-instruction-a-hollow-promise.

19. Larry Cuban, *Hugging the Middle: How Teachers Teach in an
Era of Testing and Accountability* (New York: Teachers College Press,
2009). See also National Center for Education Statistics, "Schools and
Staffing Survey," 2011–2012, Table 5, http://nces.ed.gov/surveys/sass/.

20. Samuel E. Abrams, "The Mismeasure of Teaching Time" (Center for Benefit-Cost Studies of Education, Teachers College, Columbia University, January 2015), 13–15, http://cbcse.org/wordpress/wp
-content/uploads/2015/01/The-MismeasureofTeachingTime-SA
-1.14.15.pdf?utm_source=Announcement%3A+The+Mismeasure
+of+Teaching+Time&utm_campaign=The+Mismeasure+of+Teaching
+Time&utm_medium=email.

21. Linda Darling-Hammond and Frank Adamson, *Beyond the
Bubble Test: How Performance Assessments Support 21st Century
Learning* (San Francisco: Jossey-Bass, 2014), 7.

DESEGREGATION (1957–1970)

1. Larry Cuban, *Urban Chiefs Under Fire* (Chicago: University of
Chicago Press, 1976), 59–65.

2. Sheila Curran Bernard and Sarah Mondale, *School: The Story
of American Public Education* (Boston: Beacon Press, 2001), 118.

3. Melba Patillo Beals, *Warriors Don't Cry: A Searing Memoir of
the Battle to Integrate Little Rock's Central High* (New York: A Washington Square Press Publication of Pocket Books, 1995), 119–120,
121–123.

4. Nikole Hannah-Jones, "Segregation Now," ProPublica, April
16, 2014, http://www.propublica.org/article/segregation-now-full-text.

5. Dana Goldstein, *The Teacher Wars: A History of America's Most
Embattled Profession* (New York: Doubleday, 2014) 111.

6. Goldstein, *Teacher Wars*, 112.

7. Cuban, *Urban Chiefs Under Fire*, 70–80.

8. Bernard and Mondale, *School*, 158.

9. Bernard and Mondale, *School*, 162.

10. Bernard and Mondale, *School*, 127.

11. San Francisco State University Leonard Library, The San
Francisco State College Strike Collection, http://www.library.sfsu
.edu/about/collections/strike/choronology.html.

12. David Tyack, *One Best System: A History of American Urban Education* (Cambridge, MA: Harvard University Press, 1974), 282.

13. Anya Kamenetz, *The Test: Why Our Schools Are Obsessed with Standardized Testing—But You Don't Have to Be* (New York: PublicAffairs, 2015), 66.

CHAPTER 5: PABLO

1. Gay, Lesbian and Straight Education Network, *The Experience of Lesbian, Gay, Bisexual and Transgendered Youth in Our Schools* (New York: Gay, Lesbian and Straight Education Network, 2011), 15–18.

2. Emily Bazelon, *Sticks and Stones: Defeating the Culture of Bullying and Rediscovering the Power of Character and Empathy* (New York: Random House, 2013), 77.

3. Erika Eichelberger, "Obama's Executive Action Will Protect 5 Million Undocumented Immigrants," *Mother Jones*, November 20, 2014, http://www.motherjones.com/politics/2014/11/obama-executive-action-immigration-senate.

4. California Healthy Kids Survey: Mission High Secondary 2013–2014 Main Report, 2, 11, 20. California Healthy Kids Survey: San Francisco Unified Secondary 2013–2014 Main Report, 2, 11, 20.

5. Scott Seider, *Character Compass: How Powerful School Culture Can Point Students Toward Success* (Cambridge, MA: Harvard University Press, 2012), 219–220.

CHAPTER 6: PRINCIPAL GUTHERTZ

1. Anya Kamenetz, *The Test: Why Our Schools Are Obsessed with Standardized Testing—But You Don't Have to Be* (New York: PublicAffairs, 2015), 91–94.

2. California Department of Education, "Executive Summary Explaining the Academic Performance Index," http://www.cde.ca.gov/ta/ac/ap/documents/apiexecsummary.pdf.

3. San Francisco Unified District School Accountability Report Card. For 2008 data, see page 4: http://orb.sfusd.edu/sarcs/sa08-pdf/sa08-725.pdf. For 2014 data, see page 15: http://www.sfusd.edu/assets/sfusd-staff/rpa/sarcs2/sarc-725.pdf.

4. San Francisco Unified School District, "Student Satisfaction Survey 2013," 41. See also "Family Survey 2013," 104.

5. Daniel J. Losen and Tia Elena Martinez, "Out of School and Off Track: The Overuse of Suspensions in American Middle and High Schools," The Civil Rights Project at UCLA, April 8, 2013, http://civilrightsproject.ucla.edu/resources/projects/center-for-civil-rights-remedies/school-to-prison-folder/federal-reports/out-of-school-and-off-track-the-overuse-of-suspensions-in-american-middle-and-high-schools.

6. Some closures are a result of demographic shifts or are used as a way to deal with budget deficits. The number of yearly school closures can be found at National Center for Education Statistics, Institute of Education Sciences, http://nces.ed.gov/fastfacts/display.asp?id=619.

7. Pennsylvania Clearinghouse for Education Research, "Issue Brief on School Closings Policy," March 2013, 2–5, http://www.researchforaction.org/wp-content/uploads/2013/03/RFA-PACER-School-Closing-Policy-Brief-March-2013.pdf.

8. Elaine Woo, "Tired of Having Little Say, Teachers Pushing for Shared Authority," *Los Angeles Times*, April 23, 1989, http://articles.latimes.com/1989-04-23/news/mn-1753_1_united-teachers-los-angeles-president-teachers-in-los-angeles-school-district.

9. Jenny Anderson, "Curious Grade for Teachers: Nearly All Pass," *New York Times*, March 30, 2013. http://www.nytimes.com/2013/03/31/education/curious-grade-for-teachers-nearly-all-pass.html?pagewanted=all&_r=2&.

10. Glenda L. Partee, "Retaining Teachers of Color in Our Public Schools," The Center for American Progress, June 2014. http://cdn.americanprogress.org/wp-content/uploads/2014/06/Partee-TeachersOfColor-report2.pdf.

11. Linda Darling-Hammond, *Redesigning Schools: What Matters and What Works* (Stanford, CA: School Redesign Network at Stanford University, 2002), 33.

The Standards and Accountability Movement (1980–Present)

1. Kathy Emory, "The Business Roundtable and Systemic Reform: How Corporate-Engineered High-Stakes Testing Has Eliminated Community Participation in Developing Educational Goals and Policies" (PhD diss., UC Davis, 2002), 180–190, http://www.education

anddemocracy.org/Emery_dissertation.html. See also Nanette Asimov, "S.F. School Board Illegally Barred Press: Mission High Students Had Requested Meeting to Discuss Complaints," *San Francisco Chronicle*, January 15, 1994.

2. Emory, "Business Roundtable and Systemic Reform," 188, 194.

3. Emory, "Business Roundtable and Systemic Reform," 194.

4. Sheila Curran Bernard and Sarah Mondale, *School: The Story of American Public Education* (Boston: Beacon Press, 2001), 177. See also Dana Goldstein, *Teacher Wars: A History of America's Most Embattled Profession* (New York: Doubleday, 2014), 165–170.

5. Goldstein, *Teacher Wars*, 165–184.

6. Goldstein, *Teacher Wars*, 187.

7. Goldstein, *Teacher Wars*, 209, 213.

8. Goldstein, *Teacher Wars*, 165, 187.

9. Kristina Rizga, "Everything You've Heard About Failing Schools Is Wrong," *Mother Jones* (September/October 2012), http://www.motherjones.com/media/2012/08/mission-high-false-low-performing-school.

10. "National K–12 Testing Landscape," *Education Week*, February 20, 2015, http://www.edweek.org/ew/section/multimedia/map-the-national-k-12-testing-landscape.html.

11. Tom Loveless, "How Well Are American Students Learning?" Brookings Institution, 2012, http://www.brookings.edu/~/media/newsletters/0216_brown_education_loveless.pdf.

12. Bernard and Mondale, *School*, 180.

CHAPTER 7: MS. McKAMEY

1. Susan Frey, "San Francisco Unified Eliminates 'Willful Defiance' as a Reason to Expel or Suspend Students," EdSource, February 26, 2014, http://edsource.org/2014/san-francisco-unified-eliminates-willful-defiance-as-a-reason-to-expel-or-suspend-students/58105#.VLwnx0tKmlI. "An EdSource analysis of the 30 largest districts found huge disparities in their reliance on willful defiance to suspend students, with some districts citing it as the reason for more than two-thirds of their suspensions."

2. "MetLife Survey of the American Teacher: Collaborating for Student Success," MetLife Foundation, April 2010, 72, http://files.eric.ed.gov/fulltext/ED509650.pdf.

3. David Farbman, "The Case for Improving and Expanding Time in School: A Review of Key Research and Practice," National Center on Time and Learning, April 2012, 7–8, http://www.timeand learning.org/?q=caseformoretime.

EPILOGUE

1. US Department of Education, Institute of Education Sciences, National Center for Education Statistics, "Number and Percentage of Public School Students Eligible for Free or Reduced-price Lunch, by State: Selected Years, 2000–01 through 2011–12," http://nces.ed.gov /programs/digest/d13/tables/dt13_204.10.asp. See also Prudence L. Carter and Kevin Wellner, "It's the Opportunity Gap, Stupid," *Daily News*, May 13, 2013.

2. Prudence L. Carter and Kevin G. Wellner, eds., *Closing the Opportunity Gap: What America Must Do to Give Every Child an Even Chance* (New York: Oxford University Press, 2013), 79.

3. "School Finance," *Education Week*, 2015, http://www.edweek .org/media/school-finance-education-week-quality-counts-2015.pdf.

4. Carter and Wellner, *Closing the Opportunity Gap*.

5. Allie Bidwell, "Coalition Wants New School Accountability," *US News & World Report*, October 28, 2014, http://www.usnews .com/news/articles/2014/10/28/teachers-unions-education-advocacy -groups-call-for-new-accountability-system.

6. Anya Kamenetz, *The Test: Why Our Schools Are Obsessed with Standardized Testing—But You Don't Have to Be* (New York: Public Affairs, 2015), 77.

7. Kamenetz, *The Test*, 78.

8. Carter and Welner, *Closing the Opportunity Gap*, 118–122, 217–227. See also David T. Conley, "A New Era for Educational Assessment," Students at the Center: Deeper Learning Research Series, Jobs for the Future, October 2014, 12–26, http://jff.org/publications/new-era -educational-assessment.

9. Linda Darling-Hammond, Gene Wilhoit, and Linda Pettinger, "Accountability for College and Career Readiness: Developing a New Paradigm," *Education Policy Analysis Archives* 22, no. 86 (August 18, 2014), http://epaa.asu.edu/ojs/article/view/1724.

10. Kentucky also broadened its school performance index measures, but most states continue to rely almost exclusively on test

scores alone to measure school quality as this book goes to print. "Data Dashboards: Accounting for What Matters," Alliance for Excellent Education, January 2015, 2.

11. Louis Freedberg, "State Board Approves School Funding Rules," EdSource, November 17, 2014, http://edsource.org/2014/state -board-approves-school-funding-rules/70108#.VMRVrEtKmlI.

12. For a breakdown of potential metrics, see California Office to Reform Education, "School Quality Improvement System," http:// coredistricts.org/school-quality-improvement-system/.

13. "Design Your Dream Teaching Job," Teaching Ahead: A Roundtable, *Education Week*, March 27, 2013, http://blogs.edweek .org/teachers/teaching_ahead/design-your-dream-teaching-job/.

14. Darling-Hammond, Wilhoit, and Pettinger, "Accountability for College and Career Readiness," 7–12.

15. Liz Riggs, "Why Do Teachers Quit?" *The Atlantic*, October 18, 2013, http://www.theatlantic.com/education/archive/2013/10/why -do-teachers-quit/280699/.

16. Diane Ravitch, *The Death and Life of the Great American School System: How Testing and Choice Are Undermining Education* (New York: Basic Books, 2010), 195–222. See also Bob Herbert, "The Plot Against Public Education," *Politico.com*, October 6, 2014. http:// www.politico.com/magazine/story/2014/10/the-plot-against-public -education-111630.html#.VPDixbPF9L5.

17. Carter and Wellner, *Closing the Opportunity Gap*, 150.

18. SFSUD, "All SFUSD High Schools to Offer Ethnic Studies Classes," December 10, 2014, http://www.sfusd.edu/en/news/current -news/2014-news-archive/12/all-sfusd-high-schools-to-offer-ethnic -studies-classes.html.

19. San Francisco Unified District Video Archive, 12/9/14 meeting video, December 9, 2014, http://sanfrancisco.granicus.com/View Publisher.php?view_id=47.

Index

Abrams, Samuel A., 111
Academic Progress Index (API), 155, 156
accountability, 12, 121, 163, 164, 170, 188, 203
achievement gaps, 11, 79, 91, 160, 166, 170, 175, 176, 178, 179, 187, 188, 225, 226, 236–237
reducing, 202–203
activism, 91, 117, 119–120
African Americans, 10–11, 17, 41, 54, 56, 66, 76, 102, 105, 119, 120, 135, 179, 185, 198, 200–201, 220, 225, 226, 230, 233–234
African American English, 51–52
African American history, 23–24
dropout rates of, 173–174
educators, 50–51, 67, 116, 120
enrolled in college at Mission High, 156
first student in previously segregated school, 117
graduation rates for, 156
in higher tracked classes, 197
viewed as inferior, 199–200, 202
segregated black schools, 67–68
suspensions/expulsions of, 156, 157, 200, 236
as suspect, 236, 237
videos of interviews with, 173
See also Black Student Union; civil rights movement; racism; Tulsa Race Riot of 1921
Aim High nonprofit, 235, 238
Alexie, Sherman, 147, 194
analysis, 49, 61, 195–196, 226
collective analysis of students' work, 203, 205, 209, 210
Anders, Max, 195, 207–208
Angelou, Maya, 7, 158
antisegregation lawsuits, 19
anxiety, 102, 109
API. See Academic Progress Index
Arabolos, Lupe, 185–187
Aristide, Jean-Bertrand, 42, 194
arrests, 190
art, 36, 68, 116, 155
Asian Americans, 16–17, 105, 120, 185, 230. See also China; Chinese American students

Associated Press-America Online news poll, 101
associative learning, 37–38
attendance, 56, 64, 138, 156, 170, 176, 181, 203, 213, 224, 226
attention deficit disorder, 161
autonomy, 80, 107. *See also under* teachers

Baker, Ella, 24
Ball, Aretha, 51, 52
Bay Area Writing Project (BAWP), 34, 53–54
Bazelon, Emily, 139
Beals, Melba Pattillo, 117
Because Writing Matters (NWP), 53
Belvedere Junior High (East Los Angeles), 162
Benjamin Franklin High School (East Harlem), 66
Best Buddies program, 154
biases, 140, 145
Bill Wilson Center (San Jose), 168–170
Bi Rite Creamery, 181
Black, Paul, 14
Black Lives Matter (protests), 220
Black Student Union, 144, 153, 159
Blythe, Gentle, 157
Boaler, Jo, 81–82, 97–98, 105
boycotts, 19, 40, 118
Bradley, Fran, 199
brains, 37, 38, 86
bribes, 73
Bringing the War Home (Varon), 41
Brookings Institute, 105, 190

Brown, Michael, 159
Brown v. Board of Education, 19, 91, 117–118
Brown, Willie, 186
budgeting issues, 154, 155, 163, 166, 169, 180
bullying, 129, 130, 134, 135, 139, 140, 141
  antibullying policies, 145
Bush, George, Sr., 169
Bush, Jeb, 11
Bush administration, 11
business-inspired model, 11, 187. *See also* corporate factory model

CACSEA. *See* Center for Applied Cultural Studies and Educational Achievement California, 3, 139, 191
  California High School Exit Exam, 179
  California Standards Test (CST), 3, 9, 20, 25, 103, 183
  Department of Education, 20
  Latino student majority in, 12
  University of California at Berkeley, 77, 83
  See also San Francisco
Carlos (student), 131–132, 144
Castro, Sal, 15
Catching Up or Leading the Way (Zhao), 80
Catholic Church, 130
Center for American Progress, 166
Center for Applied Cultural Studies and Educational Achievement (CACSEA), 50–51, 52

Central Americans, 76, 78. *See also* El Salvador; Guatemala
charter schools, 155, 188, 189
cheating scandals, 190
Chicago, 65, 68, 159
  Chicago Teachers Federation, 72
child labor, 64
Child Protective Services, 138
China, 17, 77, 91
  American delegation visit to, 78–79
  Chinese American students, 73–88, 119, 153
  elementary education in, 86
  high test scores but low ability in, 80
  learning math in, 83–84
  sending kids to American high schools, 81
  standardized testing in, 73, 74, 75, 78, 79, 80
civil rights movement, 12, 19, 40, 42, 116, 118, 172
  pre-civil rights era, 67
Claire Lilienthal middle school, 230
classroom management, 51, 162, 172, 207, 216. *See also* discipline
clothes, 128–129, 150, 151, 153
clubs, 139–140, 142, 143, 146, 153–154, 155. *See also* gays: Gay-Straight Student Alliance; Latinos: Latino Club
coaching, 195, 203
  district-assigned coaches, 208

See also McKamey, Pirette: coaching other teachers
Coalition of Small Essential Schools, 104
Cohen, Elizabeth, 104
college enrollments, 20, 155–156, 160, 176, 179
colonialism, 43
Columbia University, 40–41, 111
Columbine shootings in 1999, 145
coming out, 123, 125, 132, 136–137, 142
  National Coming Out Day, 140
Common Core, 93, 112, 188, 190, 191, 217
community schools, 65, 66–67, 68, 77, 159, 186
competition/competitiveness, 77, 132
computers, 112, 189, 191
Congress for Racial Equality (CORE), 40, 118
Constitution, 24
Cooper, Anna Julia, 67, 117
CORE. *See* Congress for Racial Equality
corporal punishment, 64
corporate factory model, 64–65, 68. *See also* business-inspired model
Covello, Leonard, 66, 67
"coyotes" (smugglers), 6
Creating Innovators (Wagner), 81
creativity, 79, 80, 81
Crisostomo, Paula, 15, 16
critical thinking, 74, 79, 81, 147
Cuban, Larry, 11, 35, 69, 110–111, 115, 121, 191

Cubberley, Ellwood, 69
cultural pluralism, 66
curricula, 64–65, 66, 68, 69, 70,
    79, 80, 101, 104, 115, 155,
    162, 163, 170
  collaborative planning for, 178
  demands for new, 119, 188, 190
  high curriculum standards
    and student achievement,
    190–191
  LGBTQ content in, 136
  test-oriented, 165 (*see also* tests/
    testing: teaching to the test)

Darling-Hammond, Linda, 14,
    171, 172
Darrell (student), 33–34, 36, 38,
    40, 60–62
Dartmouth College, 90, 91
debates, 2, 22
decision making, 70, 72, 73, 78,
    101, 163, 164, 166, 238
deficit model, 52, 109, 119, 177
Delpit, Lisa, 79, 102, 172
del Rio, Dolores, 23
democracy, 65, 72
deportations, 13, 25
desegregation, 115–121. *See also*
    segregation
detention centers, 25
Dewey, John, 65, 68, 115
Dieckmann, Jack, 92–93
direct instruction, 217
disabled students, 95, 100, 119,
    140, 145, 154
discipline, 45, 115, 169, 189, 190,
    216–217. *See also* classroom
    management

disidentification, 105
diversity, 154, 166. *See also under*
    Mission High
domestic violence, 29
"Do Now" review exercise, 28,
    95, 96
Douglass, Frederick, 24
DREAM Act, 143, 144
dropouts, 65, 186, 226
  dropout rates for African Ameri-
    cans, 173–174
  dropout rates for Latinos, 2
drugs, 4, 236
DuBois, W. E. B., 24, 60, 116–117,
    120
due process, 25
Dweck, Carol, 101

Education in China (report), 79
Education Trust, 12
Eisenhower, Dwight D., 116, 118
Elementary and Secondary
    Education Act (ESEA), 120,
    121
El Salvador, 1, 42, 152
  Civil War in, 23
  San Juan Las Minas in, 3–6
Emory, Kathy, 185, 186
engagement. *See* student
    engagement
engineering, 74, 85
ESEA. *See* Elementary and
    Secondary Education Act
Esters, Mac, 208–209, 211
Etaat, Shideh, 210, 211, 214
ethnic groups, 66, 202
expectations, 52, 109, 110, 162,
    175, 209, 217, 232, 233

faculty meetings, 206–207
fashion, 129, 131
Faubus, Orval, 118
Fedorchuk, Deborah, 132–133,
    133–134
feedback, 48, 54, 199, 214
    teachers receiving, 204, 206
feminism, 133
Finland, 50, 111
firings, 12, 155, 166, 167, 170,
    177, 186
Fordham Institute, 110
Forero, Valerie, 156
formative assessments, 14
Fourteenth and Fifteenth
    Amendments, 24, 25
Fox, Brian, 180, 182, 184
Fructuoso, Iz and Ed, 158, 180
Fulop, Rebecca, 179, 209, 211,
    212
funding for schools, 68, 69–70,
    91, 92, 104, 112, 118, 153,
    154–155, 171, 188, 191
    Title I, 120–121
    See also grants

Gaggero, Ronald, 158–159
gangs, 7. *See also* Mara Salvatru-
    cha gang
Garcia, Juan, 156
Garner, Eric, 159, 220, 221
Gates, Bill, 11, 189
    Gates Foundation, 170
gays, 56, 123
    gay marriage, 132
    Gay, Lesbian & Straight
        Education Network,
        139

Gay-Straight Student Alli-
    ance (GSA), 124, 134–136,
    139–140, 142, 144, 154, 159
    See also coming out; LGBTQ
        issues; Pablo (student)
GDP. *See* gross domestic product
George (student), 73–88
Ghana, 47
Glaser, Robert, 14–15
global economy, 79, 81
God, 130
Goldstein, Dana, 67, 68, 118
Gomez, Veronica, 158–159
grades, 11, 35, 53, 56, 77, 103,
    104, 105, 111, 113, 131, 137,
    138, 147, 148, 157, 170, 174,
    181–182, 198, 203, 205, 214,
    226, 227, 232, 233
    of African Americans/Latinos,
        173, 176
    GPAs, 181, 200, 235
graduation rates, 156, 170, 176
grammar, 8, 9, 18, 51, 53, 146
grants, 101, 104, 154–155, 170,
    189. *See also* funding for
        schools
Groefsema, Blair, 95, 100
gross domestic product (GDP),
    187
group work, 131, 164, 171, 183.
    See also under math
GSA. *See* gays: Gay-Straight Stu-
    dent Alliance
Guatemala, 124, 125, 128, 130,
    133, 137
guns, 224
Guthertz, Eric, 7, 12, 124, 151,
    153–184

Guthertz, Eric *(continued)*
  becoming assistant principal
    and principal, 175–176
  evaluated by teachers, 179
  family history of, 160–161
  new school opened by, 168–169

Haiti Action Committee, 42–43
Haley, Margaret, 72
Hampton, Fred, 42
Hannah-Jones, Nikole, 118
Hansberry, Lorraine, 60
Harlem community in New York,
    41
Hayden, Robert, 150
Hiebert, James, 66
high school enrollments, 64
Hilliard, Asa, III, 51
history, 116
  and LGBTQ movements, 136
  proficiency in, 9, 12–13
  as shaped by many different
    people, 43
homeless teens, 168–169
homework, 98, 114, 181
hooks, bell, 219
House of Air park, 181
housing policies, 118
Hsu, Stanley, 90–91
Hsu, Taica, 82–83, 87, 88,
    89–114, 134, 138, 143–144,
    150, 151, 182, 201
  applying for grants, 101
  as co-chair of math department,
    104
  and friend's sister Megan, 89,
    90
  parents of, 90–91

strength as a teacher, 108–109
Hugging the Middle (Cuban), 35
human capital, 191

ICE. *See* US Immigration and
    Customs Enforcement
immigrants, 6, 63, 69, 70, 135,
    151
India, 79
industrialization, 63
inequality, 41, 63, 71, 105, 117
In Search of Memory (Kandel), 37
intelligence, 101–102
inventions, 63
IQ testing, 68, 71, 72, 103
Israel, Neiel, 219–220

Jamal (student), 193–194
Japan, 50, 104, 111
Jesmyn (student), 15, 17, 28–30,
    31–33, 39, 200, 201, 209,
    223–239
  being late for classes, 224
  boyfriend Travis, 227, 239
  feeling at peace, 231–232
  middle school attended by, 230,
    231
  mother of, 224, 227
  neighborhoods of, 227, 230
  research paper of, 223,
    225–226, 235–237
  speech at graduation, 238
J. Eugene McAteer High School
    (San Francisco), 55
Joaquin (student), 94, 96, 100,
    107, 181–182
Johnson, Lyndon, 120
Judd, Charles, 68

Kamenetz, Anya, 71, 121
Kandel, Eric R., 37
Kendrick (student), 56–59
Kennedy, Robert, 121
Khan, Salman, 82
Kim (student), 142, 143–144
King, Martin Luther, Jr., 43
KIPP charter school chain, 189
Kopp, Wendy, 11
Kozol, Jonathon, 91

Labaree, David F., 69–70, 71, 79
Laboratory School, University of
    Chicago, 65–66, 68
Lady Gaga, 125, 142, 149
LeMoine, Noma, 51, 120
Lange, Dorothea, 30–31
Language issues, 1, 18, 51, 139,
    156, 157, 164
    African American English,
        51–52
    English language proficiency in
        China, 80
    Second Language programs,
        119
    speaking Spanish at home/in
        class, 10, 16
    and taking multiple choice tests,
        20–21
    teacher interventions concern-
        ing, 134, 135
    See also Mission High: classes
        for Spanish-speaking new-
        comers; writing
Latinos, 10–11, 12, 56, 119, 120,
    126, 143, 162, 173, 176, 179
    and civil rights movement, 19
    as high school dropouts, 2

Latino Club, 7, 24, 77, 143, 153,
    159, 185
"Latinos in America in the
    1920s" (paper by Maria), 23
    and menial labor, 16
    proficiency in history, 9
    suspensions/expulsions of, 157
Lau v. Nichols, 119
Lee, Betty, 76
Leonardo da Vinci, 130, 149
lesson plans, 46–47, 55, 98, 108,
    111, 169, 216
    teachers planning together, 171,
        177, 178, 191, 204, 210
LGBTQ issues, 124, 135, 144, 152
    harassment of students, 139,
        141–142
    See also gays
Lili'uokalani (Queen of Hawaii), 34
Little Rock, Arkansas, 117
London, Jack, 216
Los Angeles, 15
Lotan, Rachel, 104
Loveless, Tom, 105
Lowell High (San Francisco),
    74–75, 75–76, 77
Luther Burbank Middle School
    (San Francisco), 44–45,
    48–49, 54, 180
    NWP workshop at, 52–53
LYRIC organization, 138–139

McDaniel, Mark A., 38
McKamey, Pirette, 45–51, 52, 53,
    54–56, 106, 108–109, 120,
    135, 146–150, 172, 173, 175,
    176, 177, 191–221, 225, 226,
    233, 239

McKamey, Pirette *(continued)*
  on analysis, 195
  coaching other teachers, 56,
    157, 207, 208–209, 215–221
  collecting/returning students'
    work, 213–214
  mother of, 198
  "Quests" unit taught by, 46,
    193–194, 215
  as writer, 197, 198, 199
Maher, Mary, 99, 104
*Make It Stick: The Science of
  Successful Learning* (Roediger
  and McDaniel), 38
Mali, 47
Mara Salvatrucha gang (MS-13),
    4, 5–6
Maria (student), 1–26, 31
  and aunt Angelica, 3–5, 6
  bus trip to California from
    El Salvador, 6
  mother of, 3, 6
  as proficient in history, 12–13
  self-confidence of, 8, 9, 13, 22
  as writer, 13, 18, 19, 22, 23,
    24, 27
Martin, Trayvon, 143, 225,
    235–237
Martinez, Erik, 138
math, 2, 36, 78–79, 115, 116, 164,
    213
  algebra, 76, 82, 89, 94, 105, 112
  calculus, 92
  Complex Instruction program
    for, 104, 107, 108
  engagement of students in, 101,
    103, 109, 110, 111
  exponential functions, 83, 84

  group work in, 85, 86, 87–88,
    95, 96, 99, 104, 106–107,
    108, 112
  as hated in high school, 101
  multiplication, 8, 89, 90, 102
  open-ended problems, 96–97
  personalized instruction in,
    109–110
  procedural teaching of, 82, 103,
    107, 110
  test scores in, 188, 189
  thinking conceptually/visually
    about, 87, 90, 92–93, 93–94,
    103, 104, 107, 108, 110, 111
  in variety of formats, 97–98
media, 41, 116, 176, 189
memory/memorization, 35, 36,
    37, 53, 65, 82, 83, 84, 92, 93,
    97, 103
Mendez v. Westminster, 19, 27
mentoring, 162, 199, 201, 210
  Mentoring Circles, 154,
    180–184
metrics, 12, 73
Mexican Americans, 71, 72, 76
Michelle (student), 134
middle class, 71, 73
Migrant Mother (photograph),
    30–31
militarism, 41
Million Hoodie March (New
    York), 237
Mirkinson, Judith, 40, 42
Mission High, 1, 12, 55–56, 75,
    84, 93, 161, 226–227
  after-school programs at, 7, 154
  classes for Spanish-speaking
    newcomers, 2, 7, 132, 146

classroom interactions at, 85
diversity of, 76–77, 146,
    166–167, 185
Dolores Park near, 7, 160–161
Drag Show at, 123–128,
    140–141, 142, 144, 151, 152
founding of, 63
Hoodie Day at, 237
as low performing, 3, 14, 25
museum at, 158, 160
rewards for students at, 181,
    183
role in community, 159 (*see also*
    community schools)
with strong/effective GSA
    chapter, 140 (*see also* gays:
    Gay-Straight Student
    Alliance)
video of staff members, 175
Mogannam, Sam, 183
Monroe Doctrine, 33
Morocco, 153
Morrison, Toni, 216, 219
Moses, Bob, 120
motivation, 61, 88, 110, 173–174,
    232
of teachers, 203–204
MS-13. *See* Mara Salvatrucha
    gang
M Street High School (Washing-
    ton, D.C.), 67–68
"Multicultural and Anti-Racist
    Teaching," 171–172
music, 36, 68, 116, 155

NAACP. *See* National Association for the Advancement of
Colored People

National Association for the
    Advancement of Colored
    People (NAACP), 117, 118
National Council of La Raza, 12
National Defense Education Act,
    116
National Educators Association,
    72
National Hoodie Day, 143
National Writing Project (NWP),
    52–54
*Nation at Risk, A: The Impera-
    tive for Educational Reform*
    (report), 187–188
NCLB. *See* No Child Left Behind
    Act
neuroplasticity, 38
neuroscientists, 37
newspapers/magazines, student-
    run, 77
New York Times, 14–15
Nicaragua, 42
Nobel Prizes, 80
No Child Left Behind Act
    (NCLB), 10, 11, 120, 159,
    188
    and teaching reading vs. writ-
        ing, 49
    and teaching to the test, 35–36
NWP. *See* National Writing
    Project

Obama, Barack, 154, 189, 190,
    237
O'Brien, Tim, 195–197
OECD (Organization for Eco-
    nomic Co-Operation and
    Development), 111

One Best System, The: A History of American Urban Education (Tyack), 65
One World Schoolhouse, The (Khan), 82

Pablo (student), 123–152
  Aunt Maria, 130–131
  coming out, 132, 136, 137
  cousin Vicky, 128–129
  friend Claudia, 136, 138
  friend Mario, 125
  mother of, 126–127, 128, 133, 137, 150
  as vice president of Mission High's GSA, 141–142
  as writer, 133, 147–149
PARCC consortium, 190
parents of color, 119, 188
Pavon, Jose Luis, 185
performance assessments, 164
Perry, Theresa, 67
perseverance, 212, 214
Phan, Charles, 158
Philippines, 38
photography, 30–31, 158
Pledge of Resistance group, 42
Plessy v. Ferguson, 19, 24
poetry, 210–211, 220–221
poverty, 68, 120, 188
principals, 24, 54, 55, 66, 67, 163, 170, 180, 185. *See also* Guthertz, Eric
problem solving, 81, 88
professional learning communities, 204

progressives, 63–72, 115, 118
  Administrative Progressives, 64–65, 67, 68, 69, 70–71, 116, 187, 191
  Child-centered Progressives, 64, 65, 66, 69–70
Prohibition, 28–30
Project Double Discovery, 42
protests, 15, 24, 40, 41, 185, 186, 190, 220. *See also* strikes; walkouts
Puerto Ricans, 66
punctuation, 53, 146, 148

race, discussions about, 166, 219–220, 237
Race to the Top initiative, 154–155, 188, 189
racial profiling, 236
racism, 41, 71, 121, 134, 135, 139, 140, 141, 219, 220, 221, 237
  antiracist teaching, 173, 175, 178
Raisin in the Sun, A (Hansberry), 60
rape, 5, 32
Rasheed (student), 94–95, 99, 100, 101, 106–107, 112–113, 181–182
Ratliff, Alan, 140
reading, 36, 48, 49, 116, 149
  taught before writing, 53
  test scores in, 188, 189
Reagan, Ronald, 187
recession, 155
"Reconstruction Defeated," (paper by Maria), 24
Reconstruction era, 24, 60

reforms, 49, 55, 63, 68, 70, 80, 82, 106, 186, 191
 as incremental, 176
 teacher-led, 177
 top-down strategy for, 172
remedial courses, 105
resilience, 13, 15, 62, 79, 103, 139, 199
respect, 67, 91, 103, 142, 144, 154, 172, 179, 206, 207, 209, 234
Reyes, Cat, 156
Rhee, Michelle, 11, 24
rhythm of classroom activities, 51
rigor, 218
Ritalin, 161
Rock, Chris, 219
Roediger, Henry L., III, 38
Rojas, Bill, 185, 186, 187
Roosevelt, Franklin D., 43
Roth, Robert, 15, 16, 17–18, 20, 21, 22, 27–62, 120, 172, 176, 201, 207, 224, 225, 228–229, 233, 234, 239
 as activist, 40, 42, 44
 coaching other teachers, 56, 157
 at Columbia University, 40–41, 42
 writings of, 34, 54

safety nets, 160, 169
Sam, Michael, 56–58
San Francisco, 1, 35, 44, 55, 74–75, 118, 160, 161
 Castro district, 124
 City College of San Francisco, 235, 238
 Presidio in, 231

San Francisco State University's Black Student Union, 119
San Francisco State University's College of Ethnic Studies, 120
San Francisco Teachers Residency, 167
Santana, Carlos, 7, 77, 158
SAS. *See* Student Afro-American Society
SAT. *See* Scholastic Aptitude Test
scaffolding (for assignments), 210–211
scholarships, 3, 74
Scholastic Aptitude Test (SAT), 72
school closings, 12, 24, 26, 155, 159, 188
school culture outside of classrooms, 157
School Improvement Grant (SIG), 104, 154
Schools: The Story of American Public Education (Spring), 116
science, 36, 53, 78–79, 115, 116, 190
 scientific approach to education, 64–65, 68–69, 71
SDS. *See* Students for a Democratic Society
segregation, 91–92, 105
 psychological damage of, 117
 See also desegregation
Seider, Scott, 145
self-doubt, 109
self-esteem/self-confidence, 75, 105, 107, 199, 202, 212, 233
self-reflection, 203

Senegal, 47
sexism, 134, 140, 145
sexual abuse, 25
Shahan, Emily, 92–93
Shame of the Nation, The: The Restoration of Apartheid Schooling in America (Kozol), 91
Singapore, 80
single parents, 61
slavery, 43, 60, 67
SMARTER consortium, 190
Soares, Dayna, 111, 158, 167, 204, 206, 209–210, 210–211
social change, 43, 63
social exclusion, 141
social justice, 45, 92, 159
social studies, 36, 44, 51, 55, 61, 177–178
Someone Has to Fail: The Zero-Sum Game of Public Schooling (Labaree), 69
South Korea, 80
Soviet Union, 115, 116
Spears, Harold, 115
special education, 154. *See also* disabled students
sports, 76, 79, 116
Spring, Joel, 116
Sputnik, 115
stability, 54, 55, 165, 180
standardized tests, 10–11, 11–12, 13, 23, 34, 71, 72, 79, 110–111, 121, 154, 159–160, 170, 184, 186, 187
    dangers of, 14–15, 81–82, 189–190
    sample tests for, 20–21

vs. tests created by teachers, 36–37, 165
    See also California: California Standards Test; tests/testing
Standards and Accountability Movement, 185–191
Stanford Graduate School of Education, 92, 104
Steele, Claude, 102, 106, 109, 117, 172, 225
Step-to-College program, 186
stereotypes, 16–17, 67, 78, 140, 143, 199
    stereotype threat, 102, 172
sterilization, forced, 71
Stewart, Ms. (attendance liaison), 224
Stigler, James W., 66
strikes, 63, 119–120, 163
Student Advisory Council, 154
Student Afro-American Society (SAS), 41
student discussions, 215, 218, 220. *See also* student engagement
student engagement, 51, 108, 109, 110, 154, 177, 198, 203, 206, 211, 212, 217, 234. *See also* math: engagement of students in; student discussions
student power, 41
Students for a Democratic Society (SDS), 40–41, 42
suicides, 25, 142
Sula (Morrison), 216, 219, 220, 221
Supreme Court, 19, 117
surveys, 104–105, 107, 110, 144, 156, 180, 182
    of teachers, 204

teachers, 7–10, 15, 25, 61, 76, 91, 108, 132, 161, 162, 178–179, 190, 199
and African American students, 233–234
assessments/tasks designed by, 14, 165
attrition among, 157
autonomy of, 72, 163
believing all students can learn, 201–202
bonuses for, 12, 203–204
caring for and supporting students, 174–175, 182, 209, 212, 215
collaborating, 203, 204–205, 209 (*see also* teachers: planning lessons together)
diversity of, 166–167
empowerment of, 164, 177
engaged with subject taught, 44, 177
evaluation of, 155, 177, 187, 189, 203–204
great teachers, 146
hours spent in classrooms, 50
ineffective teachers, 165, 166, 167
judging on broad range of students' work, 81
limitations of, 219
listening to students, 46
merit pay for, 187
and middle-achieving students, 205
and personal lives of students, 59, 232

planning lessons together, 171, 203 (*see also* lesson plans: teachers planning together)
professional development of, 163, 175, 203, 204
self-reflection of, 203
special education teachers, 95
strategies of, 205–206, 207, 208–209, 218, 220
student teachers, 195, 199
support programs for, 104
teacher-leaders, 206–207
Teachers for Social Justice, 159
teacher strikes, 163
teachers' unions, 72, 163–164, 165, 166, 167
tenure for, 165–166
tests created by, 34, 36–37, 164
as writers, 54
See also language: teacher interventions concerning; *individual teachers*
Teacher Wars, The: A History of America's Most Embattled Profession (Goldstein), 67
Teach for America, 11, 188
Teaching Gap, The: Best Ideas from the World's Best Teachers for Improving Education in the Classroom (Stigler and Hiebert), 66
Terman, Lewis, 71
tests/testing, 54, 70, 78, 81, 163, 191
business-inspired approach to, 11
essay questions on tests, 34–35

tests/testing *(continued)*
  and higher-order thinking skills,
    12
  multiple-choice, 9–10, 20–21,
    34, 35, 81, 110, 165, 189, 190
  preparing for, 33–34, 38
  students' suggestions concern-
    ing, 25–26
  teaching to the test, 21, 35–36,
    155, 165, 166
  See also standardized tests;
    teachers: tests created by
textbooks, 23, 44, 46, 79, 112,
    191
thesaurus, 32
Things They Carried, The
    (O'Brien), 195–197
Third World Liberation Front
    (TWLF), 119
Thorndike, Edward, 69
Those Winter Sundays (Hayden),
    150
Thurgood Marshall High School
    (San Francisco), 35, 55
Tobie, Edna, 31–33, 239
"To Build a Fire" (London), 216
tracking, 70–71, 85–86, 92,
    105–106, 110, 118, 181, 197,
    200
Truitt, Kevin, 170, 173, 176
tuition for undocumented stu-
    dents, 8
Tulsa Race Riot of 1921, 31–33
tutors, 98, 113, 169
Two Million Minutes (documen-
    tary), 79
Tyack, David, 65, 66, 120

United Teachers Los Angeles
    (UTLA), 163–164
units (subject matter taught),
    46–47, 157, 203, 215. *See also*
    McKamey, Pirette: "Quests"
    unit taught by
Urban School Chiefs under Fire
    (Cuban), 115
US Department of Education, 145
US Immigration and Customs
    Enforcement (ICE), 25
UTLA. *See* United Teachers Los
    Angeles

Varon, Jeremy, 41
Velez, Amadis, 7–10, 13, 14, 22,
    24, 176
Vergara v. California, 165
Vietnam War, 41, 42
Villaraigosa, Antonio, 15
"Viva la Raza," 16, 17
vocabulary, 51, 53
vocational training, 11, 67, 68
  vs. intellectual development, 69

Wagner, Tony, 79, 81
Waiting for Superman (film), 24
walkouts, 119, 185
  Walkout, The (film), 15–16, 18,
    19–20, 22
War on Poverty, 120
Warren, Earl, 117
Washington, D.C., 11, 67–68, 159
Weather Underground, 42
Wells, Ida B., 24
West Africa Project (history unit),
    47

What's Math Got to Do with It?
(Boaler), 81–82, 98
"What You Pawn I Will Redeem"
(Alexie), 147, 194
"When a Black Man Walks"
(Israel), 220–221
*Whistling Vivaldi: How Stereotypes
Affect Us and What We Can
Do* (Steele), 225
White, Alison, 207, 215–221
William, Dylan, 14
Wintermeyer, Winni, 144
women, 29, 67, 92, 101, 102, 133
bisexual, 134
working class, 71
World War I, 71, 72
writing, 7, 9, 28, 49–50, 56–59,
61–62, 146, 163, 171, 178,
220, 221
drafts for, 32, 226
essay questions on tests,
34–35
in journals, 132–133, 168
Ms. McKamey on, 193, 197

National Writing Project
(NWP), 52–53
portfolio pieces, 58
research papers, 13, 19, 31, 36,
47, 49, 61, 147, 164, 190, 194,
205, 214 (*see also* Jesmyn:
research paper of)
skills for, 35
teaching writing across disciplines, 49
titles for, 195
as tool for mastery and intellectual growth, 48
See also McKamey, Pirette:
as writer; Maria: as writer;
Pablo: as writer; Roth, Robert: writings of

Youth Leadership Council, 154

Zelaya, Arnold, 182, 183
Zhao, Yong, 79–80
Zimmerman, George, 235, 236
zone of proximal development, 48

Winni Wintermeyer

Kristina Rizga has been writing about youth and student issues for over a decade, most recently as an education reporter for *Mother Jones*. Her writing has been published in *The Nation, The American Prospect,* and *Global Post,* among other publications. Prior to writing for *Mother Jones,* Rizga was the executive editor of *WireTap,* an award-winning political magazine for young adults. She serves on the editorial board of *The Nation* and is also a cofounder and reporter at Re:Baltica, the Baltic Center for Investigative Journalism, based in her homeland, Latvia. She lives with her husband, Mike Stern, in San Francisco.

Other Books by Karl Shapiro

Person, Place, and Thing
V-Letter and Other Poems
Essay on Rime
Trial of a Poet
A Bibliography of Modern Prosody
Poems 1940–1953
Beyond Criticism (essays)
Poems of a Jew
American Poetry (editor)
In Defense of Ignorance (essays)
Start with the Sun (with James E. Miller Jr.
    and Bernice Slote)
The Bourgeois Poet
A Prosody Handbook (with Robert Beum)
Prose Keys to Modern Poetry (editor)
Selected Poems
Edsel (fiction)
To Abolish Children (essays)
White-Haired Lover
The Poetry Wreck (essays)
Adult Bookstore
Collected Poems 1940–1978
Love and War, Art and God
New and Selected Poems 1940–1986
The Younger Son (autobiography)
Reports of My Death (autobiography)
The Old Horsefly

Edited by Stanley Kunitz
and David Ignatow

Foreword by Stanley Kunitz

Introduction by M. L. Rosenthal

University of Illinois Press   Urbana and Chicago

Karl Shapiro

The Wild Card

Selected Poems, Early and Late

Publication of this book was supported by a
grant from the Eric Mathieu King Fund of the
Academy of American Poets

Manufactured in the United States of America
1 2 3 4 5 C P 5 4 3 2 1

This book is printed on acid-free paper.

Typeset in 10/13 Janson by
Keystone Typesetting, Inc.

Library of Congress
Cataloging-in-Publication Data

Shapiro, Karl Jay, 1913–
The wild card : selected poems, early and late /
Karl Shapiro ; edited by Stanley Kunitz and
David Ignatow ; foreword by Stanley Kunitz ;
introduction by M.L. Rosenthal.
p. cm.
ISBN 0-252-02389-7 (alk. paper).
—ISBN 0-252-06689-8 (pbk. : alk. paper)
I. Kunitz, Stanley, 1905–   . II. Ignatow, David,
1914–   . III. Title.
PS3537.H27A6   1998
811'.52 — dc21   97-32579
CIP

To the memory of Susan Hanzo

— K.S.

Contents

Foreword, by Stanley Kunitz   xv

Introduction, by M. L. Rosenthal   xix

From *Person, Place, and Thing* (1942)

The Dome of Sunday   3

Washington Cathedral   5

Auto Wreck   7

Hospital   9

The Fly   11

University   13

Drug Store   15

Haircut   16

Waitress   17

Buick   18

Israfel   19

Mongolian Idiot   20

Necropolis   21

October 1   22

Epitaph for John and Richard   24

Emporium   25

Death of Emma Goldman   26

The Contraband   27

Elegy for Two Banjos   28

Scyros   30

The Glutton   32

Poet   33

Travelogue for Exiles   36

Midnight Show   37

Conscription Camp   39

The Twins   42

Nostalgia   43

A Cut Flower   44

From *V-Letter and Other Poems*   (1944)

Troop Train   47

Christmas Eve: Australia   49

Piano   50

Magician   51

Red Indian   53

Full Moon: New Guinea   54

The Gun   55

The Second-Best Bed   56

Fireworks   58

Lord, I Have Seen Too Much   59

Franklin   60

Jefferson   61

Sunday: New Guinea   62

Jew   63

Shylock   64

The Synagogue   65

The Interlude   67

The Intellectual   69

V-Letter   71

Elegy for a Dead Soldier   73

From *Trial of a Poet*   (1947)

Homecoming   81

The Conscientious Objector   83

The Progress of Faust   84

In the Waxworks   86

D.C.   88

The Convert   90

Boy-Man   92

The Southerner   94

Recapitulations   96

From *Poems 1940–1953*   (1953)

Israel   103

The Minute   104

The Figurehead   106

The Potomac   108

Going to School   109

From *Poems of a Jew*   (1958)

The Alphabet   115

Messias   116

The Confirmation   117

The First Time   119

The Murder of Moses   120

From *The Bourgeois Poet*   (1964)

Solipsism   125

The Bourgeois Poet   126

The Living Rooms of My Neighbors   127

The Wood   128

The Clearing   129

Hair   130

Beautiful Thing   131

Office Love   132

High School   133

The Child Who Is Silent   134

Generations   135

I Am an Atheist Who Says His Prayers   136

My Century   138

Amsterdam Whores   139

Jazz   140

Nebraska   141

The Cracking-Plant   142

Burlesk   143

Bouquet   144

Fox Hole   145

The Nature of Belief   146

French Poetry   147

Baudelaire in Iowa   148

Randall Jarrell   149

Clowning   150

Roethke   151

Poets' Corner   152

Glad Hand   153

Fame   154

The Funeral of Poetry   155

From *Selected Poems* (1968)

Manhole Covers   159

Calling the Child   160

Lines for a Unitarian Church   161

Bad Taste, Inc.   162

Human Nature   163

You Call These Poems?   164

Emily Dickinson and Katherine Anne Porter   165

California Winter   166

A Selection of Poems (1969–92)

There Was That Roman Poet   171

W.H.A.   172

The Old Poet   173

Mozart's Jew   174

The Humanities Building   175

Crossing Lincoln Park   177

My Father's Funeral   178

Moving In   180

A Curiosity   182

The Piano Tuner's Wife   183

At Auden's Grave   184

The Old Horsefly   187

Tennyson   188

Whitman   189

Future-Perfect   190

July 7, 1978   191

Acknowledgments   193

Foreword

Stanley Kunitz

The story of Karl Shapiro's famously brilliant literary debut, which generated more enthusiasm and acclaim than most poets experience in a lifetime, belongs to the annals of American poetry. In a memoir contributed to a festschrift for Shapiro's eightieth birthday, Hayden Carruth vividly recalls the impact of *Person, Place, and Thing* on an impressionable young college student in 1942: "I was excited by it in a way that I never had been before. . . . [I remember] how fresh, new, vigorous and pointed the poems were, how they awakened me to whole perspectives of poetic possibility that I had never suspected before. Here were poems taken from the American actuality I knew, from the technological world, cars, radios, industrial blight, the impersonality of death from machine . . . beautiful poems in a manner that I instantly recognized, the beauty of good, hard, varied metres and tough, functional rhymes" (in *Seriously Meeting Karl Shapiro*, ed. Sue Walker, 1993).

When Shapiro was awarded the Pulitzer Prize for his second collection of poems, *V-Letter* (1944), written and published while he was on military duty in the southwest Pacific, he seemed well on the way toward fulfilling Louise Bogan's prediction that "his work will become a sort of touchstone for his generation." But as his incisive introduction to the book pointedly indicated, Shapiro was in the process of evolving a quite different image of himself in his role as citizen poet:

> I have not written these poems to accord with any doctrine or system of thought or even a theory of composition. I have nothing to offer in the way of beliefs or challenges or prosody. I try to write freely, one day as a Christian, the next as a Jew, the next as a soldier who sees the gigantic slapstick of modern war. I hope I do not impersonate other poets. Certainly our contemporary man should feel divested of the stock attitudes of the last generation, the stance of the political intel-

lectual, the proletarian, the expert, the salesman, the world-traveler, the pundit-poet.

That self-analytical pronouncement anticipates the defiant litany of flamboyant paradoxes that would appear twenty years later in *The Bourgeois Poet*, beginning, "I am an atheist who says his prayers. I am an anarchist, and a full professor at that. I take the loyalty oath." Young as he was, Shapiro had an inkling that his destiny was to live as a free, quixotic, and iconoclastic spirit, a stormy presence in the house of letters. Savage wit, contradiction, and paradox would arm an imagination that had its roots in the lyric tradition. His voice would be the unappeasable voice of conscience.

Even his unprecedented appointment, at thirty-three, to the post of Consultant in Poetry to the Library of Congress (now termed Poet Laureate of the United States) did not divert him from his course or induce him to modify the blazing candor that drove his art. He was not tamed by prizes and honors or inclined by temperament to play it safe by writing predictably perfect sestinas on innocuous themes. For reasons that pertain to the life as well as to the work, Carruth acknowledges his debt and that of his generation to the bold example set by "Shapiro's poetic courage, his willingness to change, his insistence on it."

When *The Bourgeois Poet* appeared in 1964, critics who had lauded Shapiro's mastery of craft were among those who felt challenged by his dismissal of meter and rhyme as nonessential and artificial impediments to the poetic process. "All things remain to be simplified," he wrote. "I must break free of the poetry trap." A surprising number of fellow-poets were not amused by his obituary quip on the current state of the art: "I didn't go to the funeral of poetry. I stayed home and watched it on television." Satiric, erotic, outrageous, apocalyptic, *The Bourgeois Poet* is simultaneously a book of self-revelation, a poet's zigzag manifesto, and a cry of the heart against the ills of an age. Yes, this was a work for which he paid dearly, but it was worth the cost, and it remains triumphant.

"What would American poetry be like, to deserve the name?" Shapiro has asked; and he has replied, with a nod to Walt Whitman, "It would be nonsensical, hilarious, and obscene like us. Absurd like us." All American poetry, he contends, tries to measure up to *Leaves of Grass*. His own poem in homage to Whitman is small in scale, but its grand and, indeed, "hilarious" finale exemplifies the relaxed style, vernacular tone, and esprit of the best of his later, mostly neglected verse:

> Two hundred pounds of genius and hype,
> Nature-mystic who designed his tomb

Solid as an Egyptian pyramid,
American to the soles of his boots,
Outspoken as Christ or Madame Blavatsky,
Messiah, Muse of the Modern, Mother!

There are times when the risks that Shapiro takes in the course of his poems seem on the verge of becoming unmanageable, but he has a way of overriding difficulties through the sheer momentum of his creative energy. In a game where aces are wild he has a gambler's faith that luck is on the side of those who dare.

As we prepare to go to press, my thoughts turn to my friend, the late David Ignatow, whose distinctive contribution to this undertaking is recognized on the title page. In his last communication with me, he remarked, "I must tell you how good I feel about helping to pass these poems on, so that they can be discovered again. Isn't that part of our obligation?"

Karl's own words would seem to indicate that this is a propitious time for publication. As far back as 1975, in the foreword to his selected essays *The Poetry Wreck*, he speculated that on the arrival of the millennium — now so near at hand — there will be a day of judgment for the poets of this century. "Strip away from twentieth-century poetry all the sociology and all the politics and see what is left," he wrote. "Precious little, perhaps, but something to conjure with, something our descendants will remember us by."

Here is *The Wild Card*, definitely something to conjure with.

Introduction:
"Shapiro Is All Right!"

M. L. Rosenthal

"Shapiro Is All Right!" Thus exclaimed the title of a review, years ago, of one of Karl Shapiro's books in the *New York Times Book Review*. The reviewer was William Carlos Williams, Shapiro's senior by three decades and our best-loved avant-garde model since the late 1920s. It was a bit of a surprise. The inventor of the "variable foot," experimenter *par excellence* in search of a poetry rooted in American idiom and speech-rhythms, was praising Shapiro, who had gained his early fame working in conventional forms, with debts to Auden and other British figures. The present collection shows why the younger poet won the Old Master's shout of approval.

Shapiro's rapid leap into recognition, marked by a Pulitzer award, the poetry consultantship at the Library of Congress, the editorship of *Poetry: A Magazine of Verse*, and university professorships, had seemed to take him far from Williams's embattled world. But if we look back at the pieces in his early collection *Person, Place, and Thing* (1942), we can see implicit affinities — continuities of attitude and sensibility from the two preceding decades — after all.

The particular American historical moment, in the immediate wake of the relatively Left-tending, socially critical Depression era, was also one of mobilization against the Axis powers and their ideology. Shapiro himself, serving with the army in the South Pacific when his book came out, was hardly a gung-ho flagwaver. His poem "Conscription Camp," set in Virginia, swings a double saber-slash of disgust against both the South's history and any sort of glib patriotism:

> You manufacture history like jute —
> Labor is cheap, Virginia, for high deeds,
> But in your British dream of reputation
> The black man is your conscience and your cost.
> ⋅ ⋅ ⋅ ⋅ ⋅ ⋅ ⋅ ⋅

The sunrise gun rasps in the throat of heaven;
The lungs of dawn are heavy and corrupt;
We hawk and spit; our flag walks through the air
Breathing hysteria thickly in each face.

Other pieces in *Person, Place, and Thing* reveal an anarcho-bohemian edge akin to Williams's but more emphatic in their antiracist and radical sympathies: attitudes that many young American Jews of Shapiro's generation shared with him. (The amusing, self-ironic sixth poem of his autobiographical sequence "Recapitulations," in his 1947 volume *Trial of a Poet*, describes his younger days when, as he has written, he "raved like a scarlet banner.") He had attended the University of Virginia, and his poem "University" begins, memorably: "To hurt the Negro and avoid the Jew / Is the curriculum."

Another early poem, "Death of Emma Goldman," described that passionate anarchist, "dark conscience of the family" (her own and humanity's), with gentle appreciation. At the same time, it reviled the people who, after her death, called her immoral because she never married her lover, Alexander Berkman:

Triumphant at the final breath,
  Their senile God, their cops,
All the authorities and friends pro tem
Passing her pillow, keeping her concerned.
But the cowardly obit was already written:
Morning would know she was a common slut.

Given the general ignorance, including that of most intellectuals, about Emma Goldman or anarchism, such poetry was hardly what won Shapiro his first success. Other reasons were far more compelling. For one thing, he was our first young American to emerge as a serious poet of World War II. For another, he had the splendid knack of being able to project a heightened vision of commonplace objects and circumstances. Many of his "civilian" poems are brilliant closeups of this sort. One example is "The Dome of Sunday," which points its lens — perhaps unfairly but "with focus sharp as Flemish-painted face / In film of varnish brightly fixed" — on the poet's prosperous Baltimore neighbors as hopelessly vulgar and self-centered. Others include "Buick," a witty, sexy, very American love song to a car, and the swift-moving, terrified "Auto Wreck." In the military context, the candidly gloomy picture of young, newly enlisted soldiers (including the poet) in "Conscription Camp" is similarly precise and evocative:

Through the long school of day, absent in heart,
Distant in every thought but self we tread,
Wheeling in blocks like large expensive toys
That never understand except through fun.

To steal aside as aimlessly as curs
Is our desire; to stare at corporals
As sceptically as boys; not to believe
The misty-eyed letter and the cheap snapshot.

Shapiro's first volume showed he could also write lyrical pieces whose feeling, despite their subtleties, had the direct appeal of folksongs. This gift has been a winning wild card for him, from the beginning to the more recent poems at the close of this collection. One moving early instance, expressing the pang of separation from home and from one's beloved in wartime, is his poem "Nostalgia." It begins:

My soul stands at the window of my room,
    And I ten thousand miles away;
My days are filled with Ocean's sound of doom,
    Salt and cloud and the bitter spray.
Let the wind blow, for many a man shall die.

My selfish youth, my books with gilded edge,
    Knowledge and all gaze down the street;
The potted plants along the window ledge
    Gaze down with selfish lives and sweet.
Let the wind blow, for many a man shall die.

My night is now her day, my day her night,
    So I lie down, and so I rise;
The sun burns close, the star is losing height,
    The clock is hunted down the skies.
Let the wind blow, for many a man shall die.

Not to labor the point, the music of pure lyricism makes a number of Shapiro's poems unforgettable, whether in a psychologically demanding piece like "The Figurehead" (about coping with a paralytic friend's "cold torture" as he lies imprisoned "on the treacherous shoals of his bed"); or in a piercing war poem like "Full Moon: New Guinea" (a Shakespearean sonnet about waiting in fear for the bombers to strike on a beautiful moonlit night); or in a tender, troubled gesture of understanding like "Mongolian Idiot."

Shapiro's celebration of the inevitable contradictions in our moral natures, his cultivation of what we might call a principled ambivalence, reaches its climax in his 1964 sequence *The Bourgeois Poet*. It is there, too, that Shapiro, a genuine virtuoso of conventional metrics, repudiates what he calls "the cosmetology of font and rule, meters laid on like fingernail enamel." "Why," he asks —

> Why the attractive packaging of stanza? Those cartons so pretty, shall I open them up? Why the un-American activity of the sonnet? Why must grown people listen to rhyme? How much longer the polite applause, the tickle in the throat?

The Bourgeois Poet, made up mainly of prose poems, provides the fullest example of Shapiro's shifted poetic values. To some extent it is a series of notebook entries whose essential rhythm is a kind of oracular musing that can rise to a lyrical pitch. Baudelaire may well be the major model for Shapiro in this form. But at times we hear reminiscences of a whole range of free inventors from Whitman through Williams, Fearing, and the Beats. The sound-patterns — shorter units, many single lines, and chantlike parallelism — echo them, and so does the recurrent mockery of fixed attitudes. But Shapiro's idiosyncratic humor and phrasing — and, even more, his introspective obsession with the ambivalence and unresolvable terror life forces upon us — keep the ultimate effect underivatively his own. Thus, section 34 in the original text begins in a series of laughingly depreciative and paradoxical self-definitions:

> I am an atheist who says his prayers.
>
> I am an anarchist, and a full professor at that. I take the loyalty oath.
>
> I am a deviate. I fondle and contribute, backscuttle and brown, father of three.

But later it opens itself to more mordant, fear-ridden utterances:

> My century, take savagery to your heart. Take wooden
> idols, walk them through the streets. Bow down to Science.
>
> My century that boils history to a pulp for newspaper, my century of
> the million-dollar portrait, century of the decipherment of
> Linear B and the old scrolls, century of the dream of penultimate
> man (he wanders among the abandoned skyscrapers of Kansas;
> he has already forgotten language), century of the turning-point
> of time, the human wolf pack and the killing light.

To re-read Shapiro's work in the unfolding, expanding scroll of his entire career is to see its manysidedness as never before. His is the essential, relentlessly self-scrutinizing modern Jewish sensibility. He was hard on his own people in "The Dome of Sunday" and yet expressed in "Israel" his giddy joy at the founding of the Jewish state — *and yet,* for the most part, shares the secular, antidogmatic mentality that permeates the leading thought of our era, when, indeed, "The best lack all conviction, while the worst / Are full of passionate intensity." (The lines are of course Yeats's, whom Shapiro once parodied, cleverly and affectionately, in his poem "Going to School." What they imply is very much what Shapiro meant in the passage about "my century" quoted in the preceding paragraph.)

And more intimately, he is also a poet who deals with desolation as well as joy in love and marriage, and who would be as toughminded as he often claims to be if only his humanity did not stand in the way. He may have begun his exuberantly ugly poem "The Fly" with the apostrophe "O hideous little bat, the size of snot." But that masterpiece of revulsion is at least counterbalanced by the concluding sonnet of a little group called "The Interlude," which in its way sums up the pathetic contradictions poets must confront and perhaps, if possible, even resolve:

> Writing, I crushed an insect with my nail
> And thought nothing at all. A bit of wing
> Caught my eye then, a gossamer so frail
>
> And exquisite, I saw in it a thing
> That scorned the grossness of the thing I wrote.
> It hung upon my finger like a sting.
>
> A leg I noticed next, fine as a mote,
> "And on this frail eyelash he walked," I said,
> "And climbed and walked like any mountain-goat."
>
> And in this mood I sought the little head,
> But it was lost; then in my heart a fear
> Cried out, "A life — why beautiful, why dead!"
>
> It was a mite that held itself most dear,
> So small I could have drowned it with a tear.

From
Person, Place, and Thing
(1942)

The Dome of Sunday

With focus sharp as Flemish-painted face
In film of varnish brightly fixed
And through a polished hand-lens deeply seen,
Sunday at noon through hyaline thin air
Sees down the street,
And in the camera of my eye depicts
Row-houses and row-lives:
Glass after glass, door after door the same.
Face after face the same, the same,
The brutal visibility the same;

As if one life emerging from one house
Would pause, a single image caught between
Two facing mirrors where vision multiplies
Beyond perspective,
A silent clatter in the high-speed eye
Spinning out photo-circulars of sight.

I see slip to the curb the long machines
Out of whose warm and windowed rooms pirouette
Shellacked with silk and light
The hard legs of our women.
Our women are one woman, dressed in black.
The carmine printed mouth
And cheeks as soft as muslin-glass belong
Outright to one dark dressy man,
Merely a swagger at her curvy side.
This is their visit to themselves:
All day from porch to porch they weave
A nonsense pattern through the even glare,
Stealing in surfaces
Cold vulgar glances at themselves.

And high up in the heated room all day
I wait behind the plate glass pane for one,
Hot as a voyeur for a glimpse of one,
The vision to blot out this woman's sheen;
All day my sight records expensively
Row-houses and row-lives.

But nothing happens; no diagonal
With melting shadow falls across the curb:
Neither the blinded negress lurching through fatigue,
Nor exiles bleeding from their pores,
Nor that bright bomb slipped lightly from its rack
To splinter every silvered glass and crystal prism,
Witch-bowl and perfume bottle
And billion candle-power dressing-bulb,
No direct hit to smash the shatter-proof
And lodge at last the quivering needle
Clean in the eye of one who stands transfixed
In fascination of her brightness.

Washington Cathedral

From summer and the wheel-shaped city
That sweats like a swamp and wrangles on
Its melting streets, white mammoth Forums,
And political hotels with awnings, caryatids;
Past barricaded embassies with trees
That shed trash and parch his eyes,
To here, the acres of superior quiet,
Shadow and damp, the tourist comes,
And, cooled by stones and darkness, stares.

Tall as a lover's night, the nave
Broods over him, irradiates,
And stars of color out of painted glass
Shoot downward on apostles and on chairs
Huddled by hundreds under altar rails.
Yet it is only Thursday; there are no prayers,

But exclamations. The lady invokes by name
The thousand-odd small sculptures, spooks,
New angels, pitted roods; she gives
The inventory of relics to his heart
That aches with history and astonishment:
He gives a large coin to a wooden coffer.

Outside, noon blazes in his face like guns.
He goes down by the Bishop's walk, the dial,
The expensive grass, the Byzantine bench,
While stark behind him a red naked crane
Hangs over the unfinished transept,
A Cubist hen rivalling the Gothic School.

Whether he sees the joke; whether he cares;
Whether he tempts a vulgar miracle,
Some deus ex machina, this is his choice,
A shrine of whispers and tricky penumbras.
    Therefore he votes again for the paid
Clergy, the English hint, the bones of Wilson
Crushed under tons of fake magnificence.
    Nor from the zoo of his instincts
    Come better than crude eagles: now
He cannot doubt that violent obelisk
And Lincoln whittled to a fool's colossus.
This church and city triumph in his eyes.
He is only a good alien, nominally happy.

Auto Wreck

Its quick soft silver bell beating, beating,
And down the dark one ruby flare
Pulsing out red light like an artery.
The ambulance at top speed floating down
Past beacons and illuminated clocks
Wings in a heavy curve, dips down,
And brakes speed, entering the crowd.
The doors leap open, emptying light;
Stretchers are laid out, the mangled lifted
And stowed into the little hospital.
Then the bell, breaking the hush, tolls once,
And the ambulance with its terrible cargo
Rocking, slightly rocking, moves away,
As the doors, an afterthought, are closed.

We are deranged, walking among the cops
Who sweep glass and are large and composed.
One is still making notes under the light.
One with a bucket douches ponds of blood
Into the street and gutter.
One hangs lanterns on the wrecks that cling,
Empty husks of locusts, to iron poles.

Our throats were tight as tourniquets,
Our feet were bound with splints, but now,
Like convalescents intimate and gauche,
We speak through sickly smiles and warn
With the stubborn saw of common sense,
The grim joke and the banal resolution.
The traffic moves around with care,
But we remain, touching a wound
That opens to our richest horror.
Already old, the question Who shall die?
Becomes unspoken Who is innocent?

For death in war is done by hands;
Suicide has cause and stillbirth, logic;
And cancer, simple as a flower, blooms.
But this invites the occult mind,
Cancels our physics with a sneer,
And spatters all we knew of denouement
Across the expedient and wicked stones.

Hospital

Inside or out, the key is pain. It holds
The florist to your pink medicinal rose,
The nickname to the corpse. One wipes it from
Blue German blades or drops it down the drain;
The novelist with a red tube up his nose
Gingerly pets it. Nurse can turn it off.

This is the Oxford of all sicknesses.
Kings have lain here and fabulous small Jews
And actresses whose legs were always news.
In this black room the painter lost his sight,
The crippled dancer here put down her shoes,
And the scholar's memory broke, like an old clock.

These reached to heaven and inclined their heads
While starchy angels reached them into beds:
These stooped to hell to labor out their time,
Or choked to death in seas of glaucous slime:
All tasted fire, and then, their hate annealed,
Ate sad ice-cream and wept upon a child.

What church is this, what factory of souls
Makes the bad good and fashions a new nose,
And the doctors reel with Latin and even the dead
Expect the unexpected? For O the souls
Fly back like heavy homing-birds to roost
In long-racked limbs, filling the lonely boughs.

The dead cry *life* and stagger up the hill;
But is there still the incorrigible city where
The well enjoy their poverty and the young
Worship the gutter? Is Wednesday still alive
And Tuesday wanting terribly to sin?
Hush, there are many pressing the oak doors,

Saying, "Are boys and girls important fears?
Can you predict the elections by my guts?"
But the rubber gloves are deep in a deep wound,
Stitching a single heart. These far surpass
Themselves, their wives, and the removed goiter;
Are, for the most part, human but unbandaged.

The Fly

O hideous little bat, the size of snot,
With polyhedral eye and shabby clothes,
To populate the stinking cat you walk
The promontory of the dead man's nose,
Climb with the fine leg of a Duncan-Phyfe
   The smoking mountains of my food
     And in a comic mood
  In mid-air take to bed a wife.

Riding and riding with your filth of hair
On gluey foot or wing, forever coy,
Hot from the compost and green sweet decay,
Sounding your buzzer like an urchin toy —
You dot all whiteness with diminutive stool,
   In the tight belly of the dead
     Burrow with hungry head
  And inlay maggots like a jewel.

At your approach the great horse stomps and paws
Bringing the hurricane of his heavy tail;
Shod in disease you dare to kiss my hand
Which sweeps against you like an angry flail;
Still you return, return, trusting your wing
   To draw you from the hunter's reach
     That learns to kill to teach
  Disorder to the tinier thing.

My peace is your disaster. For your death
Children like spiders cup their pretty hands
And wives resort to chemistry of war.
In fens of sticky paper and quicksands
You glue yourself to death. Where you are stuck
   You struggle hideously and beg,
     You amputate your leg
  Imbedded in the amber muck.

But I, a man, must swat you with my hate,
Slap you across the air and crush your flight,
Must mangle with my shoe and smear your blood,
Expose your little guts pasty and white,
Knock your head sidewise like a drunkard's hat.
    Pin your wings under like a crow's,
       Tear off your flimsy clothes
    And beat you as one beats a rat.

Then like Gargantua I stride among
The corpses strewn like raisins in the dust,
The broken bodies of the narrow dead
That catch the throat with fingers of disgust.
I sweep. One gyrates like a top and falls
    And stunned, stone blind, and deaf
       Buzzes its frightful F
    And dies between three cannibals.

University

To hurt the Negro and avoid the Jew
Is the curriculum. In mid-September
The entering boys, identified by hats,
Wander in a maze of mannered brick
    Where boxwood and magnolia brood
    And columns with imperious stance
    Like rows of ante-bellum girls
        Eye them, outlanders.

In whited cells, on laws equipped for peace,
Under the arch, and lofty banister,
Equals shake hands, unequals blankly pass;
The exemplary weather whispers, "Quiet, quiet"
    And visitors on tiptoe leave
    For the raw North, the unfinished West,
    As the young, detecting an advantage,
        Practice a face.

Where, on their separate hill, the colleges,
Like manor houses of an older law,
Gaze down embankments on a land in fee,
The Deans, dry spinsters over family plate,
    Ring out the English name like coin,
    Humor the snob and lure the lout.
    Within the precincts of this world
        Poise is a club.

But on the neighboring range, misty and high,
The past is absolute: some luckless race
Dull with inbreeding and conformity
Wears out its heart, and comes barefoot and bad
    For charity or jail. The scholar
    Sanctions their obsolete disease;
    The gentleman revolts with shame
        At his ancestor.

And the true nobleman, once a democrat,
Sleeps on his private mountain. He was one
Whose thought was shapely and whose dream was broad;
This school he held his art and epitaph.
    But now it takes from him his name,
    Falls open like a dishonest look,
    And shows us, rotted and endowed,
      Its senile pleasure.

Drug Store

I do remember an apothecary,
And hereabouts 'a dwells

It baffles the foreigner like an idiom,
And he is right to adopt it as a form
Less serious than the living-room or bar;
      For it disestablishes the café,
Is a collective, and on basic country.

Not that it praises hygiene and corrupts
The ice-cream parlor and the tobacconist's
Is it a center; but that the attractive symbols
      Watch over puberty and leer
Like rubber bottles waiting for sick-use.

Youth comes to jingle nickels and crack wise;
The baseball scores are his, the magazines
Devoted to lust, the jazz, the Coca-Cola,
      The lending-library of love's latest.
He is the customer; he is heroized.

And every nook and cranny of the flesh
Is spoken to by packages with wiles.
"Buy me, buy me," they whimper and cajole;
      The hectic range of lipsticks pouts,
Revealing the wicked and the simple mouth.

With scarcely any evasion in their eye
They smoke, undress their girls, exact a stance;
But only for a moment. The clock goes round;
      Crude fellowships are made and lost;
They slump in booths like rags, not even drunk.

Haircut

O wonderful nonsense of lotions of Lucky Tiger,
Of savory soaps and oils of bottle-bright green,
The gold of liqueurs, the unguents of Newark and Niger,
Powders and balms and waters washing me clean;

In mirrors of marble and silver I see us forever
Increasing, decreasing the puzzles of luminous spaces
As I turn, am revolved and am pumped in the air on a lever,
With the backs of my heads in chorus with all of my faces.

Scissors and comb are mowing my hair into neatness,
Now pruning my ears, now smoothing my neck like a plain;
In the harvest of hair and the chaff of powdery sweetness
My snow-covered slopes grow dark with the wooly rain.

And the little boy cries, for it hurts to sever the curl,
And we too are quietly bleating to part with our coat.
Does the barber want blood in a dish? I am weak as a girl,
I desire my pendants, the fatherly chin of a goat.

I desire the pants of a bear, the nap of a monkey
Which trousers of friction have blighted down to my skin.
I am bare as a tusk, as jacketed up as a flunkey,
With the chest of a moth-eaten camel growing within.

But in death we shall flourish, you summer-dark leaves of my head,
While the flesh of the jaw ebbs away from the shores of my teeth;
You shall cover my sockets and soften the boards of my bed
And lie on the flat of my temples as proud as a wreath.

Waitress

Whoever with the compasses of his eyes
Is plotting the voyage of your steady shape
As you come laden through the room and back
And rounding your even bottom like a Cape
Crooks his first finger, whistles through his lip
Till you arrive, all motion, like a ship,

He is my friend — consider his dark pangs
And love of Niger, naked indigence,
Dance him the menu of a poem and squirm
Deep in the juke-box jungle, green and dense.
Surely he files his teeth, punctures his nose,
Carves out the god and takes off all his clothes.

For once, the token on the table's edge
Sufficing, proudly and with hair unpinned
You mounted the blueplate, stretched out and grinned
Like Christmas fish and turkey pink and skinned,
Eyes on the half-shell, loin with parsley stuck,
Thigh-bones and ribs and little toes to suck.

I speak to you, ports of the northern myth,
This dame is carved and eaten. One by one,
God knows what hour, her different parts go home,
Lastly her pants, and day or night is done;
But on the restaurant the sign of fear
Reddens and blazes — "English spoken here."

Buick

As a sloop with a sweep of immaculate wing on her delicate spine
And a keel as steel as a root that holds in the sea as she leans,
Leaning and laughing, my warm-hearted beauty, you ride, you ride,
You tack on the curves with parabola speed and a kiss of goodbye,
Like a thoroughbred sloop, my new high-spirited spirit, my kiss.

As my foot suggests that you leap in the air with your hips of a girl,
My finger that praises your wheel and announces your voices of song,
Flouncing your skirts, you blueness of joy, you flirt of politeness,
You leap, you intelligence, essence of wheelness with silvery nose,
And your platinum clocks of excitement stir like the hairs of a fern.

But how alien you are from the booming belts of your birth and the smoke
Where you turned on the stinging lathes of Detroit and Lansing at night
And shrieked at the torch in your secret parts and the amorous tests,
But now with your eyes that enter the future of roads you forget;
You are all instinct with your phosphorous glow and your streaking hair.

And now when we stop it is not as the bird from the shell that I leave
Or the leathery pilot who steps from his bird with a sneer of delight,
And not as the ignorant beast do you squat and watch me depart,
But with exquisite breathing you smile, with satisfaction of love,
And I touch you again as you tick in the silence and settle in sleep.

Israfel

la tombe de Poe éblouissante

Picture the grave in his diabolical dream
Where death would come with clues and scenery,
The bulbous forehead and the crooked mouth
Leaking a poison, the translucent hands.

Perhaps like Juliet he could come alive
To hate Longfellow and to outrage life,
But dare not from his wretched rusty stone,
Landmark for girls developing in slums.

Here he is local color, another crank;
Pawnshops and whores and sour little bars
Accept him. Neither alarming nor prophetic,
He pleases like a wop or a jack-o-lantern.

Others uptown forgive his nasty eyes
Because he was sick and had a mind to err;
But he was never dirty like Hawthorne,
But boyish with his spooks and funerals

And clammy virgins. What else were his codes
But diagrams of hideouts of the mind
Plugged up with corpses and expensive junk,
Prosopopoeia to keep himself at bay?

Think of him as a cicerone with data
False as a waxworks and that understood
Ask pitifully for pain. Or think that now
Four cities claim him as France recommended.

Mongolian Idiot

A dog that spoke, a monster born of sheep
We mercilessly kill, and kill the thought,
Yet house the parrot and let the centaur go,
These being to their nature and those not.
We laugh at apes, that never quite succeed
      At eating soup or wearing hats.

Adam had named so many but not this,
This that would name a curse when it had come,
Unfinished man, or witch, or myth, or sin,
Not ever father and never quite a son.
Ape had outstripped him, dog and darling lamb
      And all the kindergarten beasts.

Enter the bare room of his mind and count
His store of words with letters large and black;
See how he handles clumsily those blocks
With swans and sums; his colored picture books.
At thirty-five he squeals to see the ball
      Bounce in the air and roll away.

Pity and fear we give this innocent
Who maimed his mother's beautiful instinct;
But she would say, "My body had a dog;
I bore the ape and nursed the crying sheep.
He is my kindness and my splendid gift
      Come from all life and for all life."

Necropolis

Even in death they prosper; even in the death
Where lust lies senseless and pride fallow
The mouldering owners of rents and labor
Prosper and improve the high hill.

For theirs is the stone whose name is deepest cut,
Theirs the facsimile temple, theirs
The iron acanthus and the hackneyed Latin,
The boxwood rows and all the birds.

And even in death the poor are thickly herded
In intimate congestion under streets and alleys.
Look at the standard sculpture, the cheap
Synonymous slabs, the machined crosses.

Yes, even in death the cities are unplanned.
The heirs govern from the old centers;
They will not remove. And the ludicrous angels,
Remains of the poor, will never fly
But only multiply in the green grass.

October 1

That season when the leaf deserts the bole
And half-dead see-saws through the October air
Falling face-downward on the walks to print
The decalcomania of its little soul —
Hardly has the milkman's sleepy horse
On wooden shoes echoed across the blocks,
When with its back jaws open like a dredge
The van comes lumbering up the curb to someone's door and knocks.

And four black genii muscular and shy
Holding their shy caps enter the first room
Where someone hurriedly surrenders up
The thickset chair, the mirror half awry,
Then to their burdens stoop without a sound.
One with his bare hands rends apart the bed,
One stuffs the china-barrel with stale print,
Two bear the sofa toward the door with dark funereal tread.

The corner lamp, the safety eye of night,
Enveloped in the sun blinks and goes blind
And soon the early risers pick their way
Through kitchenware and pillows bolt upright.
The bureau on the sidewalk with bare back
And wrinkling veneer is most disgraced,
The sketch of Paris suffers in the wind,
Only the bike, its nose against the wall, does not show haste.

Two hours — the movers mop their necks and look,
Filing through dust and echoes back and forth.
The halls are hollow and all the floors are cleared
Bare to the last board, to the most secret nook;
But on the street a small chaos survives
That slowly now the leviathan ingests,
And schoolboys and stenographers stare at
The truck, the house, the husband in his hat who stands and rests.

He turns with miserable expectant face
And for the last time enters. On the wall
A picture-stain spreads from the nail-hole down.
Each object live and dead has left its trace.
He leaves his key; but as he quickly goes
This question comes behind: Did someone die?
Is someone rich or poor, better or worse?
What shall uproot a house and bring this care into his eye?

Epitaph for John and Richard

There goes the clock; there goes the sun;
Greenwich is right with Arlington;
The signal's minutes are signifying
That somebody old has finished dying,
That somebody young has just begun.

What do you think you earned today
Except the waste, except the pay,
Except the power to be spending?
And now your year is striking, ending,
What do you think you have put away?

Only a promise, only a life
Squandered in secret with a wife
In bedtime feigning and unfeigning;
The blood has long since ceased complaining;
The clock has satisfied the strife.

They will not cast your honored head
Or say from lecterns what you said,
But only keep you with them all
Committed in the City Hall;
Once born, once married, and once dead.

Emporium

He must have read Aladdin who rubbed his head
And brought this out of space; some genie came
With bolts of lawn and rugs of heavy red,
Shoes for white boxes, gems for velvet trays;
For who could authorize in his right name
Such pricelessness of time and recklessness of days?

Not Faust, who longed for Hell, would sell his light
For moving stairs and mirrors set in miles
Where wives might wander with their sex in sight;
Rage and rat's-logic this man must have known
Who built these buttresses on rotted piles,
Initialed every brick, and carved his lips in stone.

As if the ancient principle obtained
And solvent time would underwrite his debt,
Or the strong face of flesh were not profaned
For mannikins with hair of cloth-of-gold;
As if no tongue had ever questioned yet
Who buys and who is bought, who sells and who is sold.

But those politely dressed in normal drab
Shall think of him remotely, think with shame
How of their skill, their goodness and their gab
He trained his joys to be obsequious Jews;
At last not even wives shall goad his name
To feats of wealth, humility, and sickness-news;

So that, with rounded ruins honored, like Stonehenge,
Time shall have time, and he his impotent revenge.

Death of Emma Goldman

Triumphant of the final breath,
 Their senile God, their cops,
All the authorities and friends pro tem
Passing her pillow, keeping her concerned.
But the cowardly obit was already written:
Morning would know she was a common slut.

Russians who stood for tragedy
 Were sisters all around;
Dark conscience of the family, down she lay
To end the career of passion, brain a bruise;
And mother-wonder filled her like a tide,
Rabid and raging discipline to bear.

In came the monarchist, a nurse,
 And covered up her eyes;
Volkstaat of hate took over: suddenly
The Ego gagged, the Conscious overpowered,
The Memory beaten to a pulp, she fell.
It remained to hide the body, or make it laugh.

Yet not to sink her name in coin
 Like Caesar was her wish,
To come alive like Frick, conjecture maps,
Or speak with kings of low mentality,
But to be left alone, a law to scorn
Of all, and none more honored than the least.

This way she died, though premature
 Her clarity for others;
For it was taught that, listening, the soul
Lost track and merged with trespasses and spies
Whose black renown shook money like a rat
And showed up grass a mortmain property.

The Contraband

I dreamed I held a poem and knew
The capture of a living thing.
Boys in a Grecian circle sang
And women at their harvesting.

Slowly I tried to wake and draw
The vision after, word by word,
But sleep was covetous: the song
The singers and the singing blurred.

The paper flowers of everynight
All die. Day has no counterpart,
Where memory writes its boldface wish
And swiftly punishes the heart.

Elegy for Two Banjos

Haul up the flag, you mourners,
        Not half-mast but all the way;
The funeral is done and disbanded;
        The devil's had the final say.

O mistress and wife too pensive,
        Pallbearers and priestly men,
Put your black clothes in the attic,
        And get up on your feet again.

Death did his job like a scholar,
        A most unusual case,
Death did his job like a gentleman;
        He barely disturbed the face.

You packed him in a handsome carton,
        Set the lid with silver screws;
You dug a dark pit in the graveyard
        To tell the white worms the news.

Now you've nothing left to remember,
        Nothing but the words he wrote,
But they'll never let you remember,
        Only stick like a bone in your throat.

O if I'd been his wife or mistress,
        His pallbearer or his parish priest,
I'd have kept him at home forever —
        Or as long as bric-a-brac at least.

I would have burned his body
        And salvaged a sizable bone
For a paper-weight or a door-stop
        Or a garden flagstone.

I would have heaped the fire
        And boiled his beautiful skull.
It was laden like a ship for travels
        And now is but an empty hull.

I would have dried it off in linens,
        Polished it with a chamois cloth
Till it shone like a brand-new quarter
        And felt smooth as the nose of a moth.

Or I'd have hung it out in the garden
        Where everything else is alive,
Put a queen bee in the brain case
        So the bees could build a hive.

Maybe I'd have wired the jawbone
        With a silver spring beneath,
Set it in the cradle with baby
        So baby could rattle the teeth.

O you didn't do right by William
        To shove him down that filthy hole,
Throw him a lot of tears and Latin
        And a cheap "God bless your soul."

You might as well leave off mourning,
        His photograph is getting dim,
So you'd better take a long look at it
        For it's all you'll ever see of him.

Haul up the flag, you mourners,
        Not half-mast but all the way;
The funeral is done and disbanded;
        The devil's had the final say.

Scyros

snuffle and sniff and handkerchief

The doctor punched my vein
The captain called me Cain
Upon my belly sat the sow of fear
With coins on either eye
The President came by
And whispered to the braid what none could hear

High over where the storm
Stood steadfast cruciform
The golden eagle sank in wounded wheels
White Negroes laughing still
Crept fiercely on Brazil
Turning the navies upward on their keels

Now one by one the trees
Stripped to their naked knees
To dance upon the heaps of shrunken dead
The roof of England fell
Great Paris tolled her bell
And China staunched her milk and wept for bread

No island singly lay
But lost its name that day
The Ainu dived across the plunging sands
From dawn to dawn to dawn
King George's birds came on
Strafing the tulips from his children's hands

Thus in the classic sea
Southeast from Thessaly
The dynamited mermen washed ashore
And tritons dressed in steel
Trolled heads with rod and reel
And dredged potatoes from the Aegean floor

Hot is the sky and green
Where Germans have been seen
The moon leaks metal on the Atlantic fields
Pink boys in birthday shrouds
Loop lightly through the clouds
Or coast the peaks of Finland on their shields

That prophet year by year
Lay still but could not hear
Where scholars tapped to find his new remains
Gog and Magog ate pork
In vertical New York
And war began next Wednesday on the Danes.

The Glutton

The jowls of his belly crawl and swell like the sea
When his mandibles oily with lust champ and go wide;
Eternal, the springs of his spittle leak at the lips
Suspending the tongue like a whale that rolls on the tide,

His hands are as rotten fruit. His teeth are as corn.
Deep are the wells of his eyes and like navels, blind,
Dough is the brain that supplies his passion with bread,
Dough is the loose-slung sack of his great behind,

Will his paps become woman's? He dreams of the yielding of milk,
Despising the waste of his stool that recalls him to bread;
More than passion of sex and the transverse pains of disease
He thinks of starvation, the locked-up mouth of the dead.

I am glad that his stomach will eat him away in revenge,
Digesting itself when his blubber is lain in the earth.
Let the juice of his gluttony swallow him inward like lime
And leave of his volume only the mould of his girth.

Poet

Il arrive que l'esprit demande la poesie

Left leg flung out, head cocked to the right,
Tweed coat or army uniform, with book,
Beautiful eyes, who is this walking down?
Who, glancing at the pane of glass looks sharp
And thinks it is not he — as when a poet
Comes swiftly on some half-forgotten poem
And loosely holds the page, steady of mind,
        Thinking it is not his?

And when will *you* exist? — Oh, it is I,
Incredibly skinny, stooped, and neat as pie,
Ignorant as dirt, erotic as an ape,
Dreamy as puberty — with dirty hair!
Into the room like kangaroo he bounds,
Ears flopping like the most expensive hound's;
His chin receives all questions as he bows
        Mouthing a green bon-bon.

Has no more memory than rubber. Stands
Waist-deep in heavy mud of thought and broods
At his own wetness. When he would get out,
To his surprise he lifts in air a phrase
As whole and clean and silvery as a fish
Which jumps and dangles on his damned hooked grin,
But like a name-card on a man's lapel
        Calls him a conscious fool.

And child-like he remembers all his life
And cannily constructs it, fact by fact,
As boys paste postage stamps in careful books,
Denoting pence and legends and profiles,
Nothing more valuable. — And like a thief.
His eyes glassed over and congealed with guilt,
Fondles his secrets like a case of tools,
        And waits in empty doors.

By men despised for knowing what he is,
And by himself. But he exists for women.
As dolls to girls, as perfect wives to men,
So he to women. And to himself a thing,
All ages, epicene, without a trade.
To girls and wives always alive and fated;
To men and scholars always dead like Greek
        And always mistranslated.

Towards exile and towards shame he lures himself,
Tongue winding on his arm, and thinks like Eve
By biting apple will become most wise.
Sentio ergo sum: he feels his way
And words themselves stand up for him like Braille
And punch and perforate his parchment ear.
All language falls like Chinese on his soul,
        Image of song unsounded.

This is the coward's coward that in his dreams
Sees shapes of pain grow tall. Awake at night
He peers at sounds and stumbles at a breeze.
And none holds life less dear. For as a youth
Who by some accident observes his love
Naked and in some natural ugly act,
He turns with loathing and with flaming hands,
        Seared and betrayed by sight.

He is the business man, on beauty trades,
Dealer in arts and thoughts who, like the Jew,
Shall rise from slums and hated dialects
A tower of bitterness. Shall be always strange,
Hunted and then sought after. Shall be sat
Like an ambassador from another race
At tables rich with music. He shall eat flowers,
Chew honey and spit out gall. They shall all smile
        And love and pity him.

His death shall be by drowning. In that hour
When the last bubble of pure heaven's air
Hovers within his throat, safe on his bed,
A small eternal figurehead in terror,
He shall cry out and clutch his days of straw
Before the blackest wave. Lastly, his tomb
Shall list and founder in the troughs of grass
            And none shall speak his name.

Travelogue for Exiles

Look and remember. Look upon this sky;
Look deep and deep into the sea-clean air,
The unconfined, the terminus of prayer.
Speak now and speak into the hallowed dome.
What do you hear? What does the sky reply?
The heavens are taken: this is not your home.

Look and remember. Look upon this sea;
Look down and down into the tireless tide.
What of a life below, a life inside,
A tomb, a cradle in the curly foam?
The waves arise; sea-wind and sea agree
The waters are taken: this is not your home.

Look and remember. Look upon this land,
Far, far across the factories and the grass.
Surely, there, surely, they will let you pass.
Speak then and ask the forest and the loam.
What do you hear? What does the land command?
The earth is taken: this is not your home.

Midnight Show

The year is done, the last act of the vaudeville,
The last top hat and patent leather tappity-tap
Enclosed in darkness. Pat. Blackout. Only the organ
Groans, groans, its thousand golden throats in love;
While blue lowlight suffuses mysteries of sleep
Through racks of heads, and smoothly parts the gauzy veil
That slips, the last pretense of peace, into the wings.

With a raucous crash the music rises to its feet,
And pouring from the hidden eye like God the Light
The light white-molten cold fills out the vacant field
With shattered cities, striped ships, and maps with lines
That crawl — symbols of horror, symbols of obscenity;
A girl astride a giant cannon, holding a flag;
Removal of stone and stained-glass saints from a known cathedral;

And the Voice, the loving and faithful pointer, trots beside
Reel after reel, taking death in its well-trained stride.
The Voice, the polite, the auctioneer, places his hints
Like easy bids. The lab assistant, the Voice, dips
Their pity like litmus papers into His rancid heart. —
Dream to be surfeited, nerves clogged up with messages,
And, backed up at the ganglion, the news refused.

Dream to be out in snow where every corner Santa,
Heart of one generation's dreams, tinkles a bell.
We know him too. He is the Unemployed, but clowns
As the Giver, receiving pennies in a cast-iron pot.
Dream to be cold with Byrd at the world's bottom. Dream
To be warm in the Vatican, photographing a manuscript.
Dream to be there, a cell in Europe's poisoned blood.

Revulsion cannot rouse our heads for pride or protest.
The eye sees as the camera, a clean moronic gaze,
And to go is not impossible but merely careless.
O wife, what shall we tell the children that we saw?
O son, what shall we tell our father? And O my friend,
What shall we tell our senses when the lights go up
And noiselessly the golden curtains crash together!

Conscription Camp

Your landscape sickens with a dry disease
Even in May, Virginia, and your sweet pines
Like Frenchmen runted in a hundred wars
Are of a child's height in these battlefields.

For Wilson sowed his teeth where generals prayed
— High-sounding Lafayette and sick-eyed Lee —
The loud Elizabethan crashed your swamps
Like elephants and the subtle Indian fell,

Is it for love, you ancient-minded towns,
That on the tidy grass of your great graves
And on your roads and riverways serene
Between the corn with green flags in a row,

Wheat amorous as hair and hills like breasts
Each generation, ignorant of the last,
Mumbling in sheds, embarrassed to salute,
Comes back to choke on etiquette of hate?

You manufacture history like jute —
Labor is cheap, Virginia, for high deeds,
But in your British dream of reputation
The black man is your conscience and your cost.

Here on the plains perfect for civil war
The clapboard city like a weak mirage
Of order rises from the sand to house
These thousands and the paranoid Monroe;

The sunrise gun rasps in the throat of heaven;
The lungs of dawn are heavy and corrupt;
We hawk and spit; our flag walks through the air
Breathing hysteria thickly in each face.

Through the long school of day, absent in heart,
Distant in every thought but self we tread,
Wheeling in blocks like large expensive toys
That never understand except through fun.

To steal aside as aimlessly as curs
Is our desire; to stare at corporals
As sceptically as boys; not to believe
The misty-eyed letter and the cheap snapshot.

To cross the unnatural frontier of your name
Is our free dream, Virginia, and beyond,
White and unpatriotic in our beds,
To rise from sleep like driftwood out of surf.

But stricter than parole is this same wall
And these green clothes, a secret on the fields,
In towns betray us to the arresting touch
Of lady-wardens, good and evil wives.

And far and fabulous is the word "Outside"
Like "Europe" when the midnight liners sailed,
Leaving a wake of ermine on the tide
Where rubies drowned and eyes were softly drunk.

Still we abhor your news and every voice
Except the Personal Enemy's, and songs
That pumped by the great central heart of love
On tides of energy at evening come.

Instinctively to break your compact law
Box within box, Virginia, and throw down
The dangerous bright habits of pure form
We struggle hideously and cry for fear.

And like a very tired whore who stands
Wrapped in the sensual crimson of her art
High in the tired doorway of a street
And beckons half-concealed the passerby,

The sun, Virginia, on your Western stairs
Pauses and smiles away between the trees,
Motioning the soldier overhill to town
To his determined hungry burst of joy.

The Twins

Likeness has made them animal and shy.
See how they turn their full gaze left and right,
Seeking the other, yet not moving close;
Nothing in their relationship is gross,
But soft, conspicuous, like giraffes. And why
Do they not speak except by sudden sight?

Sisters kiss freely and unsubtle friends
Wrestle like lovers; brothers loudly laugh:
These in a dreamier bondage dare not touch.
Each is the other's soul and hears too much
The heartbeat of the other; each apprehends
The sad duality and the imperfect half.

The one lay sick, the other wandered free,
But like a child to a small plot confined
Walked a short way and dumbly reappeared.
Is it not all-in-all of what they feared,
The single death, the obvious destiny
That maims the miracle their will designed?

For they go emptily from face to face,
Keeping the instinctive partnership of birth
A ponderous marriage and a sacred name;
Theirs is the pride of shouldering each the same
The old indignity of Esau's race
And Dromio's denouement of tragic mirth.

Nostalgia

My soul stands at the window of my room,
    And I ten thousand miles away;
My days are filled with Ocean's sound of doom,
    Salt and cloud and the bitter spray.
Let the wind blow, for many a man shall die.

My selfish youth, my books with gilded edge,
    Knowledge and all gaze down the street;
The potted plants upon the window ledge
    Gaze down with selfish lives and sweet.
Let the wind blow, for many a man shall die.

My night is now her day, my day her night,
    So I lie down, and so I rise;
The sun burns close, the star is losing height,
    The clock is hunted down the skies.
Let the wind blow, for many a man shall die.

Truly a pin can make the memory bleed,
    A word explode the inward mind
And turn the skulls and flowers never freed
    Into the air, no longer blind.
Let the wind blow, for many a man shall die.

Laughter and grief join hands. Always the heart
    Clumps in the breast with heavy stride;
The face grows lined and wrinkled like a chart,
    The eyes bloodshot with tears and tide.
Let the wind blow, for many a man shall die.

A Cut Flower

I stand on slenderness all fresh and fair,
I feel root-firmness in the earth far down,
I catch in the wind and loose my scent for bees
That sack my throat for kisses and suck love.
What is the wind that brings thy body over?
Wind, I am beautiful and sick. I long
For rain that strikes and bites like cold and hurts.
Be angry, rain, for dew is kind to me
When I am cool from sleep and take my bath.

Who softens the sweet earth about my feet,
Touches my face so often and brings water?
Where does she go, taller than any sunflower
Over the grass like birds? Has she a root?
These are great animals that kneel to us,
Sent by the sun perhaps to help us grow.
I have seen death. The colors went away,
The petals grasped at nothing and curled tight.
Then the whole head fell off and left the sky.

She tended me and held me by my stalk.
Yesterday I was well, and then the gleam,
The thing sharper than frost cut me in half.
I fainted and was lifted high. I feel
Waist-deep in rain. My face is dry and drawn.
My beauty leaks into the glass like rain.
When first I opened to the sun I thought
My colors would be parched. Where are my bees?
Must I die now? Is this a part of life?

From
V-Letter and
Other Poems
(1944)

.

Troop Train

It stops the town we come through. Workers raise
Their oily arms in good salute and grin.
Kids scream as at a circus. Business men
Glance hopefully and go their measured way.
And women standing at their dumbstruck door
More slowly wave and seem to warn us back,
As if a tear blinding the course of war
Might once dissolve our iron in their sweet wish.

Fruit of the world, O clustered on ourselves
We hang as from a cornucopia
In total friendliness, with faces bunched
To spray the streets with catcalls and with leers.
A bottle smashes on the moving ties
And eyes fixed on a lady smiling pink
Stretch like a rubber-band and snap and sting
The mouth that wants the drink-of-water kiss.

And on through crummy continents and days,
Deliberate, grimy, slightly drunk we crawl,
The good-bad boys of circumstance and chance,
Whose bucket-helmets bang the empty wall
Where twist the murdered bodies of our packs
Next to the guns that only seem themselves.
And distance like a strap adjusted shrinks,
Tighten across the shoulder and holds firm.

Here is a deck of cards; out of this hand
Dealer, deal me my luck, a pair of bulls,
The right draw to a flush, the one-eyed jack.
Diamonds and hearts are red but spades are black,
And spades are spades and clubs are clovers — black.
But deal me winners, souvenirs of peace.
This stands to reason and arithmetic,
Luck also travels and not all come back.

Trains lead to ships and ships to death or trains,
And trains to death or trucks, and trucks to death,
Or trucks lead to the march, the march to death,
Or that survival which is all our hope;
And death leads back to trucks and trains and ships,
But life leads to the march, O flag! at last
The place of life found after trains and death —
Nightfall of nations brilliant after war.

Christmas Eve: Australia

The wind blows hot. English and foreign birds
And insects different as their fish excite
The would-be calm. The usual flocks and herds
Parade in permanent quiet out of sight,
And there one crystal like a grain of light
Sticks in the crucible of day and cools.
A cloud burnt to a crisp at some great height
Sips at the dark condensing in deep pools.

I smoke and read my Bible and chew gum,
Thinking of Christ and Christmas of last year,
And what those quizzical soldiers standing near
Ask of the war and Christmases to come,
And sick of causes and the tremendous blame
Curse lightly and pronounce your serious name.

Piano

The perfect ice of the thin keys must break
And fingers crash through stillness into sound,
And through the mahogany darkness of the lake
Splinter the muteness where all notes are found.
O white face floating upwards amidst hair!
Sweet hands entangled in the golden snare,
        Escape, escape, escape,
     Or in the coils of joy be drowned.

What is the cabinet that holds such speech
And is obedient to caresses strange
As tides that stroke the long-deserted beach,
And gales that scourge the Peruvian mountain range?
O flesh of wood with flanks aglow with suns,
O quivering as at the burst of monstrous guns,
        Subside, subside, subside,
     Or into dust and atoms change.

Nor can the note-shaped heart, nor can the ear
Withstand your praise, O numbers more appalling
Than ringed and voyaging on the atmosphere
Those heavy flocks of fallen angels falling;
You strike with fists of heaven against the void
Where all but choiring music is destroyed,
        And light, and light, and light,
     Bursts into voice forever calling.

Magician

Tall in his top hat, tall and alone in the room
Of aerial music, electric light
And the click of tables, the mephistophelian man
Toys with a wand and the wonders happen — for whom
And to what end the gleam of the shellacked
Trick within trick, as plain as black and white,
And all too clever, all too matter-of-fact
Like the sudden neatness of a shutting fan?

And somewhat sinister, like a millionaire
Or a poet or a street-corner quack
With a dollar bottle of cure . . . We are drawn to his eye
Only to stop at the eye we dare not dare;
We suspect and believe; *he* looks us out of face
And seems to say that magic is the knack
Of showing the result without a trace
Of the cause, end without means, what without why.

If now the amusing audience could see
His mangey unicorn that crops
The shabby velvet of his weariness,
An inch from the abyss of villainy,
The applause would freeze, the dust settle like snow,
And long before the asbestos curtain drops
Even the children would get up to go,
Be sick in the lobby, sob with young distress;

But fortunately they cannot. We proceed
Beyond the fire-eating, doves,
Padlocks, confetti, disappearing ropes,
To personal murder, the necessary deed
Of sawing a woman in half. We want her heart.
The sable executioner in gloves
Labors, but hoc est corpus! quite apart
She stands; we applaud our disappointed hopes.

And backstage somewhere, peeling his moustache,
He muses that he is an honest man
And wonders dramatically why. Deep in his ear
At times there sounds the subterranean plash
Of Alf and Phlegeton where tides revolve
With eyes of evil. There he first began;
There is the task he can no longer solve
But only wait for till his dying year.

Red Indian

To Jim Powell

Purest of breed of all the tribes
That trekked from time and took the Trail of Tears
There to the plain beyond the bribes
Of best advantage, past the rifle's reach,
Where instinct rests and action disappears
And the skulls of cattle bleach.

High in the plateaus of their soul
The silence is reshaped like rocks by wind,
Their eyes are beads that pay their toll,
Record the race-long heritage of grief,
At altitudes where memory is thinned,
Frown like a wrinkled chief.

The painted feather still upright
They walk in concrete Tulsa dark and mute,
Their bravest blankets slashing bright
The afternoon of progress and of wives;
Their children glow like some primordial fruit
Cut from the branch by knives.

Bark-smooth as spears and arrow-straight
They watch the world like winter trees and grow;
Forests of them revive and wait,
In timeless hibernation dream and stir.
These are the lives that love the soundless snow
And wear the wind like fur.

Because their pride of nation leaps,
The august rivers where they yelled and died
Move with a blood that never sleeps.
Because their nature suffers the arrest
Of seed, their silence crowds us like a tide
And moves their mournful quest.

Full Moon: New Guinea

These nights we fear the aspects of the moon,
Sleep lightly in the radiance falling clear
On palms and ferns and hills and us; for soon
The small burr of the bombers in our ear
Tickles our rest; we rise as from a nap
And take our helmets absently and meet,
Prepared for any spectacle or mishap,
At trenches fresh and narrow at our feet.

Look up, look up, and wait and breathe. These nights
We fear Orion and the Cross. The crowd
Of deadly insects caught in our long lights
Glitter and seek to burrow in a cloud
Soft-minded with high explosive. Breathe and wait,
The bombs are falling darkly for our fate.

The Gun

You were angry and manly to shatter the sleep of your throat;
The kiss of your blast is upon me, O friend of my fear,
And I savour your breath like a perfume as salt and austere
As the scent of the thunder of heaven that brims in the moat!

I grip you. We lie on the ground in the thongs of our clasp
And we stare like the hunter who starts at a tenuous cry;
We have wounded the wind with a wire and stung in the sky
A white hole that is small and unseen as the bite of the asp.

The smooth of your cheek — Do you sight from the depth of your eye
More faultless than vision, more true than the aiming of stars?
Is the heart of your hatred the target of redness of Mars
Or the roundness of heart of the one who must stumble and die?

O the valley is silent and shocked. I absolve from your name
The exaction of murder, my gun. It is I who have killed.
It is I whose enjoyment of horror is fine and fulfilled.
You are only the toy of my terror, my emblem of blame.

Come with me. We shall creep for his eyes like the sweat of my skin,
For the wind is repaired and the fallen is calling for breath.
You are only the means of the practical humor of death
Which is savage to punish the dead for the sake of my sin!

The Second-Best Bed

In the name of the almighty God, amen,
   I, William Shakespeare, take my pen
   And do bequeath in perfect health
To Christ my soul and to my kin my wealth
      When I am dead.
      And to Anne, good dame,
      I bequeath my name,
A table, a chair, and the second-best bed.

To Judith a hundred fifty pounds I give,
   The same if three more years she live,
   And the broad-edge silver bowl. To Joan
My hose and clothes and all the suits I own
      Both blue and red.
      And to Anne, good dame,
      I bequeath my name,
A table, a chair, and the second-best bed.

Ten pounds to beggars for their drink and board,
   To Mr. Thomas Cole my sword,
   To Richard Burbage, Cundell, Nash,
Heminge and Hamlet one pound six in cash,
      And to her I wed
      Who is Anne, good dame,
      I bequeath my name,
A table, a chair, and the second-best bed.

To Joan also my Stratford house I will,
   For sisters shall not go with nil,
   And to her sons five pounds apiece
To be paid within a year of my decease.
      And as I have said
      To Anne, good dame,
      I bequeath my name,
A table, a chair, and the second-best bed.

Last, to my daughter, born Susanna Hall,
   My barns and stables, lands and all,
   Tenements, orchards, jewels, and wares,
All these forever for herself and heirs,
      Till all are dead;
      But to Anne, good dame,
      I bequeath my name,
A table, a chair, and the second-best bed.

Good wife, bad fortune is to blame
That I bequeath, when I am dead,
To you my honor and my name,
A table, a chair, and the second-best bed.

Fireworks

In midsummer darkness when primeval silences close
On the women in linen and children and husbands in blouses
We gather in laughter and move with a current that flows
Through the intimate suburbs of ice-cream and talkative houses

To a fabulous field of the night of the rainbows of ages
Where blindness is dyed with the blooms and the tints of desire,
And the wars of our boyhood rise up from the oldest of pages
With heroes erected on billboards of fuses and wire.

In the garden of pleistocene flowers we wander like Alice
Where seed sends a stalk in the heavens and pops from a pod
A blue blossom that hangs on the distance and opens its chalice
And falls in the dust of itself and goes out with a nod.

How the hairy tarantulas crawl in the soft of the ether
Where showers of lilies explode in the jungle of creepers;
How the rockets of sperm hurtle up to the moon and beneath her
Deploy for the eggs of the astral and sorrowful sleepers!

And the noble bombardment that bursts in the depth of our ears
Lifts the hair of our heads and interprets in absolute noises
The brimstone of total destruction, the doom of our years.
O the Judgment that shatters the rose of our secrets and poises!

In Niagaras of fire we leak in the luminous aura
And gasp at the portrait of Lincoln alive on the lattice.
Our history hisses and spits in the burning Gomorrah,
The volcanoes subside; we are given our liberty gratis.

Lord, I Have Seen Too Much

Lord, I have seen too much for one who sat
In quiet at his window's luminous eye
And puzzled over house and street and sky,
Safe only in the narrowest habitat;
Who studied peace as if the world were flat,
The edge of nature linear and dry,
But faltered at each brilliant entity
Drawn like a prize from some magician's hat.

Too suddenly this lightning is disclosed:
Lord, in a day the vacuum of Hell,
The mouth of blood, the ocean's ragged jaw,
More than embittered Adam ever saw
When driven from Eden to the East to dwell,
The lust of godhead hideously exposed!

Franklin

The star of Reason, Ben, reposed in you
Octagon spectacles, a sparking kite,
Triggers and jiggers, bobbins, reels and screws,
And aphorisms spelled in black and white.

Wiseacre, editor, and diplomat,
First of the salesmen, hero of the clerk,
The logic of invention led to bells
Joyous for George and terrible for Burke.

Poor Richard prospers and the grocery man
Has your disarming prose and pays his tax.
Sir, what is the reason for this bird
That sings and screams and coos and crows and quacks?

Two-penny buns, a whistle for the boy,
Rare Ben, the printer's devil used you well.
Lenin and Freud embroider left and right
And Curtis beats The Independence Bell.

Jefferson

If vision can dilate, my noble lord,
Farther than porticos, Italian cells,
Newtonian gardens, Haydn, and cuisine,
Tell us, most serious of all our poets,
Why is the clock so low?

I see the tender gradient of your will;
Virginia is the Florence of your soul,
Yes, ours. The architecture of your hands
Quiets ambition and revives our skill
And buys our faithlessness.

So temperate, so remote, so sure of phrase,
Your music sweeps a continent, a sphere,
Fashions a modern language for a war
And by its cadence makes responsible
Our million names to you.

When you were old the god of government
Seemed to recede a pace, and you were glad.
You watched the masons through your telescope
Finish your school of freedom. Death itself
Stood thoughtful at your bed.

And now the surfaces of mind are rubbed
Our essence starts like serum from our eyes.
How can you not assume the deities
That move behind the bloodshot look and lean
Like saints and Salem devils?

Sunday: New Guinea

The bugle sounds the measured call to prayers,
The band starts bravely with a clarion hymn,
From every side, singly, in groups, in pairs,
Each to his kind of service comes to worship Him.

Our faces washed, our hearts in the right place,
We kneel or stand or listen from our tents;
Half-naked natives with their kind of grace
Move down the road with balanced staffs like mendicants.

And over the hill the guns bang like a door
And planes repeat their mission in the heights.
The jungle outmaneuvers creeping war
And crawls within the circle of our sacred rites.

I long for our disheveled Sundays home,
Breakfast, the comics, news of latest crimes,
Talk without reference, and palindromes,
Sleep and the Philharmonic and the ponderous *Times*.

I long for lounging in the afternoons
Of clean intelligent warmth, my brother's mind,
Books and thin plates and flowers and shining spoons,
And your love's presence, snowy, beautiful, and kind.

Jew

The name is immortal but only the name, for the rest
Is a nose that can change in the weathers of time or persist
Or die out in confusion or model itself on the best.

But the name is a language itself that is whispered and hissed
Through the houses of ages, and ever a language the same,
And ever and ever a blow on our heart like a fist.

And this last of our dream in the desert, O curse of our name,
Is immortal as Abraham's voice in our fragment of prayer
Adonai, Adonai, for our bondage of murder and shame!

And the word for the murder of God will cry out on the air
Though the race is no more and the temples are closed of our will
And the peace is made fast on the earth and the earth is made fair;

Our name is impaled in the heart of the world on a hill
Whether we suffer to die by the hands of ourselves, and to kill.

Shylock

Ho, no, no, no, no, my meaning in saying he is a good
man is to have you understand me, that he is sufficient.
— *The Merchant of Venice*

Home from the court he locked the door and sat
In the evil darkness, suddenly composed.
The knife shone dimly on the table and his eyes
Like candles in an empty room
Shone hard at nothing. Yet he appeared to smile.

Then he took up his talith and his hat
And prayed mechanically and absently closed
His fingers on the knife. If he could realize
His actual defeat or personal doom
He must die or change or show that he was vile.

Nevertheless he would remain and live,
Submit to baptism, pay his fines,
Appear in the Rialto as early as tomorrow,
Not innocently but well aware
That his revenge is an accomplished fact.

And poverty itself would help to give
Humility to his old designs.
His fallen reputation would help borrow
A credit of new hate; for nothing will repair
This open breach of nature, cruel and wracked.

His daughter lies with swine, and the old rat
Tubal will be obsequious
To buy off his disgrace and bargain on his shame.
Despair can teach him nothing at all:
Gold he hates more than he hates Jesus' crown.

The logic of Balthasar will fall flat
On heaven's hearing. Incurious
As to the future, totally clear of blame,
He takes his ledgers out of the wall
And lights them with a taper and sits down.

The Synagogue

The synagogue dispirits the deep street,
Shadows the face of the pedestrian,
It is the adumbration of the Wall,
The stone survival that laments itself,
Our old entelechy of stubborn God,
Our calendar that marks a separate race.

The swift cathedral palpitates the blood,
The soul moves upward like a wing to meet
The pinnacles of saints. There flocks of thanks
In nooks of holy tracery arrive
And rested take their message in mid-air
Sphere after sphere into the papal heaven.

The altar of the Hebrews is a house,
No relic but a place, Sinai itself,
Not holy ground but factual holiness
Wherein the living god is resident.
Our scrolls are volumes of the thundered law
Sabbath by sabbath wound by hand to read.

He knows Al-Eloah to whom the Arab
Barefooted falls on sands, on table roofs,
In latticed alleys underneath the egg
On wide mosaics, when the crier shrills.
O profitable curse, most sacred rug,
Your book is blindness and your sword is rust.

And Judenhetze is the course of time;
We were rebellious, all but Abraham,
And skulked like Jonah, angry at the gourd.
Our days are captives in the minds of kings,
We stand in tens disjointed on the world
Grieving the ribbon of a coast we hated.

Some choose the ethics of belief beyond
Even particular election. Some
In bland memorial churches modify
The architecture of the state, and heaven
Disfranchised watches, caput mortuum,
The human substance eating, voting, smiling.

The Jew has no bedecked magnificat
But sits in stricken ashes after death,
Refusing grace; his grace is flowerless,
He gutters in the tallow of his name.
At Rome the multiplying tapers sing
Life endless in the history of art.

And Zion womanless refuses grace
To the first woman as to Magdalene,
But half-remembers Judith or Rahab,
The shrewd good heart of Esther honors still,
And weeps for almost sacred Ruth, but doubts
Either full harlotry or the faultless birth.

Our wine is wine, our bread is harvest bread
That feeds the body and is not the body.
Our blessing is to wine but not the blood
Nor to sangreal the sacred dish. We bless
The whiteness of the dish and bless the water
And are not anthropophagous to him.

The immanent son then came as one of us
And stood against the ark. We have no prophets,
Our scholars are afraid. There have been friars,
Great healers, poets. The stars were terrible.
At the Sadducee court he touched our panic;
We were betrayed to sacrifice this man.

We live by virtue of philosophy,
Past love, and have our devious reward.
For faith he gave us land and took the land,
Thinking us exiles of all humankind.
Our name is yet the identity of God
That storms the falling altar of the world.

The Interlude

I

Much of transfiguration that we hear,
The ballet of the atoms, the second law
Of thermo-dynamics, Isis, and the queer

Fertilization of fish, the Catholic's awe
For the life-cycle of the Nazarene,
His wife whom sleeping Milton thought he saw;

Much of the resurrection that we've seen
And taken part in, like the Passion Play,
All of autumnal red and April green,

To those who walk in work from day to day,
To economic and responsible man,
All, all is substance. Life that lets him stay

Uses his substance kindly while she can
But drops him lifeless after his one span.

II

What lives? the proper creatures in their homes?
A weed? the white and giddy butterfly?
Bacteria? necklaces of chromosomes?

What lives? the breathing bell of the clear sky?
The crazed bull of the sea? Andean crags?
Armies that plunge into themselves to die?

People? A sacred relic wrapped in rags,
The ham-bone of a saint, the winter rose,
Do these? — And is there not a hand that drags

The bottom of the universe for those
Who still perhaps are breathing? Listen well,
There lives a quiet like a cathedral close

At the soul's center where substance cannot dwell
And life flowers like music from a bell.

III

Writing, I crushed an insect with my nail
And thought nothing at all. A bit of wing
Caught my eye then, a gossamer so frail

And exquisite, I saw in it a thing
That scorned the grossness of the thing I wrote.
It hung upon my finger like a sting.

A leg I noticed next, fine as a mote,
"And on this frail eyelash he walked," I said,
"And climbed and walked like any mountain-goat."

And in this mood I sought the little head,
But it was lost; then in my heart a fear
Cried out, "A life — why beautiful, why dead!"

It was a mite that held itself most dear,
So small I could have drowned it with a tear.

The Intellectual

What should the wars do with these jigging fools?

The man behind the book may not be man,
His own man or the book's or yet the time's,
But still be whole, deciding what he can
In praise of politics or German rimes;

But the intellectual lights a cigarette
And offers it lit to the lady, whose odd smile
Is the merest hyphen — lest he should forget
What he has been resuming all the while.

He talks to overhear, she to withdraw
To some interior feminine fireside
Where the back arches, beauty puts forth a paw
Like a black puma stretching in velvet pride,

Making him think of cats, a stray of which
Some days sets up a howling in his brain,
Pure interference such as this neat bitch
Seems to create from listening disdain.

But talk is all the value, the release,
Talk is the very fillip of an act,
The frame and subject of the masterpiece
Under whose film of age the face is cracked.

His own forehead glows like expensive wood,
But back of it the mind is disengaged,
Self-sealing clock recording bad and good
At constant temperature, intact, unaged.

But strange, his body is an open house
Inviting every passerby to stay;
The city to and fro beneath his brows
Wanders and drinks and chats from night to day.

Think of a private thought, indecent room
Where one might kiss his daughter before bed!
Life is embarrassed; shut the family tomb.
Console your neighbor for his recent dead;

Do something! die in Spain or paint a green
Gouache, go into business (Rimbaud did),
Or start another Little Magazine,
Or move in with a woman, have a kid.

Invulnerable, impossible, immune,
Do what you will, your will will not be done
But dissipate the light of afternoon
Till evening flickers like the midnight sun,

And midnight shouts and dies: I'd rather be
A milkman walking in his sleep at dawn
Bearing fat quarts of cream, and so be free,
Crossing alone and cold from lawn to lawn.

I'd rather be a barber and cut hair
Than walk with you in gilt museum halls,
You and the puma-lady, she so rare
Exhaling her silk soul upon the walls.

Go take yourselves apart, but let me be
The fault you find with everyman. I spit,
I laugh, I fight; and you, *l'homme qui rît*,
Swallow your stale saliva, and still sit.

V-Letter

I love you first because your face is fair,
        Because your eyes Jewish and blue,
Set sweetly with the touch of foreignness
Above the cheekbones, stare rather than dream.
Often your countenance recalls a boy
        Blue-eyed and small, whose silent mischief
Tortured his parents and compelled my hate
        To wish his ugly death.
Because of this reminder, my soul's trouble,
And for your face, so often beautiful,
        I love you, wish you life.

I love you first because you wait, because
        For your own sake, I cannot write
Beyond these words. I love you for these words
That sting and creep like insects and leave filth.
I love you for the poverty you cry
        And I bend down with tears of steel
That melt your hand like wax, not for this war
        The droplets shattering
Those candle-glowing fingers of my joy,
But for your name of agony, my love,
        That cakes my mouth with salt.

And all your imperfections and perfections
        And all your magnitude of grace
And all this love explained and unexplained
Is just a breath. I see you woman-size
And this looms larger and more goddess-like
        Than silver goddesses on screens.
I see you in the ugliness of light,
        Yet you are beautiful,
And in the dark of absence your full length
Is such as meets my body to the full
        Though I am starved and huge.

You turn me from these days as from a scene
    Out of an open window far
Where lies the foreign city and the war.
You are my home and in your spacious love
I dream to march as under flaring flags
    Until the door is gently shut.
Give me the tearless lesson of your pride,
    Teach me to live and die
As one deserving anonymity,
The mere devotion of a house to keep
    A woman and a man.

Give me the free and poor inheritance
    Of our own kind, not furniture
Of education, nor the prophet's pose,
The general cause of words, the hero's stance,
The ambitions incommensurable with flesh,
    But the drab makings of a room
Where sometimes in the afternoon of thought
    The brief and blinding flash
May light the enormous chambers of your will
And show the gracious Parthenon that time
    Is ever measured by.

As groceries in a pantry gleam and smile
    Because they are important weights
Bought with the metal minutes of your pay,
So do these hours stand in solid rows,
The dowry for a use in common life.
    I love you first because your years
Lead to my matter-of-fact and simple death
    Or to our open marriage,
And I pray nothing for my safety back,
Not even luck, because our love is whole
    Whether I live or fail.

Elegy for a Dead Soldier

I

A white sheet on the tail-gate of a truck
Becomes an altar; two small candlesticks
Sputter at each side of the crucifix
Laid round with flowers brighter than the blood,
Red as the red of our apocalypse,
Hibiscus that a marching man will pluck
To stick into his rifle or his hat,
And great blue morning-glories pale as lips
That shall no longer taste or kiss or swear.
The wind begins a low magnificat,
The chaplain chats, the palmtrees swirl their hair,
The columns come together through the mud.

II

We too are ashes as we watch and hear
The psalm, the sorrow, and the simple praise
Of one whose promised thoughts of other days
Were such as ours, but now wholly destroyed,
The service record of his youth wiped out,
His dream dispersed by shot, must disappear.
What can we feel but wonder at a loss
That seems to point at nothing but the doubt
Which flirts our sense of luck into the ditch?
Reader of Paul who prays beside this fosse,
Shall we believe our eyes or legends rich
With glory and rebirth beyond the void?

III

For this comrade is dead, dead in the war,
A young man out of millions yet to live,
One cut away from all that war can give,
Freedom of self and peace to wander free.
Who mourns in all this sober multitude
Who did not feel the bite of it before
The bullet found its aim? This worthy flesh,
This boy laid in a coffin and reviewed —
Who has not wrapped himself in this same flag,
Heard the light fall of dirt, his wound still fresh,
Felt his eyes closed, and heard the distant brag
Of the last volley of humanity?

IV

By chance I saw him die, stretched on the ground,
A tattooed arm lifted to take the blood
Of someone else sealed in a tin. I stood
During the last delirium that stays
The intelligence a tiny moment more,
And then the strangulation, the last sound.
The end was sudden, like a foolish play,
A stupid fool slamming a foolish door,
The absurd catastrophe, half-prearranged,
And all the decisive things still left to say.
So we disbanded, angrier and unchanged,
Sick with the utter silence of dispraise.

V

We ask for no statistics of the killed,
For nothing political impinges on
This single casualty, or all those gone,
Missing or healing, sinking or dispersed,
Hundreds of thousands counted, millions lost.
More than an accident and less than willed
Is every fall, and this one like the rest.
However others calculate the cost,
To us the final aggregate is *one*,
One with a name, one transferred to the blest;
And though another stoops and takes the gun,
We cannot add the second to the first.

VI

I would not speak for him who could not speak
Unless my fear were true: he was not wronged,
He knew to which decision he belonged
But let it choose itself. Ripe in instinct,
Neither the victim nor the volunteer,
He followed, and the leaders could not seek
Beyond the followers. Much of this he knew;
The journey was a detour that would steer
Into the Lincoln Highway of a land
Remorselessly improved, excited, new,
And that was what he wanted. He had planned
To earn and drive. He and the world had winked.

VII

No history deceived him, for he knew
Little of times and armies not his own;
He never felt that peace was but a loan,
Had never questioned the idea of gain.
Beyond the headlines once or twice he saw
The gathering of a power by the few
But could not tell their names; he cast his vote,
Distrusting all the elected but not law.
He laughed at socialism; *on mourrait*
Pour les industriels? He shed his coat
And not for brotherhood, but for his pay.
To him the red flag marked the sewer main.

VIII

Above all else he loathed the homily,
The slogan and the ad. He paid his bill,
But not for Congressmen at Bunker Hill.
Ideals were few and those there were not made
For conversation. He belonged to church
But never spoke of God. The Christmas tree,
The Easter egg, baptism, he observed,
Never denied the preacher on his perch,
And would not sign Resolved That or Whereas.
Softness he had and hours and nights reserved
For thinking, dressing, dancing to the jazz.
His laugh was real, his manners were homemade.

IX

Of all men poverty pursued him least;
He was ashamed of all the down and out,
Spurned the panhandler like an uneasy doubt,
And saw the unemployed as a vague mass
Incapable of hunger or revolt.
He hated other races, south or east,
And shoved them to the margin of his mind.
He could recall the justice of the Colt,
Take interest in a gang-war like a game.
His ancestry was somewhere far behind
And left him only his peculiar name.
Doors opened, and he recognized no class.

X

His children would have known a heritage,
Just or unjust, the richest in the world,
The quantum of all art and science curled
In the horn of plenty, bursting from the horn,
A people bathed in honey, Paris come,
Vienna transferred with the highest wage,
A World's Fair spread to Phoenix, Jacksonville,
Earth's capital, the new Byzantium,
Kingdom of man — who knows? Hollow or firm,
No man can ever prophesy until
Out of our death some undiscovered germ,
Whole toleration or pure peace is born.

XI

The time to mourn is short that best becomes
The military dead. We lift and fold the flag,
Lay bare the coffin with its written tag,
And march away. Behind, four others wait
To lift the box, the heaviest of loads.
The anesthetic afternoon benumbs,
Sickens our senses, forces back our talk.
We know that others on tomorrow's roads
Will fall, ourselves perhaps, the man beside,
Over the world the threatened, all who walk:
And could we mark the grave of him who died
We would write this beneath his name and date:

EPITAPH

Underneath this wooden cross there lies
A Christian killed in battle. You who read,
Remember that this stranger died in pain;
And passing here, if you can lift your eyes
Upon a peace kept by a human creed,
Know that one soldier has not died in vain.

From
Trial of a Poet
(1947)

Homecoming

Lost in the vastness of the void Pacific
My thousand days of exile, pain,
Bid me farewell. Gone is the Southern Cross
To her own sky, fallen a continent
Under the wave, dissolved the bitterest isles
In their salt element,
And here upon the deck the mist encloses
My smile that would light up all darkness
And ask forgiveness of the things that thrust
Shame and all death on millions and on me.

We bring no raw materials from the East
But green-skinned men in blue-lit holds
And lunatics impounded between-decks;
The mighty ghoul-ship that we ride exhales
The sickly-sweet stench of humiliation,
And even the majority, untouched by steel
Or psychoneurosis, stare with eyes in rut,
Their hands a rabble to snatch the riches
Of glittering shops and girls.

Because I am angry at this kindness which
Is both habitual and contradictory
To the life of armies, now I stand alone
And hate the swarms of khaki men that crawl
Like lice upon the wrinkled hide of earth,
Infesting ships as well. Not otherwise
Could I lean outward piercing fog to find
Our sacred bridge of exile and return.
My tears are psychological, not poems
To the United States; my smile is prayer.

Gnawing the thin slops of anxiety,
Escorted by the groundswell and by gulls,
In silence and with mystery we enter
The territorial waters. Not till then
Does that convulsive terrible joy, more sudden
And brilliant than the explosion of a ship,
Shatter the tensions of the heaven and sea
To crush a hundred thousand skulls
And liberate in that high burst of love
The imprisoned souls of soldiers and of me.

The Conscientious Objector

The gates clanged and they walked you into jail
More tense than felons but relieved to find
The hostile world shut out, the flags that dripped
From every mother's windowpane, obscene
The bloodlust sweating from the public heart,
The dog authority slavering at your throat.
A sense of quiet, of pulling down the blind
Possessed you. Punishment you felt was clean.

The decks, the catwalks, and the narrow light
Composed a ship. This was a mutinous crew
Troubling the captains for plain decencies,
A Mayflower brim with pilgrims headed out
To establish new theocracies to west,
A Noah's ark coasting the topmost seas
Ten miles above the sodomites and fish.
These inmates loved the only living doves.

Like all men hunted from the world you made
A good community, voyaging the storm
To no safe Plymouth or green Ararat;
Trouble or calm, the men with Bibles prayed,
The gaunt politicals construed our hate.
The opposite of all armies, you were best
Opposing uniformity and yourselves;
Prison and personality were your fate.

You suffered not so physically but knew
Maltreatment, hunger, ennui of the mind.
Well might the soldier kissing the hot beach
Erupting in his face damn all your kind.
Yet you who saved neither yourselves nor us
Are equally with those who shed the blood
The heroes of our cause. Your conscience is
What we come back to in the armistice.

The Progress of Faust

He was born in Deutschland, as you would suspect,
And graduated in magic from Cracow
In Fifteen Five. His portraits show a brow
Heightened by science. The eye is indirect,
As of bent light upon a crooked soul,
And that he bargained with the Prince of Shame
For pleasures intellectually foul
Is known by every court that lists his name.

His frequent disappearances are put down
To visits in the regions of the damned
And to the periodic deaths he shammed,
But, unregenerate and in Doctor's gown,
He would turn up to lecture at the fair
And do a minor miracle for a fee.
Many a life he whispered up the stair
To teach the black art of anatomy.

He was as deaf to angels as an oak
When, in the fall of Fifteen Ninety-four,
He went to London and crashed through the floor
In mock damnation of the playgoing folk.
Weekending with the scientific crowd,
He met Sir Francis Bacon and helped draft
"Colours of Good and Evil" and read aloud
An obscene sermon at which no one laughed.

He toured the Continent for a hundred years
And subsidized among the peasantry
The puppet play, his tragic history;
With a white glove he boxed the devil's ears
And with a black his own. Tired of this,
He published penny poems about his sins,
In which he placed the heavy emphasis
On the white glove which, for a penny, wins.

Some time before the hemorrhage of the Kings
Of France, he turned respectable and taught;
Quite suddenly everything that he had thought
Seemed to grow scholars' beards and angels' wings.
It was the Overthrow. On Reason's throne
He sat with the fair Phrygian on his knees
And called all universities his own,
As plausible a figure as you please.

Then back to Germany as the sages' sage
To preach comparative science to the young
Who came from every land in a great throng
And knew they heard the master of the age.
When for a secret formula he paid
The Devil another fragment of his soul,
His scholars wept, and several even prayed
That Satan would restore him to them whole.

Backwardly tolerant, Faustus was expelled
From the Third Reich in Nineteen Thirty-nine.
His exit caused the breaching of the Rhine,
Except for which the frontier might have held.
Five years unknown to enemy and friend
He hid, appearing on the sixth to pose
In an American desert at war's end
Where, at his back, a dome of atoms rose.

In the Waxworks

At midday when the light rebukes the world,
Searching the seams of faces, cracks of walls
And each fault of the beautiful,
Seized by a panic of the street I fled
Into a waxworks where the elite in crime
And great in fame march past in fixed parade.
How pale they were beneath their paint, how pure
The monsters gleaming from the cubicles!

When, as in torsion, I beheld
These malformations of the evil mind
I grew serene and seemed to fall in love,
As one retiring to a moving picture
Or to a gallery of art. I saw
The basest plasm of the human soul
Here turned to sculpture, fingering,
Kissing, and corrupting life.

So back and forth among the leers of wax
I strutted for the idols of the tribe,
Aware that I was on display, not they,
And that I had come down to pray,
As one retires to a synagogue
Or to a plaster saint upon the wall.
Why were these effigies more dear to me
Than haughty mannikins in a window-shop?

I said a rosary for the Presidents
And fell upon my knees before
The Ripper and an exhibit of disease
Revolting more in its soft medium
Than in the flesh. I stroked a prince's hand,
Leaving a thumbprint in the palm. I swore
Allegiance to the suicide whose wrists
Of tallow bled with admirable red.

Why were these images more dear to me
Than faïence dolls or gods of smooth Pentelikon?
Because all statuary turns to death
And only half-art balances.
The fetish lives, idolatry is true,
The crude conception of the putrid face
Sticks to my heart. This criminal in wan
Weak cerement of translucent fat

Is my sweet saint. O heretic, O mute,
When broils efface the Metropolitan
And swinish man from some cloaca creeps
Or that deep midden, his security,
Coming to you in brutish admiration
May he look soft into your eyes;
And you, good wax, may you not then despise
Our sons and daughters, fallen apes.

D.C.

The bad breed of the natives with their hates
That border on a Georgian night,
The short vocabulary, the southern look
That writes a volume on your past, the men
Freeholders of the city-state, the women
Polite for murder — these happen to be;
The rest arrive and never quite remain.

The rest live with an easy homelessness
And common tastelessness, their souls
Weakly lit up by blazing screens and tales
Told by a newspaper. Holidays the vast
Basilicas of the railroad swallow up
Hundreds of thousands, struggling in the tide
For home, the one identity and past.

The noble riches keep themselves, the miles
Of marble breast the empty wind,
The halls of books and pictures manufacture
Their deep patinas, the fountains coldly splash
To the lone sailor, the boulevards stretch out
Farther than Arlington, where all night long
One living soldier marches for the dead.

Only the very foreign, the very proud,
The richest and the very poor
Hid in their creepy purlieus white or black
Adore this whole Augustan spectacle,
And chancelleries perceive the porch of might
Surmounted by the dome in which there lies
No Bonaparte, no Lenin, but a floor.

Yet those who govern live in quaintness, close
In the Georgian ghetto of the best;
What was the simplest of the old becomes
The exquisite palate of the new. Their names
Are admirals and paternalists, their ways
The ways of Lee who, having lost the slaves,
Died farther south, a general in the wrong.

The Convert

Deep in the shadowy bethel of the tired mind,
Where spooks and death lights ride, and Marys, too,
Materialize like senseless ectoplasm
Smiling in blue, out of the blue,
Quite gradually, on a common afternoon,
With no more inner fanfare than a sigh,
With no cross in the air, drizzle of blood,
Beauty of blinding voices from up high,
The man surrenders reason to the ghost
And enters church, via the vestry room.

The groan of positive science, hiss of friends,
Substantiate what doctors call
His rather shameful and benign disease,
But ecumenical heaven clearly sees
His love, his possibilities.
O victory of the Unintelligence,
What mystic rose developing from rock
Is more a miracle than this overthrow?
What Constitution ever promised more
Than his declared insanity?

Yet he shall be less perfect than before,
Being no longer neutral to the Book
But answerable. What formerly were poems,
Precepts, and commonplaces now are laws,
Dantean atlases, and official news.
The dust of ages settles on his mind
And in his ears he hears the click of beads
Adding, adding, adding like a prayer machine
His heartfelt sums. Upon his new-found knees
He treasures up the gold of never-ending day.

All arguments are vain — that Notre Dame
Has plumbing, Baptists shoot their fellowmen,
Hindus are pious, nuns have Cadillacs.
Apologetics anger him who is
The living proof of what he newly knows;
And proudly sorrowing for those who fail
To read his simple summa theologica,
He prays that in the burning they be spared,
And prays for mercy as the south wind blows,
And for all final sins that tip the scale.

Peace on a hundred thousand temples falls
With gently even light, revealing some
With wounded walls and missing faces, some
Spared by the bombardier, and some by God.
In mournful happiness the clerics move
To put the altars back, and the new man,
Heartbroken, walks among the broken saints,
Thinking how heavy is the hand that hates,
How light and secret is the sign of love
In the hour of many significant conversions.

Boy-Man

England's lads are miniature men
To start with, grammar in their shiny hats,
And serious: in America who knows when
Manhood begins? Presidents dance and hug
And while the kind King waves and gravely chats
American wets on England's old green rug.

The boy-man roars. Worry alone will give
This one the verisimilitude of age.
Those white teeth are his own, for he must live
Longer, grow taller than the Texas race.
Fresh are his eyes, his darkening skin the gauge
Of bloods that freely mix beneath his face.

He knows the application of the book
But not who wrote it; shuts it like a shot.
Rather than read he thinks that he will look,
Rather than look he thinks that he will talk,
Rather than talk he thinks that he will not
Bother at all; would rather ride than walk.

His means of conversation is the joke,
Humor his language underneath which lies
The undecoded dialect of the folk.
Abroad he scorns the foreigner: what's old
Is worn, what's different bad, what's odd unwise.
He gives off heat and is enraged by cold.

Charming, becoming to the suits he wears,
The boy-man, younger than his eldest son,
Inherits the state; upon his silver hairs
Time like a panama hat sits at a tilt
And smiles. To him the world has just begun
And every city waiting to be built.

Mister, remove your shoulder from the wheel
And say this prayer, "Increase my vitamins,
Make my decisions of the finest steel,
Pour motor oil upon my troubled spawn,
Forgive the Europeans for their sins,
Establish them, that values may go on."

The Southerner

He entered with the authority of politeness
And the jokes died in the air. A well-made blaze
Grew round the main log in the fireplace
Spontaneously. I watched its brightness
Spread to the altered faces of my guests.
They did not like the Southerner. I did.
A liberal felt that someone should forbid
That soft voice making its soft arrests.

As when a Negro or a prince extends
His hand to an average man, and the mind
Speeds up a minute and then drops behind,
So did the conversation of my friends.
I was amused by this respectful awe
Which those hotly deny who have no prince.
I watched the frown, the stare, and the wince
Recede into attention, the arms thaw.

I saw my southern evil memories
Raped from my mind before my eyes, my youth
Practicing caste, perfecting the untruth
Of staking honor on the wish to please.
I saw my honor's paradox:
Grandpa, the saintly Jew, keeping his beard
In difficult Virginia, yet endeared
Of blacks and farmers, although orthodox.

The nonsense of the gracious lawn,
The fall of hollow columns in the pines,
Do these deceive more than the rusted signs
Of Jesus on the road? Can they go on
In the timeless manner of all gentlefolk
There in a culture rotted and unweeded
Where the black yoni of the South is seeded
By crooked men in denims thin as silk?

They do go on, denying still the fall
Of Richmond and man, who gently live
On the street above the violence, fugitive,
Graceful, and darling, who recall
The heartbroken country once about to flower,
Full of black poison, beautiful to smell,
Who know how to conform, how to compel,
And how from the best bush to receive a flower.

Recapitulations

I

I was born downtown on a wintry day
    And under the roof where Poe expired;
Tended by nuns my mother lay
    Dark-haired and beautiful and tired.

Doctors and cousins paid their call,
    The rabbi and my father helped.
A crucifix burned on the wall
    Of the bright room where I was whelped.

At one week all my family prayed,
    Stuffed wine and cotton in my craw;
The rabbi blessed me with a blade
    According to the Mosaic Law.

The white steps blazed in Baltimore
    And cannas and white statuary.
I went home voluble and sore
    Influenced by Abraham and Mary.

II

At one the Apocalypse had spoken,
Von Moltke fell, I was housebroken.

At two how could I understand
The murder of Archduke Ferdinand?

France was involved with history,
I with my thumbs when I was three.

A sister came, we neared a war,
Paris was shelled when I was four.

I joined in our peach-kernel drive
For poison gas when I was five.

At six I cheered the big parade,
Burned sparklers and drank lemonade.

At seven I passed at school though I
Was far too young to say *Versailles*.

At eight the boom began to tire,
I tried to set our house on fire.

The Bolsheviks had drawn the line,
Lenin was stricken, I was nine.

— What evils do not retrograde
To my first odious decade?

III

Saints by whose pages I would swear,
    My Zarathustra, Edward Lear,
Ulysses, Werther, fierce Flaubert,
    Where are my books of yesteryear?

Sixteen and sixty are a pair;
    We twice live by philosophies;
My marginalia of the hair,
    Are you at one with Socrates?

Thirty subsides yet does not dare,
    Sixteen and sixty bang their fists.
How is it that I no longer care
    For Kant and the Transcendentalists?

Public libraries lead to prayer,
    EN APXH ἦν ὁ λόγος — still
Eliot and John are always there
    To tempt our admirari nil.

IV

I lived in a house of panels,
    Victorian, darkly made;
A virgin in bronze and marble
    Leered from the balustrade.

The street was a tomb of virtues,
    Autumnal for dreams and haunts;
I gazed from the polished windows
    Toward a neighborhood of aunts.

Mornings I practiced piano,
    Wrote elegies and sighed;
The evenings were conversations
    Of poetry and suicide.

Weltschmerz and mysticism,
    What tortures we undergo!
I loved with the love of Heinrich
    And the poison of Edgar Poe.

V

My first small book was nourished in the dark,
Secretly written, published, and inscribed.
Bound in wine-red, it made no brilliant mark.
Rather impossible relatives subscribed.

The best review was one I wrote myself
Under the name of a then-dearest friend.
Two hundred volumes stood upon my shelf
Saying my golden name from end to end.

I was not proud but seriously stirred;
Sorrow was song and money poetry's maid!
Sorrow I had in many a ponderous word,
But were the piper and the printer paid?

VI

The third-floor thoughts of discontented youth
Once saw the city, hardened against truth,
Get set for war. He coupled a last rime
And waited for the summons to end time.

It came. The box-like porch where he had sat,
The four bright boxes of a medium flat,
Chair he had sat in, glider where he lay
Reading the poets and prophets of his day,

He assigned abstractly to his dearest friend,
Glanced at the little street hooked at the end,
The line of poplars lately touched with spring,
Lovely as Laura, breathless, beckoning.

Mother was calm, until he left the door;
The trolley passed his sweetheart's house before
She was awake. The Armory was cold,
But naked, shivering, shocked he was enrolled.

It was the death he never quite forgot
Through the four years of death, and like as not
The true death of the best of all of us
Whose present life is largely posthumous.

VII

We waged a war within a war,
    A cause within a cause;
The glory of it was withheld
    In keeping with the laws
Whereby the public need not know
The pitfalls of the status quo.

Love was the reason for the blood:
    The black men of our land
Were seen to walk with pure white girls
    Laughing and hand in hand.
This most unreasonable state
No feeling White would tolerate.

We threw each other from the trams,
    We carried knives and pipes,
We sacrificed in self-defense
    Some of the baser types,
But though a certain number died
You would not call it fratricide.

The women with indignant tears
      Professed to love the Blacks,
And dark and wooly heads still met
      With heads of English flax.
Only the cockney could conceive
Of any marriage so naïve.

Yet scarcely fifty years before
      Their fathers rode to shoot
The undressed aborigines,
      Though not to persecute.
A fine distinction lies in that
They have no others to combat.

By order of the high command
      The black men were removed
To the interior and north;
      The crisis thus improved,
Even the women could detect
Their awful fall from intellect.

VIII

I plucked the bougainvillaea
      In Queensland in time of war;
The train stopped at the station
      And I reached it from my door.

I have never kept a flower
      And this one I never shall
I thought as I laid the blossom
      In the leaves of *Les Fleurs du Mal.*

I read my book in the desert
   In the time of death and fear,
The flower slipped from the pages
      And fell to my lap, my dear.

I sent it inside my letter,
      The purplest kiss I knew,
And thus you abused my passion
      With "A most Victorian Jew."

From
Poems 1940–1953
(1953)

Israel

When I think of the liberation of Palestine,
When my eye conceives the great black English line
Spanning the world news of two thousand years,
My heart leaps forward like a hungry dog,
My heart is thrown back on its tangled chain,
My soul is hangdog in a Western chair.

When I think of the battle for Zion I hear
The drop of chains, the starting forth of feet
And I remain chained in a Western chair.
My blood beats like a bird against a wall,
I feel the weight of prisons in my skull
Falling away; my forebears stare through stone.

When I see the name of Israel high in print
The fences crumble in my flesh; I sink
Deep in a Western chair and rest my soul.
I look the stranger clear to the blue depths
Of his unclouded eye. I say my name
Aloud for the first time unconsciously.

Speak of the tillage of a million heads
No more. Speak of the evil myth no more
Of one who harried Jesus on his way
Saying, *Go faster.* Speak no more
Of the yellow badge, *secta nefaria.*
Speak the name only of the living land.

The Minute

The office building treads the marble dark,
The mother-clock with wide and golden dial
Suffers and glows. Now is the hour of birth
Of the tremulous egg. Now is the time of correction.
O midnight, zero of eternity,
Soon on a million bureaus of the city
Will lie the new-born minute.

The new-born minute on the bureau lies,
Scratching the glass with infant kick, cutting
With diamond cry the crystal and expanse
Of timelessness. This pretty tick of death
Etches its name upon the air. I turn
Titanically in distant sleep, expelling
From my lungs the bitter gas of life.

The loathsome minute grows in length and strength,
Bending its spring to forge an iron hour
That rusts from link to link, the last one bright,
The late one dead. Between the shining works
Range the clean angels, studying that tick
Like a strange dirt, but will not pick it up
Nor move it gingerly out of harm's way.

An angel is stabbed and is carried aloft howling,
For devils have gathered on a ruby jewel
Like red mites on a berry; others arrive
To tend the points with oil and smooth the heat.
See how their vicious faces, lit with sweat,
Worship the train of wheels; see how they pull
The tape-worm Time from nothing into thing.

I with my distant heart lie wide awake
Smiling at that Swiss-perfect engine room
Driven by tiny evils. Knowing no harm
Even of gongs that loom and move in towers
And hands as high as iron masts, I sleep,
At which sad sign the angels in a flock
Rise and sweep past me, spinning threads of fear.

The Figurehead

Watching my paralytic friend
Caught in the giant clam of himself
Fast on the treacherous shoals of his bed,
I look away to the place he had left
Where at a decade's distance he appeared
To pause in his walk and think of a limp.
One day he arrived at the street bearing
The news that he dragged an ancient foot:
The people on their porches seemed to sway.

Though there are many wired together
In this world and the next, my friend
Strains in his clamps. He is all sprung
And locked in the rust of inner change.
The therapist who plucks him like a harp
Is a cold torture: the animal bleats
And whimpers on its far seashore
As she leans to her find with a smooth hunger.

Somewhere in a storm my pity went down:
It was a wooden figurehead
With sea-hard breasts and polished mouth.
But women wash my friend with brine
From shallow inlets of their eyes,
And women rock my friend with waves
That pulsate from the female moon.
They gather at his very edge and haul
My driftwood friend toward their fires.

Speaking of dancing, joking of sex,
I watch my paralytic friend
And seek my pity in those wastes where he
Becomes my bobbing figurehead.
Then as I take my leave I wade
Loudly into the shallows of his pain,
I splash like a vacationer,
I scare his legs and stir the time of day
With rosy clouds of sediment.

The Potomac

The thin Potomac scarcely moves
But to divide Virginia from today;
   Rider, whichever is your way
You go due south and neither South improves;
Not this, of fractured columns and queer rents
   And rags that charm the nationalist,
Not that, the axle of the continents,
Nor the thin sky that flows unprejudiced
This side and that, cleansing the poisoned breath.

   For Thomas died a Georgian death
And now the legion bones of Arlington
   Laid out in marble alphabets
Stare on the great tombs of the capitol
   Where heroes calcified and cool
   Ponder the soldier named Unknown
Whose lips are guarded with live bayonets.

   Yet he shall speak though sentries walk
And columns with their cold Corinthian stalk
   Shed gold-dust pollen on Brazil
   To turn the world to Roman chalk;
Yet he shall speak, yet he shall speak
   Whose sulphur lit the flood-lit Dome,
   Whose hands were never in the kill,
Whose will was furrows of Virginia loam.

But not like London blown apart by boys
Who learned the books of love in English schools,
His name shall strike the fluted columns down;
These shall lie buried deep as fifty Troys,
The money fade like leaves from green to brown,
And embassies dissolve to molecules.

Going to School

(Phi Beta Kappa poem, Harvard)

What shall I teach in the vivid afternoon
With the sun warming the blackboard and a slip
Of cloud catching my eye?
Only the cones and sections of the moon
Out of some flaking page of scholarship,
Only some foolish heresy
To counteract the authority of prose.
The ink runs freely and the dry chalk flows
Into the silent night of seven slates
Where I create the universe as if
It grew out of some old rabbinic glyph
Or hung upon the necessity of Yeats.

O dry imaginations, drink this dust
That grays the room and powders my coat sleeve,
For in this shaft of light
I dance upon the intellectual crust
Of our own age and hold this make-believe
Like holy-work before your sight.
This is the list of books that time has burned,
These are the lines that only poets have learned,
The frame of dreams, the symbols that dilate;
Yet when I turn from this dark exercise
I meet your bright and world-considering eyes
That build and build and never can create.

I gaze down on the garden with its green
Axial lines and scientific pond
And watch a man in white
Stiffly pursue a butterfly between
Square hedges where he takes it overhand
Into the pocket of his net.
Ah psyche, sinking in the bottled fumes,
Dragging your slow wings while the hunt resumes.
I say, "He placed an image on the pool
Of the Great Mind to float there like a leaf
And then sink downward to the dark belief
Of the Great Memory of the Hermetic School."

I say, "Linnaeus drowned the names of flowers
With the black garlands of his Latin words;
The gardens now are his,
The drug-bright blossoms of the glass are ours.
I think a million taxidermist's birds
Sing in the mind of Agassiz
Who still retained one image of the good,
Who said a fish is but a thought of God.
— This is the flat world circled by its dogs,
This is the right triangle held divine
Before bald Euclid drew his empty line
And shame fell on the ancient astrologues."

The eyes strike angles on the farther wall,
Divine geometry forms upon the page,
I feel a sense of shame.
Then as the great design begins to pall
A cock crows in a laboratory cage
And I proceed. "As for the name,
It is the potency itself of thing,
It is the power-of-rising of the wing;
Without it death and feathers, for neither reed
Of Solomon nor quill of Shakespeare's goose
Ever did more or less than to deduce
Letter from number in our ignorant creed."

And what if he who blessed these walls should walk
Invisibly in the room? — My conscience prates,
"The great biologist
Who read the universe in a piece of chalk
Said all knowledge is good, all learning waits,
And wrong hypotheses exist
To order knowledge and to set it right.
We burn, he said, that others may have light.
These are the penetralia of the school
Of the last century. Under a later sky
We call both saint and fool to prophesy
The second cycle brimming at the full."

Then the clock strikes and I erase the board,
Clearing the cosmos with a sweep of felt,
Voiding my mind as well.
Now that the blank of reason is restored
And they go talking of the crazy Celt
And ghosts that sipped his muscatel,
I must escape their laughter unaware
And sidle past the question on the stair
To gain my office. Is the image lost
That burned and shivered in the speculum
Or does it hover in the upper room?
Have I deceived the student or the ghost?

Here in the quiet of the book-built dark
Where masonry of volumes walls me in
I should expect to find,
Returning to me on a lower arc,
Some image bodying itself a skin,
Some object thinking forth a mind.
This search necessitates no closer look.
I close my desk and choose a modern book
And leave the building. Low, as to astound,
The sun stands with its body on the line
That separates us. Low, as to combine,
The sun touches its image to the ground.

From
Poems of a Jew
(1958)

The Alphabet

The letters of the Jews as strict as flames
Or little terrible flowers lean
Stubbornly upwards through the perfect ages,
Singing through solid stone the sacred names.
The letters of the Jews are black and clean
And lie in chain-line over Christian pages.
The chosen letters bristle like barbed wire
That hedge the flesh of man,
Twisting and tightening the book that warns.
These words, this burning bush, this flickering pyre
Unsacrifices the bled son of man
Yet plaits his crown of thorns.

Where go the tipsy idols of the Roman
Past synagogues of patient time,
Where go the sisters of the Gothic rose,
Where go the blue eyes of the Polish women
Past the almost natural crime,
Past the still speaking embers of ghettos,
There rise the tinder flowers of the Jews.
The letters of the Jews are dancing knives
That carve the heart of darkness seven ways.
These are the letters that all men refuse
And will refuse until the king arrives
And will refuse until the death of time
And all is rolled back in the book of days.

Messias

Alone in the darkling apartment the boy
Was reading poetry when the doorbell rang;
The sound sped to his ear and winged his joy,
The book leaped from his lap on broken wing.

Down the gilt stairwell then he peered
Where an old man of patriarchal race
Climbed in an eastern language with his beard
A black halo around his paper face.

His glasses spun with vision and his hat
Was thick with fur in the August afternoon;
His silk suit crackled heavily with light
And in his hand a rattling canister shone.

Bigger he grew and softer the root words
Of the hieratic language of his heart,
And faced the boy, who flung the entrance wide
And fled in terror from the nameless hurt.

Past every door like a dead thing he swam,
Past the entablatures of the kitchen walls,
Down the red ringing of the fire escape
Singing with sun, to the green grass he came,

Sickeningly green, leaving the man to lurch
Bewildered through the house and seat himself
In the sacrificial kitchen after his march,
To study the strange boxes on the shelf.

There mother found him mountainous and alone,
Mumbling some singsong in a monotone,
Crumbling breadcrumbs in his scholar's hand
That wanted a donation for the Holy Land.

The Confirmation

When mothers weep and fathers richly proud
Worship on Sunday morning their tall son
And girls in white like angels in a play
    Tiptoe between the potted palms
    And all the crimson windows pray,
        The preacher bound in black
Opens his hands like pages of a book
    And holds the black and crimson law
    For every boy to look.

Last night between the chapters of a dream,
The photograph still sinning in the drawer,
The boy awoke; the moon shone in the yard
    On hairy hollyhocks erect
    And buds of roses pink and hard
        And on the solid wall
A square of light like movies fell to pose
    An actress naked in the night
    As hollyhock and rose.

And to confirm his sex, breathless and white
With benediction self-bestowed he knelt
Oh tightly married to his childish grip,
    And unction smooth as holy-oil
    Fell from the vessel's level lip
        Upon the altar-cloth;
Like Easter boys the blood sang in his head
    And all night long the tallow beads
    Like tears dried in the bed.

Come from the church, you parents and you girls,
And walk with kisses and with happy jokes
Beside this man. Be doubly proud, you priest,
    Once for his passion in the rose,
    Once for his body self-released;
        And speak aloud of her
Who in the perfect consciousness of joy
    Stood naked in the electric light
    And woke the hidden boy.

The First Time

Behind shut doors, in shadowy quarantine,
There shines the lamp of iodine and rose
That stains all love with its medicinal bloom.
This boy, who is no more than seventeen,
Not knowing what to do, takes off his clothes
As one might in a doctor's anteroom.

Then in a cross-draft of fear and shame
Feels love hysterically burn away,
A candle swimming down to nothingness
Put out by its own wetted gusts of flame,
And he stands smooth as uncarved ivory
Heavily curved for some expert caress.

And finally sees the always open door
That is invisible till the time has come,
And half falls through as through a rotten wall
To where chairs twist with dragons from the floor
And the great bed drugged with its own perfume
Spreads its carnivorous flower-mouth for all.

The girl is sitting with her back to him;
She wears a black thing and she rakes her hair,
Hauling her round face upward like moonrise;
She is younger than he, her angled arms are slim
And like a country girl her feet are bare.
She watches him behind her with old eyes,

Transfixing him in space like some grotesque,
Far, far from her where he is still alone
And being here is more and more untrue.
Then she turns round, as one turns at a desk,
And looks at him, too naked and too soon,
And almost gently asks: *Are you a Jew?*

The Murder of Moses

By reason of despair we set forth behind you
And followed the pillar of fire like a doubt,
To hold to belief wanted a sign,
Called the miracle of the staff and the plagues
Natural phenomena.

We questioned the expediency of the march,
Gossiped about you. What was escape
To the fear of going forward and Pharaoh's wheels?
When the chariots mired and the army flooded
Our cry of horror was one with theirs.

You always went alone, a little ahead,
Prophecy disturbed you, you were not a fanatic.
The women said you were meek, the men
Regarded you as a typical leader.
You and your black wife might have been foreigners.

We even discussed your parentage; were you really a Jew?
We remembered how Joseph had made himself a prince,
All of us shared in the recognition
Of his skill of management, sense of propriety,
Devotion to his brothers and Israel.

We hated you daily. Our children died. The water spilled.
It was as if you were trying to lose us one by one.
Our wandering seemed the wandering of your mind,
The cloud believed we were tireless,
We expressed our contempt and our boredom openly.

At last you ascended the rock; at last returned.
Your anger that day was probably His.
When we saw you come down from the mountain, your skin alight
And the stones of our law flashing,
We fled like animals and the dancers scattered.

We watched where you overturned the calf on the fire,
We hid when you broke the tablets on the rock,
We wept when we drank the mixture of gold and water.
We had hoped you were lost or had left us.
This was the day of our greatest defilement.

You were simple of heart; you were sorry for Miriam,
You reasoned with Aaron, who was your enemy.
However often you cheered us with songs and prayers
We cursed you again. The serpent bit us,
And mouth to mouth you entreated the Lord for our sake.

At the end of it all we gave you the gift of death.
Invasion and generalship were spared you.
The hand of our direction, resignedly you fell,
And while officers prepared for the river-crossing
The Old God blessed you and covered you with earth.

Though you were mortal and once committed murder
You assumed the burden of the covenant,
Spoke for the world and for our understanding.
Converse with God made you a thinker,
Taught us all early justice, made us a race.

From
The Bourgeois Poet
(1964)

Solipsism

The world is my dream, says the wise child, ever so wise, not stepping on lines. I am the world, says the wise-eyed child. I made you, mother. I made you, sky. Take care or I'll put you back in my dream.

If I look at the sun the sun will explode, says the wicked boy. If I look at the moon I'll drain away. Where I stay I hold them in their places. Don't ask me what I'm doing.

The simple son was sent to science college. There he learned how everything worked.

The one who says nothing is told everything (not that he cares). The one who dreamed me hasn't put me back. The sun and the moon, they rise on time. I still don't know how the engine works; I can splice a wire. That's about it.

The dream is my world, says the sick child. I am pure as these bed sheets. (He writes fatigue on the vast expanses.) I'm in your dream, says the wicked boy. The simple son has been decorated for objectivity. He who says nothing is still being told.

De Sade looks down through the bars of the Bastille. They have stepped up the slaughter of nobles.

The Bourgeois Poet

The bourgeois poet closes the door of his study and lights his pipe. Why am I in this box, he says to himself (although it is exactly as he planned). The bourgeois poet sits down at his inoffensive desk — a door with legs, a door turned table — and almost approves the careful disarray of books, papers, magazines and such artifacts as thumbtacks. The bourgeois poet is already out of matches and gets up. It is too early in the morning for any definite emotion and the B.P. smokes. It is beautiful in the midlands: green fields and tawny fields, sorghum the color of red morocco bindings, distant new neighborhoods, cleanly and treeless, and the Veterans Hospital fronted with a shimmering Indian Summer tree. The Beep feels seasonal, placid as a melon, neat as a child's football lying under the tree, waiting for whose hands to pick it up.

The Living Rooms of My Neighbors

The living rooms of my neighbors are like beauty parlors, like night-club powder rooms, like international airport first-class lounges. The bathrooms of my neighbors are like love nests — Dufy prints, black Kleenex, furry towels, toilets so highly bred they fill and fall without a sigh (why is there no bidet in so-clean America?). The kitchens of my neighbors are like cars: what gleaming dials, what toothy enamels, engines that click and purr, idling the hours away. The basements of my neighbors are like kitchens; you could eat off the floor. Look at the furnace, spotless as a breakfront, standing alone, prize piece, the god of the household.

But I'm no different. I arrange my books with a view to their appearance. Some highbrow titles are prominently displayed. The desk in my study is carefully littered; after some thought I hang a diploma on the wall, only to take it down again. I sit at the window where I can be seen. What do my neighbors think of me — I hope they think of me. I fix the light to hit the books. I lean some rows one way, some rows another.

A man's house is his stage. Others walk on to play their bit parts. Now and again a soliloquy, a birth, an adultery.

The bars of my neighbors are various, ranging from none at all to the nearly professional, leather stools, automatic coolers, a naked painting, a spittoon for show.

The businessman, the air-force captain, the professor with tenure — it's a neighborhood with a sky.

The Wood

Wood for the fireplace, wood for the floor, what is the life span? Sometimes before I lay the log on the fire I think: it's sculpture wood, it's walnut. Maybe someone would find a figure in it, as children find faces in the open fire (I never have). Then I lay it on the flames like a heretic, where it pauses a moment, then joins in the singing. There's oak in this cord too. My floor is oak. I watched them lay this floor, for a vastly slower fire. The grooved pieces are fitted together; it's more like a game than work; there are many choices. The grain falls arbitrarily, dark streaks and light, dots and dashes, swirls and striped shields.

Dead wood can last forever (is it dead)? Dead wood glows in palaces, rosy and dark as masterpieces. I worship wood, split my own logs in the driveway, using a maul and iron wedges. The cracking-apart is hard and sweet. I touch wood for my superstition, using five fingers as an extra precaution. My gods would all be wood if I had gods, not stone or gold or Peter's smooth-kissed toe.

In woodless Italy houses are built without a sound, no ring of hammer on nail or wood. All is quiet, stone laid upon stone, rubble, cement, tufa, travertine, tile. Rarely you see some show-off house of wood, exotic among the blinding stucco, soft among the cool and stony facings, the marbly infinitude.

The Clearing

In the Clearing I am at peace. Place without memory or charm. Stores practically empty of goods, schools kindly and frightened. This Clearing is a beach without a sea.

Here there is only sporadic and symbolic violence. The clouds are all the news. Each tree is grown by hand.

By degrees, those who have ambience are alienated from the Dark Towers: the German groaning for the picture galleries; the bank director who bakes his own bread; the housewife with a flair for words who has given up bathing; the itinerant pianist with ice-blue eyes; the Siberian physicist with his smug compliments; the Oxford don with the dirtiest stories; the rabbi with the mystique of the Sabbath Queen; the bearded classicist with broken arches; the veteran bomber of three world wars. I talk to the man who brings the firewood. He gives me a wedge for a present.

The citizens of Nowhere scatter in all directions.

Upon my discharge from the Army my handwriting changed. Neat slant characters gave way to square and upright. The color of the ink no longer mattered. I met a poet who printed all his words. (I thought this dangerous.) I find I can barely read the mail that comes. Sometimes I have it read to me. I tend to misunderstand the words. My answers are brief. I still wait for the mailman, a vestigial pleasure. Mail in the Clearing is lighter.

Hair

One by one my troops desert. A hair at a time. One by one and there is no return. Yesterday it was dark and soft, unnoticeable as a pore. Today it sticks up at a crazy angle, bristling with what act of rebellion. Yesterday a tendril, a decoration, a vestige of biology, today barbed wire. I count them all till I've lost count. I count from the top of my head. The revolution started in that sector.

In the sole world of the self that is how it happens. One cell revolts against the general harmony. The body's bourgeois security is threatened. The government gives a perceptible shudder. One cell alone goes off, giving the finger sign of obscenity. Urchins and panhandlers cheer him on. In a moment he is making speeches. Then the police, then the militia, soon the victorious grave.

Rising crooked on my arm, darting wickedly out of my eyebrows, blanching my chest like sun, what do you want, blackmailers, professional mourners. I see you starting down my arms like lice, infiltrating to the very wrist. How far will you go? When will order be restored. Halfway measures for fops and actors, black dye, tweezers, cuticle scissors. Shall I give you away? I know your little game. I saw it in the bath the other day. This plot would tickle Rabelais. A pubic hair turned silver gray!

Beautiful Thing

Autumn reminds me that you bit my lips, excellent nurse of the most famous hospital, with puffy eyes and advertisable rear. North of beautiful Baltimore, in valley taverns, reminiscent of imagined England, we watched from the rail fence the blessing of hounds. At the place of our date you made a pass at my just-married friend in the face of his bride. She is dark and full, a Renoir woman with Brooklyn accent. You are light and thin, lacking in humor or observation. How slowly the dark one moves while you engage her husband in jokes and hugs and public thigh-pushes, all thoroughly insincere. Till the bride's laughter congeals in her throat and suddenly she is flying hands and knives of fingernails slashing wickedly at your soft attractive face, your sleepless eyes with albino lashes.

At night in the improvised bed by the living-room fire in the stone cottage you bite and use your nails. Afterwards you want me to stay inside you the entire night, even asleep. I laugh, I beg. Instead of whispering *darling* you whisper (with such conviction) *you worm!*

Office Love

Office love, love of money and fight, love of calculated sex. The offices reek with thin volcanic metal. Tears fall in typewriters like drops of solder. Brimstone of brassieres, low voices, the whirr of dead-serious play. From the tropical tree and the Rothko in the Board Room to the ungrammatical broom closet fragrant with waxes, to the vast typing pool where coffee is being served by dainty waitresses maneuvering their hand trucks, music almost unnoticeable falls. The very telephones are hard and kissable, the electric water cooler sweetly sweats. Gold simmers to a boil in braceleted and sunburned cheeks. What ritual politeness nevertheless, what subtlety of clothing. And if glances meet, if shoulders graze, there's no harm done. Flowers, celebrations, pregnancy leave, how the little diamonds sparkle under the psychologically soft-colored ceilings. It's an elegant windowless world of soft pressures and efficiency joys, of civilized mishaps — mere runs in the stocking, papercuts.

Where the big boys sit the language is rougher. Phone calls to China and a private shower. No paper visible anywhere. Policy is decided by word of mouth like gangsters. There the power lies and is sexless.

High School

Waiting in front of the columnar high school (the old ones look like banks, or rather insurance companies) I glance over the top of my book. The bells go off like slow burglar alarms; innumerable sixteeners saunter out. There's no running as in the lower schools, none of that helpless gaiety of the small. Here comes a surly defiance. As in a ritual, each lights a cigaret just at the boundary where the tabu ends. Each chews. The ones in cars rev up their motors and have bad complexions like gangsters. The sixteeners are all playing gangster.

The sea of subjectivity comes at you like a tidal wave, splashing the cuffs of middle-aged monuments. War is written on their unwritten faces. They try out wet dreams and wandering mind. They're rubbing Aladdin's lamp in the locker room. They pray for moments of objectivity as drunkards pray for the one that puts you out. They've captured the telephone centers, the microphones, the magazine syndicates (they've left the movies to us). I wait behind the wheel and spy; it's enemy territory all right. My daughter comes, grows taller as she approaches. It's a moment of panic.

But once at night in the sweet and sour fall I dropped her off at the football game. The bowl of light lit up the creamy Corinthian columns. A cheer went up from the field so shrill, so young, like a thousand birds in a single cage, like a massacre of child-brides in a clearing, I felt ashamed and grave. The horror of their years stoned me to death.

The Child Who Is Silent

The child who is silent stands against his father, lovingly looking up at him as if to say without a trace of defiance: I will speak when I have decided. He marches around the table smiling intelligently, now and then deigning to say something, perhaps "locomotive." It is somewhat frightening, a kind of rebuff to grownups. The doctors smile and shrug. If the parents are worried they don't display it. It's only like living in the last house at the edge of the subdivision. There's a bit of farm left and a highway beyond: if someone should rattle the back door in the night . . . There is a child of two minds who says nothing and who is drinking it all in. Obviously happy, very much loved, handsome and straight, laughing and playing, withholding that gift we all abuse. In that room is a tower of books with their backs to us, eloquently quiet too. Man is a torrent of language, even in death. But visitors use longer words. The little philosopher goes about his business.

This is the town where the railroads ended, the wagon trains formed in the dry gray grass. It's this frontier of speech we are always crossing. The locomotive is ridiculously dying, lumbering off to the deep clay pits to settle among the mastodon bones. The piano is thinking of Mozart. On the very top, legs crossed, at ease, sits the blue-eyed boy who holds his peace.

Generations

The look of shock on an old friend's face after years of not meeting, as if perhaps we were in a play, dressed for one of the final acts. The make-up of the years (infant, schoolboy, lover, soldier, judge of others, patriarch and ultimate old child) is on us. Those who remain the same and those who change their jaws. One has milky moons around the eyes or knotty knuckles. Many and varied are the studies in gray. The spectrum of whites amazes.

A generation moves in stateliness. It arrives like a pageant and passes down the street. The children sit on the curbs and watch. There are dignitaries and clowns, the men with medals and the cross-carriers. The owners walk abreast for the afternoon: they carry the banner which reads: the business of the world is — business. Manacled dictators walk alone through the crowded silence: four swordsmen guard them like points of the compass. The poets arrive on burros, bumping each other. Theologians packed in a hearse peer out like sickly popes. A phalanx of technologists singing the latest love songs in marching rhythms. Movie stars escorting diplomats (it's hard to tell them apart).

Nine of the greatest novelists, of ridiculous difference in height and girth. Two modern saints on litters. The generation proceeds to the cenotaph, the only common meeting place. In side streets the coming generation, not even looking, waits its turn and practices a new and secret language. (They think it's secret: that's what's so depressing.) Their hero is also gray and still in high school. He drives a hundred miles an hour into a tree.

I Am an Atheist Who Says His Prayers

I am an atheist who says his prayers.

I am an anarchist, and a full professor at that. I take the loyalty oath.

I am a deviate. I fondle and contribute, backscuttle and brown, father of three.

I stand high in the community. My name is in *Who's Who*. People argue about my modesty.

I drink my share and yours and never have enough. I free-load officially and unofficially.

A physical coward, I take on all intellectuals, established poets, popes, rabbis, chiefs of staff.

I am a mystic. I will take an oath that I have seen the Virgin. Under the dry pandanus, to the scratching of kangaroo rats, I achieve psychic onanism. My tree of nerves electrocutes itself.

I uphold the image of America and force my luck. I write my own ticket to oblivion.

I am of the race wrecked by success. The audience brings me news of my death. I write out of boredom, despise solemnity. The wrong reason is good enough for me.

I am of the race of the prematurely desperate. In poverty of comfort I lay gunpowder plots. I lapse my insurance.

I am the Babbitt metal of the future. I never read more than half of a book. But that half I read forever.

I love the palimpsest, statues without heads, fertility dolls of the continent of Mu. I dream prehistory, the invention of dye. The palms of the dancers' hands are vermillion. Their heads oscillate like the cobra. High-caste woman smelling of earth and silk, you can dry my feet with your hair.

I take my place beside the Philistine and unfold my napkin. This afternoon I defend the Marines. I goggle at long cars.

Without compassion I attack the insane. Give them the horsewhip!

The homosexual lectures me brilliantly in the beer booth. I can feel my muscles soften. He smiles at my terror.

Pitchpots flicker in the lemon groves. I gaze down on the plains of Hollywood. My fine tan and my arrogance, my gray hair and my sneakers, O Israel!

Wherever I am I become. The power of entry is with me. In the doctor's office a patient, calm and humiliated. In the foreign movies a native, shabby enough. In the art gallery a person of authority (there's a secret way of approaching a picture. Others move off). The high official insults me to my face. I say nothing and accept the job. He offers me whiskey.

How beautifully I fake! I convince myself with men's room jokes and epigrams. I paint myself into a corner and escape on pulleys of the unknown. Whatever I think at the moment is true. Turn me around in my tracks; I will take your side.

For the rest, I improvise and am not spiteful and water the plants on the cocktail table.

My Century

All things remain to be simplified. I find I must break free
of the poetry trap.

The books I hunger for all always out, never to be returned:
illuminations, personal bibles, diatribes, chapters denied
acceptance in scripture, Tobit blinded by sparrows
muting warm dung in his eyes, immense declarations
of revolt, manuals of the practice of love.

I seek the entrance of the rabbit hole. Maybe it's the door
that has no name.

My century, take savagery to your heart. Take wooden idols,
walk them through the streets. Bow down to Science.

My century that boils history to a pulp for newspaper, my
century of the million-dollar portrait, century of the
decipherment of Linear B and the old scrolls, century
of the dream of penultimate man (he wanders among
the abandoned skyscrapers of Kansas; he has already
forgotten language), century of the turning-point of
time, the human wolf pack and the killing light.

Amsterdam Whores

Each in her well-lighted picture window, reading a book or magazine, the Amsterdam whores look quite domestic. The canals, as picturesque as expected, add their serenity. The customers stroll from window to window, back and forth, comparing merchandise. Where a curtain is drawn, business is being transacted. These are big, fine, strapping whores, heavy in the leg, blond, as is the preference. They don't display their wares, no more than crossing a leg. It's like a picture gallery, Flemish School, silent through varnish and glaze. What detail, what realism of texture, what narrative! And look at this masterpiece:

A solid blond sits in her window at an angle. She appears to be looking out, expressionless. Just back of her stands an African king in round white hat and lengthy white embroidered robe of satin, it may be. Behind him stands his servant, very straight. The king's face is a thin and noble ebony. And without looking at either African the whore holds one hand back of her shoulder, feeling the robe of the African king with eloquent fingers, weighing the heft of the silk in her thoughtful hand.

Jazz

August Saturday night on the Negro street the trolleys clang and break sweet dusty smoke. Cars hoot meaningless signals. The air is in a sweat of Jim Crow gaiety, shopping, milling, rubbing of flesh, five miles of laughter in white Baltimore. The second floor dance hall has a famous trumpet. You can't move on the floor, which rolls like waves and is in actual danger of giving way. The temperature adds to the frenzy. There is no pause in the jump and scream of the jazz, heat waves of laughter, untranslatable slang. The dancing is demonic, terpsichorean. It's like a war of pleasure. It's the joy of work. The fatigue is its own reward.

Across the street in the corner drug store where whiskey is sold and every blandishment of skin, a teeming Negress crowds at the perfume counter, big arms like haunches and bosom practically bare. She laughs with her friends above the cut-glass bottles with Frenchified names and recently invented colors. She purchases a sizable vial of some green scent, pays green dry money, unstoppers the bottle and dumps the entire load between her breasts! O glorious act of laughter in the half-serious bazaar of the Jew-store!

Nebraska

I love Nowhere where the factories die of malnutrition.

I love Nowhere where there are no roads, no rivers, no interesting Indians,

Where history is invented in the History Department and there are no centennials of anything.

Where every tree is planted by hand and has a private tutor.

Where the "parts" have to be ordered and the sky settles all questions,

Where travelers from California bitch at the backwardness and New Yorkers step on the gas in a panic,

Where the grass in winter is gray not brown,

Where the population diminishes.

Here on the boundary of the hired West, equidistant from every tourist office, and the air is washed by distance, here at last there is nothing to recommend.

May no one ever attempt a recommendation; Chicago be as far as Karachi.

Though the warriors come with rockets, may they fall off the trucks.

May the voting be light and the clouds like a cruise and the criminal boredom enter the district of hogs.

I love Nowhere where the human brag is a brag of neither time nor place,

But an elephant house of Smithsonian bones and the white cathedrals of grain,

The feeding-lots in the snow with the steers huddled in symmetrical misery, backs to the sleet,

To beef us up in the Beef State plains, something to look at.

The Cracking-Plant

From the top floor of the Tulsa hotel I gaze at the night beauty of the cracking-plant. Candlelit city of small gas flames by the thousands, what
a lovely anachronism dancing below like an adolescent's dream of
the 1880s, the holy gas redeemed from Baudelaire's mustachioed
curses. Elsewhere are the white lights of the age, but here, like a millionaire who frowns on electricity, the opulence of flame. Descend-
ing on Rome from the air at night, a similar beauty: the weak Italian
bulbs like faulty rheostats yellowly outline the baroque curves of the
Tiber, the semicircles of the monstrous Vatican, endless broken
parabolas.

The cracking-plant is equally palatial. Those oil men in the silent elevator,
like princes with their voices of natural volume, their soft hats and
their name-drops (like balloons of words in the mouths of caricatures
in political cartoons), men of many mansions. The doors of the
room are mahogany. Through one which adjoins and is locked I hear
the guttural laughter of undress, neither leisurely nor quick, indis-
tinct wording, and all is silent but a woman's moan. Now it rises
like the grip of pain; it is almost loud; it is certainly sincere, like the
pent-up grief of deep relief; now it is round, now vibrant, now it is
scaly as it grows. (Then it steps off into nothingness.)

I stand awed in my stocking-feet and move respectfully toward the window,
as a man in an art gallery moves toward a more distant masterpiece
to avoid the musical chatter of intruders. The cracking-plant sails
on through the delicate Oklahoma night, flying the thousand hot flags
of Laputa.

Burlesk

Hart Crane, though handicapped, did well with the burlesk: all but her belly
buried in the floor. Magdalene? Perhaps. In Kansas City I pay my
respects to the dying art. The theater is in ruins, the ticket-taker
only half-conscious. Wine took him long ago. The carpet in the aisle
is ripped; twice I snag my foot. The rank air smells of disinfectant.
All seats are vacant except the first two rows. These are lit up as
in a Rembrandt picture, the glowing center of the operation. I sit
down inches from the drum. It lifts my hair each second it is
smashed. The snare drum hisses and the block clicks. The cymbal
crazes.

She's halfway through, already down to the sash that hangs like a silk
muffler between her buttocks. She gyrates with an expert beat, more
round than sharp. Small-breasted, her nipples glitter with stardust—
some local ordinance. She is very pretty, not what you would expect, almost indifferently dancing her career. Cold flows from her
steady limbs; stately she spreads her thighs for the climactic grind,
when at the highest throw she slips her final string, holding one
hand over the part like a live fig leaf, and flittering her fingers off
—and we are there, and she is all but hairless.

Our faces light up with intelligence.

Bouquet

All tropic places smell of mold. A letter from Karachi smells of mold. A book I had in New Guinea twenty years ago smells of mold. Cities in India smell of mold and dung. After a while you begin to like it. The curry dishes in the fine Bombay restaurant add the dung flavor. In the villages dung patties plastered to the walls, the leaving of the cows the only cooking fuel. The smell rubs into the blood.

Paris in the winter smells of wood smoke and fruit. Near the Gare St. Lazare in the freezing dusk the crowds pour slowly down the streets in every direction. A police van the size of a Pullman car goes at a walking pace. The gendarme keeps jumping down from the rear like a streetcar conductor in the old days. He is examining identity cards of pedestrians, especially the females. A girl comes swinging along, her pocketbook in rhythm with her behind. She is bareheaded and wears a raincoat. The gendarme examines her identity card. She is motioned into the paddy wagon.

Salzburg, the castle smells of snow and peat. Baltimore, old oaken bucket. Portsmouth, Virginia, roses and diesel oil. Dublin, coal dust, saccharine whiskey, bitter bodies. Damp gusts of Siena doorways. Warehouses of Papeete, acrid smell of copra, frangipani, saltwater and mold. Smell of rotting water in Hollandia.

Unbreathable jungles, parks subtle and cool. Backstage the ballet dancers wipe their sweat; "the entire stage stinks like a stable." Sewer gas of beauty parlors. Electric smell of hair in rut. Talcum powder, earliest recollection. Rome, the armpit of the universe.

Fox Hole

Quintana lay in the shallow grave of coral. The guns boomed stupidly fifty yards away. The plasma trickled into his arm. Naked and filthy, covered with mosquitoes, he looked at me as I read his white cloth tag. How do you feel, Quintana? He looks away from my gaze. I lie: we'll get you out of here sometime today.

I never saw him again, dead or alive. Skin and bones, with eyes as soft as soot, neck long as a thigh, a cross on his breastbone not far from the dog tags. El Greco was all I could think of. Quintana lying in his shallow foxhole waiting to be evacuated. A dying man with a Spanish name equals El Greco. A truck driver from Dallas probably.

When the Japs were making the banzai charge, to add insult to death, they came at us screaming the supreme insult: *Babe Ruth, go to hell!* The Americans, on the other hand, when the Japs flew over dropping sticks of explosives, shouted into the air, as if they could hear: *Tojo, eat shit!*

Soldiers fall in love with the enemy all too easily. It's the allies they hate. Every war is its own excuse. That's why they're all surrounded with ideals. That's why they're all crusades.

The Nature of Belief

When suffering is everywhere, that is of the nature of belief. When the leaders are corrupted, Pope or Commissar, nor do the people flicker an eyelash, that is of the nature of belief. When there are anniversaries of battle or martyrdom, that is of the nature of belief. When there is the slogan Credo quia absurdum or intellectual proof of the existence of God, that is of the nature of belief. When priests pray for victory and generals invoke heaven, when prisons fill with children, that is of the nature of belief. When the word *evil* appears in newspapers, *moral* in the mouths of policemen, *culture* in the prepared speeches of politicians, all that is of the nature of belief. Belief makes blood flow. Belief infects the dead with more belief. Now it flows in our veins. Now it floats in the clouds.

French Poetry

French poetry that always goes itself one better.

French poetry of figure 5's and rust carnations.

French poetry of the tongue that tastes of women and children, spatulas and rubber plants.

French poetry of the tiniest print to be read with bifocals when snow first enters the rain with its wicked announcements of defeat.

French poetry of marginal headaches, wood fires, cold, sixteen-millimeter surrealist films, Martinique jazz and the woman across the way, utmost gravity and indestructible balance, winner of the double medallion,

Easter Island images, the monstrous solemnity of patriotic children and ribbons.

French poetry of convenience, Satanism, baroque brass keys to hospitals, and cats.

French poetry of the line drawn with the fist on the pale nuance,

Overly cultivated snows, sick castles.

French poetry of the exquisite ruins of conversation.

French poetry that upsets the stomach of the future.

Of frockless priests, glorious geometricians, child insurrectionists.

French poetry of the Statue of Liberty, battered by kisses and dentists,

Ropy veins of the feet of matrons and whores, stigmata, épée.

French poetry of the Missouri River, the Platte, Yarra, gutter water of the rue Jacob.

Gloire, Vrai, et cetera.

Baudelaire in Iowa

They held a celebration for you, Charles, in Iowa. I was asked but I regretted. It was the hundredth birthday of your book, your proper Christian book called *Flowers of Evil*. (Or is it THE *Flowers of Evil*? I never know.) And in that hymnal, how well you made yourself in the image of Poe — Poe with a cross, that's what you are, adored of the gangster age. In fact, aren't you a children's poet? Aren't you the Lewis Carroll of small vice? Your shabby Wonderland of pus and giant nipple, your cats and jewels and cheap perfumes, your licking Lesbians and make-believe Black Mass, O purulence of Original Sin. And always playing it safe in the end, like Disneyland. So many safety devices, pulleys, cranks, classical Alexandrines. It's Iowa for you, restless spirit, where elderly ladies embezzle millions in the *acte gratuite*. You'll need no naturalization papers here. And yet I loved you once, and Delacroix and Berlioz — all in my gangster age. The little boy in me loved you all, O solemn Charles, so photogenic. And this is my flower for your anniversary. I fashioned it of Mexican tin and black nail polish, little French Swinburne burning in Iowa City.

Randall Jarrell

Randall, I like your poetry terribly, yet I'm afraid to say so. Not that my praise keeps you awake — though I'm afraid it does. I can't help liking them. I even like the whine, the make-believe whiplash with the actual wire in it. Once when you reviewed me badly (you must) I wrote you: "I felt as if I had been run over but not hurt." That made you laugh. I was happy. It wasn't much of a triumph but it worked. When people ask about you I am inclined to say: He's an assassin (a word I never use). I'm inclined to say: Why are you always yourself? Your love of Rilke — if it's love — your intimacy with German and God knows what all, your tenderness and terrorization, your prose sentences — like Bernini graves, staggeringly expensive, Italianate, warm, sentences once-and-for-all. And the verses you leave half-finished in mid-air — I once knew a woman who never finished a sentence. Your mind is always at its best, your craft the finest craft "money can buy" you would say with a barb. I'm afraid of you. Who wouldn't be. But I rush to read you, whatever you print. That's news.

Clowning

Dylan wasn't dapper. Uncle Saul was a dandy. Dylan stole and borrowed. Uncle Saul likewise. Dylan stole a shirt or two and some bottles of whiskey. Uncle Saul purloined whole wardrobes, used checking accounts that didn't belong to him, charged at the best shops under others' names. Dylan wore motley, Uncle Saul silk. Dylan was short and curly. Uncle Saul wore Cuban heels to raise himself and ordered Scotch in the barber's chair. Dylan played at pinballs. Uncle won the monthly rent at poker or bridge. Dylan borrowed women. Uncle Saul hired them and kept them in love nests. Dylan's look was straight and far into your eyes. The eyes of Uncle Saul were always merry and shrewd but you couldn't see beyond their twinkle and scheme. Dylan was a civilian. Uncle wangled a commission in the Army, only to be discharged for juggling money records. Uncle Saul kept the table choking with laughter and sang falsetto and clowned in a lavender dressing gown, with masses of hair on his chest. Dylan toured America like a favorite nephew, sprinkling dynamite on the nipples of female professors. He had the discipline of a lovely knave.

Now both are dead, Dylan and Uncle Saul. Dylan was taken by the pickling of his beautiful brain. The sacred oxygen could not reach the convolutions. Uncle Saul was taken thrice by the heart, thrice by the broken personality. Uncle Saul joked in the lobby of the plush nuthouse, wearing a brilliant sportcoat and shined elegant shoes. The black hair dye had vanished; his hair was snowy white. They gave him the shock treatment until his heart exploded. Dylan lay inert with the Moses bumps on his forehead amidst the screaming of wives and the groans of lovers and drinkers. And the Beat said — iambic killed him.

Roethke

Glottal as a bottle, everybody loves you, only you don't believe it. Hulk of greenery among the desert great, your roots grab continents of sham and groan. You masticate all dictionaries and spew out one-word spitballs on the walls. You blackboard buccaneers of blah. You housel planetaria of spurt. You shoeshine flesh with hail and hurt. Psychologically, you sport.

The music flutes: you're nursing Mother Goose. You know her nasty secrets like a name (dirty old woman stinking of gin). Have you found the pickled foetuses! Does your poem purl in Polish? Who's bigger than you — those squishy dreams?

The decencies file in: such pretty girls, such beardy boys. Your rhythms that throb like ocean motors.

Now and then the darkness of stanzas. That bridge of ice-capped sawtooth monuments bites at the sky like industrial diamonds. You grit your teeth on broken glass, sing with a geographical tongue on the sly nights of Seattle. Art is a blood pudding foreign as frescoes. Where you dig down we are, we are. Under the smoky glass we are. How the flukes splash, ha-ha, baby!

Poets' Corner

As richly documented as the hell of priests, yes, there is a hell, the hell of sick poets, the hell of history. Those in whom honesty has turned to policy. Those diseased by notice. Those who invent new prosodies, with a logical or graphic notation. Those who wear the cold handcuffs of rhyme. Those who construct a religion of the beautiful, with symbols as the means and myth as the end. Those who mistake rage for intensity, symmetry for design, metaphor for focus, drunkenness for vision. Those who make an example of their lives and who commit acts of personal violence for public response. These inhabit the hell of poets.

Some die early by disease or accident. Some jump in the sea or drink lacerating poisons manufactured for toilets. Some lie in asylums with eyeballs metamorphosed to marble. (You cannot penetrate below their surface.) Some fall on their knees before two pieces of wood or a stone belly. Some join the revolutions and are gladly shot. Some become officials, laureates, men of affairs or major diplomats. Some become abstractionists, actuaries, mathematicians. Some become salesmen or lay priests, after their voluptuous poems are in print. Some become preachers in the last half of their lives, constructing faultless sermons. Some succumb to pageantry, some to algolagnia.

Glad Hand

I'm writing this poem for someone to see when I'm not looking. This is an open book. I want to be careful to startle you gently. The poem is about your looking at it, as one looks at a woman covertly. (I wonder what she's doing in this town; it's a long way from the look in her eyes.) The rings of my big notebook stand open like the rib cage of a barracuda. Careful with your fingers.

I'm writing this poem for an after-dinner friend who's using my pipe tobacco or my pen. I'd like some phrase to catch his eye. I'd like some phrase to wake him up in the early hours, as one wakes up with a fragment of a tune in his head (the melody for the day). The toilet bowls glow graciously and there's a box of the best Kleenex on the sink. I'm writing this poem for hospitality. I can't stand people who say Help Yourself. That always means Don't Be a Pig. Tired of picking the locks of poems I leave this one for all and sundry. To put your name in it would be a dirty trick.

Younger I dreamed of being a poet whose trash basket was rifled by scholars. I learned to write trash-basket poems. But this is closer to my real desire. I'm writing this poem as much for you as a poem is possible. It stands there like a half-filled glass, both coming and going. I'm a bad host. The drinks are too strong; I don't know how to carve (I say with a grin, I'm left-handed). This is a poem to sneak at a glance. (I'm writing it to mean, not be.)

Fame

What kind of notation is in my *Time* file for my life, especially my death? Will they say I died, O God? If they don't say I died how can I die? There it is fine and relevant to die, an honor so to speak, interesting as divorce.

What's in my file at the FBI? What's my symbol when they flick me out? Am I a good American or a borderline case? Can I hold my liquor? Have I ever been cleared, and if so, of what?

Dear Fame, I meet you in the damndest places. You smile, you walleyed bitch, but you look over my shoulder for a prearranged signal: something has come up on the other side of the room.

My life, my own, who is writing you on what pale punch cards? Deep-thinking machine, have you got my number?

A hundred oligarchs in identical suits are sitting around a table shaped like a uterus, alphabetizing greatness. I say to myself: all men are great. I would like to cry but have forgotten how. Now I remember: they used to come to me, those journalists with humble pencils. They begged me from their hats: say something big; give us an execution; make bad weather. I failed them badly. I couldn't grow a beard.

I guess I haven't built my ship of death. The word "image" is now in government. The doors are all closing by remote control. But when I meet the almighty Publicity Director, name-dropper of kings, I'll shake his hand and say: once I kissed Fame (mouth like an ass hole) but only for fun. He'll tear up the punch cards and think for a minute.

The Funeral of Poetry

The password of the twentieth century: Communications (as if we had to invent them). Animals and cannibals have communications; birds and bees and even a few human creatures called artists (generally held to be insane). But the bulk of humanity had to invent Communications. The Romans had the best roads in the world, but had nothing to communicate over them except other Romans. Americans have conquered world-time and world-space and chat with the four corners of the earth at breakfast. The entire solar system is in the hands of cartoonists.

I am sitting in the kitchen in Nebraska and watching a shrouded woman amble down the market in Karachi. She is going to get her morning smallpox shot. It's cold and mental love they want. It's the mystic sexuality of Communications. The girl hugs the hi-fi speaker to her belly: it pours into her openings like gravy. Money was love. Power was love. Communications now are love. In the spring Hitler arises. This is the time of trampling.

A man appears at the corner of the street; I prepare myself for hospitality. Man or angel, welcome! But I am afraid and double-lock the door. On the occasion of the death of a political party, I send an epitaph by Western Union. I didn't go to the funeral of poetry. I stayed home and watched it on television.

From
Selected Poems
(1968)

Manhole Covers

The beauty of manhole covers — what of that?
Like medals struck by a great savage khan,
Like Mayan calendar stones, unliftable, indecipherable,
Not like the old electrum, chased and scored,
Mottoed and sculptured to a turn,
But notched and whelked and pocked and smashed
With the great company names
(Gentle Bethlehem, smiling United States).
This rustproof artifact of my street,
Long after roads are melted away will lie
Sidewise in the grave of the iron-old world,
Bitten at the edges,
Strong with its cryptic American,
Its dated beauty.

Calling the Child

From the third floor I beckon to the child
Flying over the grass. As if by chance
My signal catches her and stops her dance
Under the lilac tree;
And I have flung my net at something wild
And brought it down in all its loveliness.
She lifts her eyes to mine reluctantly,
Measuring in my look our twin distress.

Then from the garden she considers me
And, gathering joy, breaks from the closing net
And races off like one who would forget
That there are nets and snares.
But she returns and stands beneath the tree
With great solemnity, with legs apart,
And wags her head at last and makes a start
And starts her humorous marching up the stairs.

Lines for a Unitarian Church

Little church of simple steel I-beams
Set among the squat midwestern houses,
You seem to say and I believe
Body and soul are one,
Man for the world and the world only,
For there is no evil.

Little church without a steeple,
Without the cross, the sword-hilt in the sky,
Without the crazed-glass staining the mystic floor,
You seem to say and I believe
Evil does not exist.

Church of laughter, church of light,
No more the gothic hell, psychotic tower,
Barb-wire star, cruel crescent, mandala,
No more the brothel of the nave, chancre of Guilt
In God's love-nest.

Instead, upon your lawn at church o'clock
A native head sunk in the earth,
A native head chin-deep in the land;
Here the eternal native welcomes you
Welcomes your earliest and best nature,
Welcomes the resurrection into touch.

Little church of friendly steel,
No higher than a human house, as strong,
Beautiful in humid Cincinnati,
Beautiful in the world, inside and out.

Bad Taste, Inc.

I

There is a shop in Paris called Bad Taste
(Le Mauvais Goût) where objets d'art,
Chiefly Victorian, are sold
To wedding couples from the States,
Interior decorators, movie stars,
Rich poets and other sophisticates.
The past peddles the past
To the latest barbarians. Nothing goes to waste:
Yesterday's newspaper, bits of string,
Forgotten comforts, masterpieces.
In Paris nothing goes to waste,
Especially Taste, especially Bad Taste.

II

In America everything goes to waste.
We waste ourselves in the hygienic sun,
We waste the future, burn it to the ground.
Waste in the States is the national industry,
All are consumers — *consume, consume!*
On to the waste pipe, the cloaca americana!

Human Nature

For months and years in a forgotten war
I rode the battle-gray Diesel-stinking ships
Among the brilliantly advertised Pacific Islands,
Coasting the sinister New Guinea Coasts,
All during the killing and hating of a forgotten war.
Now when I drive behind a Diesel-stinking bus
On the way to the university to teach
Stevens and Pound and Mallarmé,
I am homesick for war.

You Call These Poems?

In Hyderabad, city of blinding marble palaces,
White marble university,
A plaything of the Nizam, I read some poetry
By William Carlos Williams, American.
And the educated and the suave Hindus
And the well-dressed Moslems said,
"You call those things poems?
Are those things poems?"

For years I used to write poems myself
That pleased the Moslems and Hindus of culture,
Telling poems in iambic pentameter,
With a masculine inversion in the second foot,
Frozen poems with an ice-pick at the core,
And lots of allusions from other people's books.

Emily Dickinson and Katherine Anne Porter

I

Emily Dickinson's father yanked on the Baptist bell
To call the townspeople to see the sunset,
And the Baptists saw the glory of the sunset
And went home to stained-glass darkness, awfully disappointed
That something really hideous hadn't happened,
Like Hell or the atom bomb.
Old man Dickinson who also fed the sparrows over the snow
With grain from his barn (age seventy-one)
And hid until he saw them peck it up.

"And drove the fastest horse in town."

II

And when Dylan Thomas was introduced
To Katherine Anne Porter in a room full of people,
He stooped and picked her up below the thighs
And raised her to the ceiling like a drink,
And held her straight in the slack-jawed smoke-blue air
Two minutes, five minutes, seven minutes,
While everybody wondered what it meant
To toast the lady with her own body
Or hold her to the light like a plucked flower.

California Winter

It is winter in California, and outside
Is like the interior of a florist shop:
A chilled and moisture-laden crop
Of pink camellias lines the path; and what
Rare roses for a banquet or a bride,
So multitudinous that they seem a glut!

A line of snails crosses the golf-green lawn
From the rosebushes to the ivy bed;
An arsenic compound is distributed
For them. The gardener will rake up the shells
And leave in a corner of the patio
The little mound of empty snails, like skulls.

By noon the fog is burnt off by the sun
And the world's immensest sky opens a page
For the exercises of a future age;
Now jet planes draw straight lines, parabolas,
And x's, which the wind, before they're done,
Erases leisurely or pulls to fuzz.

It is winter in the valley of the vine.
The vineyards crucified on stakes suggest
War cemeteries, but the fruit is pressed,
The redwood vats are brimming in the shed,
And on the sidings stand tank cars of wine,
For which bright juice a billion grapes have bled.

And skiers from the snow line driving home
Descend through almond orchards, olive farms,
Fig tree and palm tree — everything that warms
The imagination of the wintertime.
If the walls were older one would think of Rome:
If the land were stonier one would think of Spain.

But this land grows the oldest living things,
Trees that were young when Pharaohs ruled the world,
Trees whose new leaves are only just unfurled.
Beautiful they are not; they oppress the heart
With gigantism and with immortal wings;
And yet one feels the sumptuousness of this dirt.

It is raining in California, a straight rain
Cleaning the heavy oranges on the bough,
Filling the gardens till the gardens flow,
Shining the olives, tiling the gleaming tile,
Waxing the dark camellia leaves more green,
Flooding the daylong valleys like the Nile.

A Selection
of Poems

(1969–92)

There Was That Roman Poet

There was that Roman poet who fell in love at fifty-odd.
My God, *Venus*, goddess of love, he cried,
Venus, for Christsake, for the love of God,
Don't do that to me!
Don't let me fall in love, a man of my age.
I beg you on my knobby knees, lay off.
Basta! I've had enough — not only that,
NON SUM QUALIS ERAM, Jesus Christ!
How do you know I can get it up!

The laughter of the goddess cool as hell
Pinged like a Cellini shell.
Priceless, she said, showing her teeth, clacking her castanets, stomping her
feet.
And what has age to do with that, Quintus, she said,
And put that in your Classical Dictionary . . .
And went her way in a wild odor of roses and garlic.

W.H.A.

Without him many of us would have never happened
But would have gone on being Georgians or worse;
We all recall how he galloped into verse
On Skelton's nag and easily reopened

Eighteenth-century prosody like a can of worms,
And there like Alice on a checkerboard
Careened through Marx and Freud and Kierkegaard
Dazzled and dazzling all the ideas and forms,

And camped out in the United States to wrinkle
Like an Indian squaw to await the Nobel Prize
And study savages with paleface eyes
And sit on Oxford Dictionaries and rankle.

God bless this poet who took the honest chances;
God bless the live poets whom his death enhances.

The Old Poet

Coming to the end of his dated poems in the complete edition, knowing what he did not — the date already written, how many weeks were left, the very number of minutes. I read as with a burning-glass. And so many years between the opening page and a man lingering over the final words in a foreign country — after which there is only an index.

That radiance of old poets (those who surrendered power with a smile). In his own city he renames the streets, the ships, the bars. History comes to his hand like a tame pigeon. One of his sentences hangs in the square like the plume of a volcano. Real speech, real life are un-written. Only these lines have a tendency to remain forever. Cities with poetry remember him. Cities without poetry.

Mozart's Jew

Much as I enjoy your minor immortality, Da Ponte, I marvel where you lie. New Jersey; New York; something like that. My God, Da Ponte, you gave Mozart the words for all that music. And why do you make me uneasy? Because you were a Jew, Emanuele Conegliano? Because you were a Catholic priest, harried from town to town, country to country, for your love affairs? Because you lie and cover up in your book, only to be caught red-handed? What difference does it make. You called yourself a poet, you fraud, but you had guts. Writing three plays for three different composers at once, and one of them Mozart. And his the *Don Giovanni!* Writing twelve hours on end, like a Hollywood hack. And plenty of Tokay on the table (*goût de terroir*) and lots of Seville tobacco, not to mention the sixteen-year-old girl, your mistress during this project. I like you Da Ponte. And finally bounced out of Europe itself, to open a grocery store in New Jersey, that's almost too much. And failing at it, of course. And yet I think you must have been the first to say of Mozart: the greatest composer, past, present and future. That little bit took genius to say. And the Emperor Joseph liked you. And Casanova, jailed for reading Voltaire. All of you Don Giovannis I like, and you especially, Mozart's Jew, Da Ponte.

The Humanities Building

All the bad Bauhaus comes to a head
In this gray slab, this domino, this plinth
Standing among the olives or the old oak trees,
As the case may be, and whatever the clime.
No bells, no murals, no gargoyles,
But rearing like a fort with slits of eyes
Suspicious in the aggregate, its tons
Of concrete, glaciers of no known color,
Gaze down upon us. Saint Thomas More,
Behold the Humanities Building!
                           On the top floor
Are one and a half professors of Greek,
Kicked upstairs but with the better view,
And two philosophers, and assorted Slavics;
Then stacks of languages coming down,
Mainly the mother tongue and its dissident children
(History has a building all its own)
To the bottom level with its secretaries,
Advisors, blue-green photographic light
Of many precious copying machines
Which only the girls are allowed to operate.
And all is bathed in the cool fluorescence
From top to bottom, justly distributed
Light, Innovation, Progress, Equity;
Though in my cell I hope and pray
Not to be confronted by
A student with a gun or a nervous breakdown,
Or a girl who closes the door as she comes in.

The Old Guard sits in judgment and wears ties,
Eying the New in proletarian drag,
Where the Assistant with one lowered eyelid
Plots against Tenure, dreaming of getting it;

And in the lobby, under the bulletin boards,
The Baudelairean forest of posters
For Transcendental Meditation, Audubon Group,
"The Hunchback of Notre Dame," Scientology,
Arab Students Co-op, "Case of the Curious Bride,"
Two students munch upon a single sandwich.

Crossing Lincoln Park

Dit le corbeau, jamais plus. — *Mallarmé*

Car locked, I started home across the grass,
A kind of island with a stand of oaks
Washed round on all sides by the swish of cars,
To where I lived, a hundred yards in view.
Quarried apartments rose on every hand,
Scoriac Gothic shouldering solid glass
Hemming me in, reflecting a blank sky.
Briefcase and I happily homeward strode
Through ankle-grass, when something at my shoe
Darkly turned over, what I never knew,
For down came the crow and with a sudden blow,
Its great wings beating, slashed at my face
With croak and scream and yellow beak
Screeching me out. I did not stop to think
But leapt and sprinted toward the curb, the bird
Cursing, crisscrossing, driving at my face,
Crashing my shoulders with its filthy wings.
Ugly, omnivorous offal-eating crow,
Bird of ill omen,
Eater of turd and dead fish, get thy beak
From out my heart! My eyeglasses flew off,
I stumbled forward, clutching my briefcase,
Fanning away the bird with naked hand,
Until I reached the street where solid cars
Bumper to bumper blocked my flight,
And still the crow surrounded me and struck
Till I broke through and in the door and up
The elevator to the velvet hall
And to the door and in, where your bright smile
Changed instantly to — "White!" you said.
"Your face whiter than chalk!"

My Father's Funeral

Lurching from gloomy limousines we slip
On the warm baby-blanket of Baltimore snow,
Wet flakes smacking our faces like distraught
Kisses on cheeks, and step upon the green
Carpet of artificial grass which crunches
Underfoot, as if it were eating, and come
To the canopy, a half-shelter which provides
A kind of room to enclose us all, and the hole,
And the camp chairs, and following after,
The scrolly walnut coffin
That has my father in it.

Minutes ago in the noncommittal chapel
I saw his face, not looking himself at all
In that compartment hinged to open and shut,
A vaudeville prop with a small waxen man,
"So cold," the widow said and shied away
In a wide arc of centrifugal motion,
To come again to stand like me beside,
In the flowerless room with electric candelabra.
If there is among our people any heaven,
We are rather ambiguous about it
And tend to ignore the subject.

The rabbi's eulogy is succinct,
Accurate and sincere, and the great prayer
That finishes the speech is simply praise
Of God, the god my father took in stride
When he made us learn Hebrew and shorthand,
Taught us to be superior, as befits
A nation of individual priests.
At my sister's house we neither pray nor cry
Nor sit, but stand and drink and joke,
So that one of the youngsters says
It's more like a cocktail party.

For Dylan's dandy villanelle,
For Sylvia's oath of damnation one reserves
A technical respect. To Miller's Willie
And Lewis's Babbitt I demur.
My father was writing a book on salesmanship
While he was dying; it was his book of poems.
Destined to be unpublished. He hadn't time
To master books but kept the house well stocked
With random volumes, like a ship's library,
Rows and rows of forgotten classics,
Books for the sake of having books.

My father in black knee-socks and high shoes
Holding a whip to whip a top upstreet;
My father the court stenographer,
My father in slouch hat in the Rockies,
My father kissing my mother,
My father kissing his secretary,
In the high-school yearbook captioned Yid,
In synagogue at six in the morning praying
Three hundred and sixty-five days for his mother's rest,
My father at my elbow on the bimah
And presiding over the Sabbath.

In the old forgotten purlieus of the city
A Jewish ghetto in its day, there lie
My father's father, mother and the rest,
Now only a ghetto lost to time,
Ungreen, unwhite, unterraced like the new
Cemetery to which my father goes.
Abaddon, the old place of destruction;
Sheol, a new-made garden of the dead
Under the snow. Shalom be to his life,
Shalom be to his death.

Moving In

I wish you for your birthday as you are,
Inherently happy,
The little girl always shining out of your face
And the woman standing her ground.

Wish you the seldom oceanic earthquake
Which shatters your gaze
Against some previous interior past
And rights you.

Wish you your honesty normal as a tree
Confounding the caws of intellectuals.
When I zip your dress I kiss you on the neck,
A talisman in honor of your pride.

When I hold your head in my hands
It is as of the roundness of Columbus
Thinking the world, "my hands capable of
Designing the earthly sphere."

Your fingers on the piano keys
Or the typewriter keys or on my face
Write identical transcriptions.
Nothing you do is lost in translation.

I am delighted that you loathe Christmas.
I feel the same way about Communism.
Let us live in the best possible house,
Selfish and true.

May the Verdi *Requiem* continue to knock you out
As it does me; fashionable protest art
Continue to infuriate your heart
And make you spill your drink.

Now ideology has had its day
Nothing is more important than your birthday.
Let us have a solid roof over our head
And bless one another.

A Curiosity

Tiny bees come to see what I am,
Lying in the sun at summer's end,
Writing a poem on a reclining chair.
A butterfly approaches and retreats;
Flies bang into my body by mistake,
And tinier things I can't identify;
And now and then a slow gigantic wasp
Rows on its stately voyage to the fence.
The trees are still too little to have birds;
Besides, the neighbors all have special cats
Bred for their oddity or arrogance.
A dragonfly sips at a lemon twig
After a helicopter landing. It
Appears that I am a curiosity
In my own backyard.
The dog of doubtful breed
Sleeps on the carpet of the sod,
And a bee necks with a rose.

The Piano Tuner's Wife

That note comes clear, like water running clear,
Then the next higher note, and up and up
And more and more, with now and then a chord,
The highest notes like tapping a tile with a hammer,
Now and again an arpeggio, a theme,
As if the keyboard spoke to the one key,
Saying, No interval is exactly true,
And the note whines slightly and then truly sings.

She sits on the sofa reading a book she has brought,
A ray of sunlight on her white hair.
She is here because he is blind. She drives.
It is almost a platitude to say
That she leads him from piano to piano.

And this continues for about an hour,
Building bridges from both sides of the void,
Coasting the chasms of the harmonies.

And in conclusion,
When there is no more audible dissent,
He plays his comprehensive keyboard song,
The loud proud paradigm,
The one work of art without content.

At Auden's Grave

From Vienna it's picture postcard all the way.
Where else on earth is such a land at ease!
The fat farms glistening, the polished pigs,
Each carven window box disgorging red
Geraniums, pencil pines and chestnut trees,
The gaily painted tractor rigs,
Steeples with onion domes that seem to say
Grüss Gott, come lie here in our flowerbed.

How many times did Auden take this train
Till that bright autumn day when he was borne
Back in a baggage car after his last
Recital, back to his Horatian house,
His cave of making, now the mask outworn,
The geographical visage consummated,
Back to the village, home to the country man
Without a country, home to the urban bard
Without a city he could call his own.

But suddenly a startling word
Leaps from the signpost of the country lane,
It's AUDENSTRASSE —
The poet becomes a street, the street a poet,
English with German music mated.

Here will arrive no pilgrim mob
As in Westminster Abbey, where his name
Is chiseled next to Eliot's. The sole cab
Has never heard of Auden, has to ask
Gasthaus directions, but we find him there
Ten yards away and settled with his slab,
The bracketed dates, the modest designation,
His plot planted to suffocation
In the country style of *horror vacui*.

Close by, a granite soldier stands
Bareheaded, bowed, without a gun,
Wearing his empty cartridge belt,
A blunt reminder of the First World War,
Signed *Unseren Helden* for those villagers
Who never returned and lay somewhere in France
Entre deux guerres before the next
World War should be begun
By the ultimate twentieth century hun.

Far from his foggy isle
The poet rests in self-exile.
Earth of the great composers of the wordless art
Enshrouds this master of the English tune
Not many miles from where Beethoven scrawled his will
When he could no longer hear the trill
Of the little yellow-hammer, nor the titanic storm.
In such a place Dame Kind
Released the intellectual minstrel's form.

Across the *Audenstrasse* from the grave
A bee drops from the chestnut, sips the beer,
Brings back his image to me, on a day
I bought him a tin collapsible cup to sip
His whiskey from, on some Iowa train,
Knowing his dread of that vertiginous plain.
Now all is comfy in his delectable cave.
I scatter the bee and greet him with my lip.

Whatever commentators come to say —
That life was not your bag — Edwardian —
Misogynist — Greenwich Villager —
Drifter — coward — traitorous clerk — or you,
In your own language, genteel anti-Jew —
I come to bless this plot where you are lain,
Poet who made poetry whole again.

Sandwiched between two families Auden lies,
At last one of the locals, over his grave
A cross, a battle monument, and a name
History will polish to a shine.
Down in the valley hums the Autobahn,
Up here the poet lies sleeping in a vale
That has no exits. All the same,
Right on target and just in time
A NATO fighter rips open the skies
Straight over Auden's domus and is gone.

The Old Horsefly

Unseasonable weather, says the commentator,
Seventy in Manhattan in December.
Flu bugs as big as pigeons, I advise.

I saw a bee buzzing a sidewalk florist
On Broadway under a wall of Christmas trees.

Eleven floors up in the too-warm living room
A horsefly dashes window to wall and back,
A horsefly in December in Manhattan,
Off-course like those venturesome seagulls
Flying between two rivers and two parks
When the wind is right.
                I get the flyswatter.

No entomologist, I decide
This is an old horsefly. I'll let it go,
Or is it a gadfly from the hotel row
Where carriage horses from another world
Still nod and stomp and swish their horsehair tails?

Its flight is frantic but I know that flies
That find their way in windows never find
The exit. I watch it speeding to and fro,
Disappearing, exploring other rooms
Till tired it lights on a white-painted door.

Biped approaches, raises his wand, then strikes.
Did I get it? I feel a pang — of what?

Tennyson

Like many of us he was rather disgusting
With his deliberate dirtiness, his myopia, his smell,
His undying enmity for unfavorable reviewers,
His stinginess, his coy greed for titles, money and gowns,
His contempt for Cockneys and Americans,
Sallow, greasy, handsome, the Ur-Victorian.
Stupid, as Auden called him.

And yet, one of the great songsters of the English word,
Though we still say, a century beyond,
With qualifications.
                                    And modern!
A family riddled with drugs, alcohol and insanity,
His major themes all givens or hand-me-downs,
The omnium-gatherum of *In Memoriam*
For beloved Arthur, the high-school *Idylls*,
The triumph of faulknerian *Maud*
(Though only Browning could call it great);

Yanking his son out of Cambridge to be his biographer,
The slavey wife he truly cherished,
His fear of Darwin, his desperation for everlastingness;

Beautiful tedious Alfred, nicotine drooling from his
          meerschaum pipe,
Which he invited guests to suck,
Long-lived, the very image of the English Poet
Whose songs still break out tears in the generations,
Whose prosody for practitioners still astounds,
Who crafted his life and letters like a watch.

Whitman

Like Queen Victoria, he used the regal *we*,
Meaning the disciples of *Leaves of Grass*,
The American Bible they literally believed;
Sat by the hour to photographers,
The Open Shirt frontispiece,
The Good Gray, the Jesus, the Laughing Philosopher,
The Old Poet in the crumpled highcrown hat
Gazing in rapture at the butterfly
        Perched upon his forefinger
(It turns out was a cardboard butterfly);
To Tennyson the greatest of his time,
Inviting Walt to sail to the Isle of Wight;
Our first and probably our only guru,
Whose opinion of niggers (his designation) was low,
But worshipped Lincoln, to whom he scribed
        His second greatest song;
Who opened the Closet but wouldn't come out;
Who lived in a kind of luxurious poverty,
Housekeeper, male nurse, amanuensis, carriage,
        On the bounty of admirers,
Adored as Gandhi or a Dr. Schweitzer,
Visited by Oscar Wilde and English titles,
        In Camden, New Jersey;
Two hundred pounds of genius and hype,
Nature-mystic who designed his tomb
Solid as an Egyptian pyramid,
American to the soles of his boots,
Outspoken as Christ or Madame Blavatsky,
Messiah, Muse of the Modern, Mother!

Future-Present

Remember the old days when the luxury liners
                    in narrow Manhattan
appeared piecemeal in segments at the end of east-west
                    streets,
a black-and-white section of portholes and stripes of decks
and slowly the majesty of the great red funnel,
even the olympian basso of its homing horn?
It would take a full half hour to go past,
as if in no hurry to pass into history.

But look there at the top pane of the window!
A burnished skyliner elegantly moving north,
as proud as leviathan above the suffering Hudson,
past the unfinished cathedral, over Grant's tomb,
into the blue-gray morning of the future-present.

July 7, 1978

for Sophie

You marked the day
that, sitting in a tired chair,
gazing toward the exhausted light
white and silent as the telephone
it came to you, that ray,

why scamp it, that annunciation
hundreds of masters tried to paint,
the flêche d'amour that marks the way
from the quotidian penitentiary
to your epiphany.

Jacob Boehme saw it in a ray
that struck a pewter pot,
Whitman saw it where he lay
outstretched on the uncut hair of graves.
It came to you
wholly unbidden from your inner day.

Acknowledgments

To find oneself "selected" and published without moving a finger is a foretaste of an afterlife — a quasi-illicit joy. This I owe to Stanley Kunitz, who first thought of it and then, with David Ignatow, saw it through to completion, also inspiring the late M. L. Rosenthal to write the excellent introduction. Arranging for this publication is only the latest instance of Robert Phillips's rare, supportive friendship over the years.

— K.S.

Karl Shapiro (b. 1913) is one of the most distinguished poets of America's Middle Generation, the generation of Lowell, Schwartz, Berryman, Roethke, and Bishop. Shapiro's second poetry collection, *V-Letter and Other Poems*, was awarded the Pulitzer Prize in 1945. In 1946 he was appointed Consultant in Poetry at the Library of Congress, the position now called U.S. Poet Laureate. From 1950 to 1956 he was editor of *Poetry: A Magazine of Verse*, and from 1956 to 1966 he edited *Prairie Schooner.* He was awarded the Bollingen Prize in Poetry in 1969. He has taught at Johns Hopkins University, the University of Nebraska, the University of Illinois at Chicago, and the University of California at Davis, from which he retired. He is a member of the American Academy of Arts and Letters and lives in Manhattan with his wife, the translator Sophie Wilkins.

Illinois Poetry Series

Laurence Lieberman, Editor

History Is Your Own Heartbeat
Michael S. Harper (1971)

The Foreclosure
Richard Emil Braun (1972)

The Scrawny Sonnets and Other
Narratives
Robert Bagg (1973)

The Creation Frame
Phyllis Thompson (1973)

To All Appearances: Poems New and
Selected
Josephine Miles (1974)

The Black Hawk Songs
Michael Borich (1975)

Nightmare Begins Responsibility
Michael S. Harper (1975)

The Wichita Poems
Michael Van Walleghen (1975)

Images of Kin: New and Selected
Poems
Michael S. Harper (1977)

Poems of the Two Worlds
Frederick Morgan (1977)

Cumberland Station
Dave Smith (1977)

Tracking
Virginia R. Terris (1977)

Riversongs
Michael Anania (1978)

On Earth as It Is
Dan Masterson (1978)

Coming to Terms
Josephine Miles (1979)

Death Mother and Other Poems
Frederick Morgan (1979)

Goshawk, Antelope
Dave Smith (1979)

Local Men
James Whitehead (1979)

Searching the Drowned Man
Sydney Lea (1980)

With Akhmatova at the Black Gates
Stephen Berg (1981)

Dream Flights
Dave Smith (1981)

More Trouble with the Obvious
Michael Van Walleghen (1981)

The American Book of the Dead
Jim Barnes (1982)

The Floating Candles
Sydney Lea (1982)

Northbook
Frederick Morgan (1982)

Collected Poems, 1930–83
Josephine Miles (1983)

The River Painter
Emily Grosholz (1984)

Healing Song for the Inner Ear
Michael S. Harper (1984)

The Passion of the Right-Angled Man
T. R. Hummer (1984)

Dear John, Dear Coltrane
Michael S. Harper (1985)

Poems from the Sangamon
John Knoepfle (1985)

In It
Stephen Berg (1986)

The Ghosts of Who We Were
Phyllis Thompson (1986)

Moon in a Mason Jar
Robert Wrigley (1986)

Lower-Class Heresy
T. R. Hummer (1987)

Poems: New and Selected
Frederick Morgan (1987)

Furnace Harbor: A Rhapsody of the
North Country
Philip D. Church (1988)

Bad Girl, with Hawk
Nance Van Winckel (1988)

Blue Tango
Michael Van Walleghen (1989)

Eden
Dennis Schmitz (1989)

Waiting for Poppa at the Smithtown
Diner
Peter Serchuk (1990)

Great Blue
Brendan Galvin (1990)

What My Father Believed
Robert Wrigley (1991)

Something Grazes Our Hair
S. J. Marks (1991)

Walking the Blind Dog
G. E. Murray (1992)

The Sawdust War
Jim Barnes (1992)

The God of Indeterminacy
Sandra McPherson (1993)

Off-Season at the Edge of the World
Debora Greger (1994)

Counting the Black Angels
Len Roberts (1994)

Oblivion
Stephen Berg (1995)

To Us, All Flowers Are Roses
Lorna Goodison (1995)

Honorable Amendments
Michael S. Harper (1995)

Points of Departure
Miller Williams (1995)

Dance Script with Electric Ballerina
Alice Fulton (reissue, 1996)

To the Bone: New and Selected Poems
Sydney Lea (1996)

Floating on Solitude
Dave Smith (3-volume reissue, 1996)

Bruised Paradise
Kevin Stein (1996)

Walt Whitman Bathing
David Wagoner (1996)

Rough Cut
Thomas Swiss (1997)

Paris
Jim Barnes (1997)

The Ways We Touch
Miller Williams (1997)

The Rooster Mask
Henry Hart (1998)

The Trouble-Making Finch
Len Roberts (1998)

National Poetry Series

Eroding Witness
Nathaniel Mackey (1985)
Selected by Michael S. Harper

Palladium
Alice Fulton (1986)
Selected by Mark Strand

Cities in Motion
Sylvia Moss (1987)
Selected by Derek Walcott

The Hand of God and a Few Bright
Flowers
William Olsen (1988)
Selected by David Wagoner

The Great Bird of Love
Paul Zimmer (1989)
Selected by William Stafford

Stubborn
Roland Flint (1990)
Selected by Dave Smith

The Surface
Laura Mullen (1991)
Selected by C. K. Williams

The Dig
Lynn Emanuel (1992)
Selected by Gerald Stern

My Alexandria
Mark Doty (1993)
Selected by Philip Levine

The High Road to Taos
Martin Edmunds (1994)
Selected by Donald Hall

Theater of Animals
Samn Stockwell (1995)
Selected by Louise Glück

The Broken World
Marcus Cafagña (1996)
Selected by Yusef Komunyakaa

Nine Skies
A. V. Christie (1997)
Selected by Sandra McPherson

Other Poetry Volumes

Local Men and *Domains*
James Whitehead (1987)

Her Soul beneath the Bone: Women's
Poetry on Breast Cancer
Edited by Leatrice Lifshitz (1988)

Days from a Dream Almanac
Dennis Tedlock (1990)

Working Classics: Poems on
Industrial Life
*Edited by Peter Oresick and
Nicholas Coles* (1990)

Hummers, Knucklers, and Slow
Curves: Contemporary Baseball
Poems
Edited by Don Johnson (1991)

The Double Reckoning of Christopher
Columbus
Barbara Helfgott Hyett (1992)

Selected Poems
Jean Garrigue (1992)

New and Selected Poems, 1962–92
Laurence Lieberman (1993)

The Dig and Hotel Fiesta
Lynn Emanuel (1994)

For a Living: The Poetry of Work
*Edited by Nicholas Coles and
Peter Oresick* (1995)

The Tracks We Leave: Poems on
Endangered Wildlife of North
America
Barbara Helfgott Hyett (1996)

Peasants Wake for Fellini's *Casanova*
and Other Poems
*Andrea Zanzotto; edited and translated
by John P. Welle and Ruth Feldman;
drawings by Federico Fellini and
Augusto Murer* (1997)

Moon in a Mason Jar and *What My
Father Believed*
Robert Wrigley (1997)

The Wild Card: Selected Poems, Early
and Late
*Karl Shapiro; edited by Stanley Kunitz
and David Ignatow* (1998)